ANNUAL FLOWERS

COMPLETE GARDENER'S LIBRARY™

ANNUAL

FLOWERS

Barbara
Pleasant

National Home
Gardening Club
Minnetonka, Minnesota

NATIONAL HOME
GARDENING CLUB

Annual Flowers

Printed in 2006.

Tom Carpenter
Creative Director

A. Cort Sinnes
Complete Gardener's Library Executive Editor

Julie Cisler
Book Design & Production

Michele Teigen
Book Development Coordinator

Gina Germ
Photo Editor

Chuck Crandall
Barbara Crandall
Principal Photographers

Brian Liedahl
Illustrator

Janice Cauley
Copy Editor

3 4 5 6 7 8 9 10 / 10 09 08 07 06
© 2000 National Home Gardening Club
ISBN 1-58159-061-X

National Home Gardening Club
12301 Whitewater Drive
Minnetonka, Minnesota 55343
www.gardeningclub.com

CONTENTS

ENOUGH FLOWERS FOR A LIFETIME

quick payback for the hard work of digging and planting and weeding. Then there's the thrill of seeing a flower make a go of it in an uncertain site and coming up a winner.

I also love working with seeds of all sizes and watching the determination of annuals as they bloom and bloom in an attempt to make a good crop of seeds. The first time I grew tall ageratum, which starts from a tiny seed indeed, I felt that I had accomplished more than could be possible with five flats of bedding plants. And it was no less thrilling, just this past season, to bang on stone-hard moonflower seeds with a knife, plant them, and watch the huge seedlings burst out of the ground like something from another planet.

Reseeding annuals also fascinate me, and I hope you discover at least a few that like your site and soil well enough to return year after year. Perhaps you can even turn them into a family legacy. My father and his mother before him stewarded many generations of zinnias through their gardens, and now that the torch has passed to me I tend to gloat over my "old maids." They pop up in a certain bed so profusely that there is little point in trying to use the spot to grow anything else, which is surely more of a blessing than a curse.

My most important advice on annuals is this: Keep trying new ones, keep your old favorites, and always set aside some space where different annuals can be set free to play together. Maybe that space will be a big pot, or maybe you can fill a whole bed with companionable annual flowers. Just be prepared for delightful surprises, and you will surely have a very good time.

Barbara Pleasant

Barbara Pleasant

My daughter was five years old when she began to learn what the names of the months meant. One day, as I took the kitchen wall calendar down to flip it to a new month, she asked which one it was getting to be now. "June," I said, "the month filled with all kinds of greens." She looked puzzled, then said solemnly that she loved June. "But it's not all green. There's lots of pink in June too."

And of course she was right. Where I live it's time to plant many annuals in April, with some of them earlier, in March. So by June there are plenty of colorful blooms for a five-year-old to gather and poke into her hair or weave into

the dog's collar. Maybe that was the year I filled a half dozen pots with hot pink petunias that seemed even pinker in the company of brilliant blue lobelia. Or maybe it was another particularly pink year when antique pink pansies and dianthus reigned until summer's heat signaled that it was time for a change. I can't remember, but it really doesn't matter. With annual flowers it's always time for a change, and therein lies the excitement of gardening with these adaptable, forgiving flowers.

Although I love all kinds of plants and all types of gardening, I especially love the fast pace of growing annuals. First there's the

WELCOME TO ANNUAL FLOWERS!

All gardeners pursue a unique vision of what they want their landscape to become, and that vision almost always includes colorful annuals. Within these pages you will find details about well-known workhorse flowers such as petunias and impatiens as well as very old and very new flowers that may be just the plants you are seeking to make your garden complete.

What's in a Name?

Every annual here has a botanical name, and many of them also go by common names that have nothing to do with their botanical classification. To keep your frustration level low as you seek the flowers you desire, we have listed annuals by their dominant common names in the main encyclopedia section (Chapter 4) and also included a cross-index of plant names (see pages 168-170). The main index includes botanical names along with all of the best-known common names for over 100 annual flowers.

Check the Facts

Gardeners are busy people who don't always have time to sit down and read several pages before deciding how best to handle a new plant. The "Facts to Know" box that accompanies each flower entry provides essential information at a glance about site, season, soil and germination.

Precise Photography

Because annuals are so beautiful, the pictures in this book are as important as the words! We've chosen photos that show what these flowers will look like when you put them to work in your garden. And if you're new to growing plants from seed or rooting cuttings, the how-to photographs will give you the confidence you need to ensure success.

Associating Annuals

Mixing and matching annuals will provide you with a lifetime of gardening fun, and there are two easy ways to get started. If you like, begin with a theme, such as butterfly gardening (pages 38-39) or growing flowers for cutting (pages 32-33), and work through the plant lists keyed to these special kinds of gardens. Or, if a certain plant already has captured your heart, check out the "Colorful Companions" suggestions that accompany each flower listing. You'll be well on your way to growing a garden where even seemingly opposing forces can work together with beautiful results.

High impact color is easy to achieve with vibrant annuals. Here blue ageratum give way to dianthus and dwarf gomphrena. Stately spires of Salvia farinacea, *sometimes called mealycup sage, form a beautiful backdrop.*

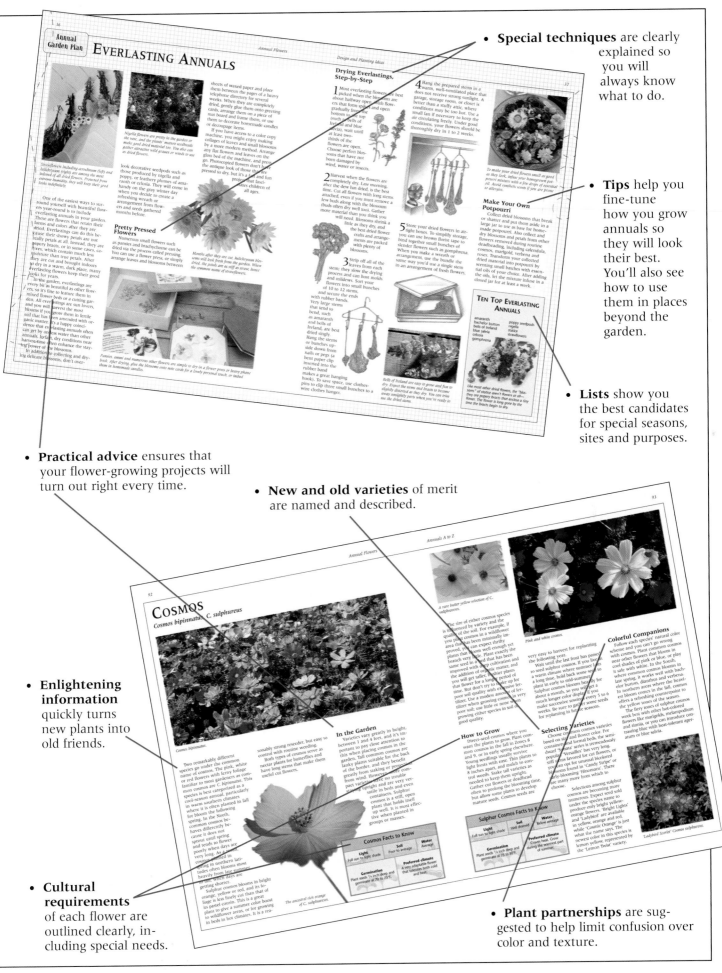

- **Special techniques** are clearly explained so you will always know what to do.

- **Tips** help you fine-tune how you grow annuals so they will look their best. You'll also see how to use them in places beyond the garden.

- **Lists** show you the best candidates for special seasons, sites and purposes.

- **Practical advice** ensures that your flower-growing projects will turn out right every time.

- **New and old varieties** of merit are named and described.

- **Enlightening information** quickly turns new plants into old friends.

- **Cultural requirements** of each flower are outlined clearly, including special needs.

- **Plant partnerships** are suggested to help limit confusion over color and texture.

◖ CHAPTER 1 ◗

ENJOYING ANNUALS

Discovering fun flowers for every site and season.

*A*nnuals can lead a garden in any season of the year, giving you the building blocks you need to bring color and life to your gardening plan. But you can also use annuals to fill voids—places and times that might otherwise go drab, were it not for those "annual" splashes of color you decided to add. Either way, annuals are for fun, for enjoyment.

Every year, annuals give you a new chance to create unique compositions of color and texture. White sweet alyssum, yellow marigolds and red begonias are the major players in this lively scene.

Grow annual flowers in pots and use them to bring color to your entryway, patio or deck. White begonias, blue bachelor buttons and multicolored lantana are but a few excellent choices for containers.

There are so many annuals you will never get bored growing them!

Pinning down an exact definition of a garden annual is not as simple as it sounds, because plants grow differently in different climates. Botanically speaking, a true annual is a plant that germinates from seed, grows to maturity, and produces flowers and mature seeds in a single season. Perennials are different in that a perennial plant can survive winter, usually in a dormant state, and then reappear in spring year after year.

Annual flowers are the fun plants of summer—and of spring and fall too. After a winter dominated by pale shades of gray, the first violas and English daisies announce the coming of spring. After that, the parade of colorful garden annuals goes on and on until a resolute late fall freeze stops the show.

From a practical point of view, annuals are often viewed as summer color plants, but they have much, much more to offer. Depending on how you use them, they can be the stellar feature flowers in your landscape or small punctuation points of texture and color—pockets of inspiring beauty to cheer your mornings, dazzle your day, or bring light and fragrance to your yard after dark. Annuals are endlessly versatile in beds or when used as edgings. They also make great container flowers. And they produce lovely blossoms for bouquets.

You can dry many annuals by hanging them in small bunches in a well ventilated place. Protected from strong sunlight, "everlasting" annuals such as blue statice or bright yellow strawflowers will hold their colors indefinitely.

A window box becomes a summer-long festival of color when planted with robust petunias. Crowding the plants helps to give the box an extra lush and full look. Regular feeding fuels strong growth and steady bloom.

What's an Annual?

The majority of flowers described in this book are true annuals, but many of them also can grow as perennials if the climate is right. Whether or not a certain flower will be annual or perennial depends on how much cold weather it can take or, in some cases, on how much heat it can survive. For example, foxglove and hollyhock are hardy perennials in all but the coldest climates, but you can grow certain varieties as annuals no matter where you live. English daisies and pansies will grow as perennials in cold climates, but they always succumb to summer's heat in warmer regions.

There also are two in-between categories to consider: hardy annuals (often called biennials) and short-lived perennials. Hardy annuals are willing and able to grow through winter and bloom in the spring, and some of them, like forget-me-nots, greatly benefit from winter's chill. Short-lived perennials (such as dianthus) often will prosper for 2 to 3 years before dying out.

However, you will have to actually grow foxgloves or forget-me-nots or dianthus before you will know which life cycle your climate affords them. In other words, start them out as annuals, and then wait and see.

These flowing ribbons of bright color began as inexpensive bedding plants. Front to back, this display is comprised of blue lobelia, multicolored verbena, white petunia, red salvia and blue salvia.

When butterflies discover a source of flower nectar, they quickly learn how to best approach the blooms to drink their fill. Flat, daisy-shaped blooms like those of cosmos provide sure footing and plenty of sweet nectar.

ANNUALS FOR ALL SEASONS

Cool-season annuals often bloom in late summer in areas where nights are consistently cool. Left to right, salpiglossis, clarkia and lobelia are combined with perennial coreopsis and chrysanthemums in a compact raised bed.

The annual flowers we know and love come from all over the world and bring with them strong preferences for certain types of weather. Originally from Peru, four o'clocks thrive in warm, steamy summers. In contrast, calendulas need consistently cool weather like that of their ancestral England, and native gaillardias want a cool start followed by summer warmth, the typical weather pattern that dominates much of the United States.

But you need not know the ancestry of every annual to know when to plant it in your garden. The simplest way to align your choice of flowers with the changing seasons is to sort annuals into groups based on their weather preferences. Here we will discuss the three main categories: cool-season annuals, warm-season annuals, and a third group called transitional annuals—exceptionally adaptable flowers that prosper in both cool and warm weather.

Cool-Season Annuals

Cool-season annuals vary in how much cold they can take, but they have in common a need for a temperature range of about 50 to 80°F while they are actively growing. The hardiest among them will survive minimum temperatures in the teens provided they are well rooted, but they do not grow much unless soil temperatures are above 45°F. And, although healthy plants will continue to bloom after the weather turns hot, the flowering period for cool-season annuals often ends prematurely under very warm growing conditions.

With most cool-season annuals that are not available as bedding plants, you should start seeds indoors and move the plants out at the earliest possible time. To avoid delays when direct-seeding cool-season annuals, prepare the beds in the fall and cover them with a thick mulch through winter. This way you will not have to wait for the soil to dry out before you start planting the first flowers of the year.

Ornamental kale can anchor beds from fall to spring in mild winter areas. Cool weather improves the color of kale's broad leaves, softened by the close company of blue forget-me-not and perennial candytuft.

COOL-SEASON ANNUALS

Modern hybrid violas, still affectionately known as johnny jump-ups, are non-stop bloomers under cool to cold conditions, but they often melt out in heat. Little whiskers mark the throat of each petite blossom.

ammi
asarina
aster
bachelor button*
brachychome
calendula
candytuft
cobbity daisy
cosmos
dianthus**
English daisy**
foxglove**
hollyhock**
kale and cabbage*
larkspur*

lobelia
mimulus
nasturtium
nigella
pansy**
poppy*
salpiglossis

schizanthus
snapdragon*
statice
stocks
sweet alyssum
sweet pea
viola**

* will grow as winter annuals in many areas
** will grow as short-lived perennials

Like many other annuals with a naturally sprawling growth habit, a mass planting of 'Pink Bouquet' hybrid verbenas will produce bright clouds of colorful blooms for most of the summer.

Zinnias appear almost elegant in the company of dwarf marigolds and rhythmic mounds of sweet alyssum, dusty miller and red begonia. Impatiens brings color and light to warm shade.

Warm-Season Annuals

These flameproof flowers thrive in heat that will melt out many cool-season annuals. Their ideal temperature range is 55 to 90°F, so they are best used as summer standouts. In many climates, you can follow fall or spring plantings of cool-season flowers with annuals from this group.

All warm-season annuals need warm soil to germinate and grow, so it's useless to plant them too early. If you do, they will sit and sulk until the weather warms. But come summer, most warm-season annuals will bloom continuously from mid-summer to frost.

Several warm-season annuals can be handled as perennials where winters are very mild, including cup and saucer vine, dahlia, four o'clock, lantana and nicotiana. Where the soil often freezes for short periods in winter, an extra helping of mulch to insulate the dormant roots from cold makes a big difference in these plants' winter survival.

Transitional Annuals

Transitional annuals are backbone plants in most annual gardens because they are so flexible when it comes to weather. Accepting of both heat and cold, they bridge the bloom gap between cool-season and warm-season flowers. Understandably, the most popular garden annuals fall into this group, including geranium, marigold, petunia and verbena. And, because the demand for them is high, most transitional annuals are easily found as spring bedding plants.

Black-eyed Susan vine is unsurpassed for covering a fence with greenery and flowers.

KNOWING YOUR CLIMATE

Throughout this book, the regional adaptability of many flowers is summarized by naming the "Zones" in which they grow during the various seasons. The zones on this hardiness zone map, based on average winter temperatures, are the standard numbered zones used in almost all gardening books, magazines, and seed catalogs. Sometimes the zone number is followed by a letter, as in Zone 6a or 6b. An "a" means that the area falls within the colder sections within the zone, and the "b" suggests warmer growing conditions than those that prevail elsewhere in the zone.

Zone 1: Below -50°F

Zone 2: -50° to -40°

Zone 3: -40° to -30°

Zone 4: -30° to -20°

Zone 5: -20° to -10°

Zone 6: -10° to 0°

Zone 7: 0° to 10°

Zone 8: 10° to 20°

Zone 9: 20° to 30°

Zone 10: 30° to 40°

Zone 11: Above 40°

USDA Plant Hardiness Zone Map, indicating areas with similar average low temperatures. This map is a necessary reference tool for every gardener.

PLANTING AFTER FROST

With annuals, the last spring frost and the first frost of fall are widely used as hallmarks around which good planting times may be planned. Use the map and table below as a general guide to average frost dates. And, because elevation and proximity to large bodies of water strongly affect the occurrence of frost, it's also wise to obtain first and last frost data from your local extension service.

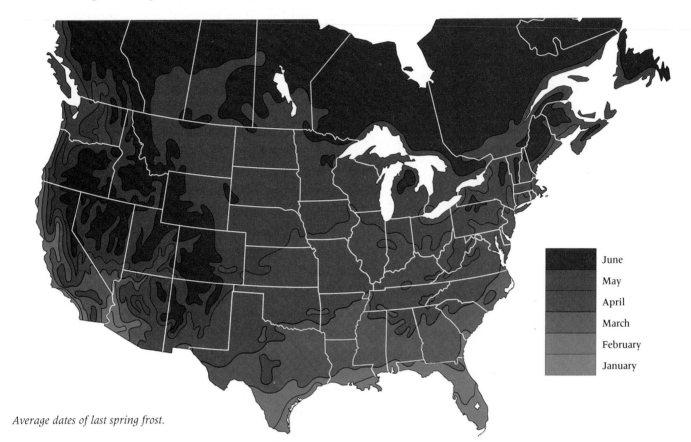

June
May
April
March
February
January

Average dates of last spring frost.

FROST DATES FOR SOME AMERICAN CITIES

Zone 3

Great Falls, MT	S-May 9	F-September 25
Grand Forks, ND	S-May 24	F-September 13

Zone 4

Albany, NY	S-May 18	F-September 24
Minneapolis, MN	S-May 17	F-September 22
Casper, WY	S-June 8	F-September 10

Zone 5

Boston, MA	S-May 7	F-October 2
Chicago, IL	S-May 17	F-September 30
St. Louis, MO	S-April 21	F-October 17
Denver, CO	S-May 18	F-September 29
Spokane, WA	S-May 23	F-September 21

Zone 6

New York, NY	S-April 14	F-October 30
Lexington, KY	S-April 29	F-October 14
Salt Lake City, UT	S-May 20	F-September 27
Las Alamos, NM	S-May 23	F-October 2
Walla Walla, WA	S-April 22	F-October 29

Zone 7

Raleigh, NC	S-April 1	F-November 6
Birmingham, AL	S-April 10	F-October 25
Oklahoma City, OK	S-April 21	F-October 14
Lubbock, TX	S-April 1	F-November 9
Chico, CA	S-March 30	F-November 16

Zone 8

Charleston, SC	S-March 28	F-November 9
Jackson, MS	S-April 17	F-October 10
Dallas, TX	S-March 18	F-November 17
Phoenix, AZ	S-March 1	F-November 30
Seattle, WA	S-April 22	F-October 29

Zone 9

Tampa, FL	S-February 9	F-December 8
New Orleans, LA	S-February 20	F-December 9
Corpus Christi, TX	S-March 9	F-November 23
Tucson, AZ	S-March 19	F-November 19
Sacramento, CA	S-March 25	F-November 17

S—*Average last spring frost.*   **F**—*Average first fall frost.*

Note – *Frost dates will vary widely from year to year. These dates are long-term averages.*

◀ CHAPTER 2 ▶

DESIGN AND PLANTING IDEAS

Breathe life into your landscape with colorful flowers.

*T*he first rule about gardening with annuals is this: There are no rules! Arrange them formally. Cast them in casual swoops and swales. Create a straight and defined border. Use annuals to make a fun and festive edge. Fill in problem spots with the right annuals for that particular microclimate … the ideas never end. Annuals can provide an answer for almost every flower gardening challenge.

Using a lot of one type of flower insures easy upkeep and makes a scene appear spacious and neat. Yellow marigolds need only occasional trimming to keep them blooming for most of the summer.

Wherever bright annuals bloom, they attract attention. This is the main thing to keep in mind when thinking about where you might grow colorful flowers in your landscape. Certainly you will want a few of your favorites near entryways, outside your kitchen window, and perhaps around the base of your mailbox. Any place that is often seen is a great place for annuals.

The style of your landscape will help you decide whether to organize your annuals into neat groupings that have a formal look or use them in more relaxed, flowing beds with curved edges. Many gardeners do both, using balanced, almost symmetrical planting plans in the front yard and a more free-and-easy style in the more private space behind the house. Generally speaking, annuals that naturally grow to a very uniform size work best in formal areas, so you might first look at ageratum, wax begonia, impatiens, petunias, gerani-ums, vinca and compact zinnias for formal areas. Larger flowers that sprawl about, such as tall

Like other bright red flowers, 'Telstar Crimson' dianthus can magically draw attention from far away. However, the blossoms are so rich with color that you may want to grow a few in pots for close viewing.

cleome, cosmos and sunflowers are better suited to informal areas or cutting gardens, where the total effect is less important than the flowers themselves.

Part of the beauty of working with annuals is that nothing is permanent. You can change designs and colors from one season to the next, or repeat schemes that you find particularly pleasing. If, on the other hand, you find yourself at mid-summer with a garden full of clashing plants that are struggling to survive, simply pull out the misfits and replace them with more promising candidates. Annual flowers offer endless flexibility and a lifetime of gardening enjoyment.

In this chapter, you will learn how to use annuals as a colorful add-on feature in an existing landscape, as well as how to use annuals to create special gardens. Depending on the design strategies

Pots overflowering with cascading lobelia use a special design trick—repeating the begonias used in nearby window boxes—to give this entryway color and texture while keeping a feeling of unity.

you use, your annuals can provide little punctuation points of color, form long ribbons that tie the landscape together, or stand alone as large swaths of dramatic energy. Use annuals to indulge your creativity and sense of adventure, and you will never tire of the fun.

When people see an curbside display like this, they'll be smiling long before they reach your front door. Here a small pot of New Guinea impatiens presides over purple lobelia, white sweet alyssum and red geraniums.

ANNUALS IN COLOR

When using mixed colors in shade, be sure to include enough white to create crisp contrast. The huge range of color choices available in impatiens makes this a simple challenge.

Cool pinks and blues impart a relaxed mood and give a scene some soft light. The differences in form between the pink pansies' flat blossoms and spikes of blue sage (Salvia farinacea) make this a dynamic team.

Annual flowers give you unlimited opportunities to experiment with both types of color from one season to the next. You can change color schemes from season to season and from year to year. Although there are but a few hard-and-fast rules for working with color, several common threads are apparent in beautiful landscape pictures painted with annual flowers. As you study these possibilities, don't lose track of the most important factor in finding your way through the color maze: following your own personal preferences.

Keying Color to the Season

One way to organize your color choices in annual flowers is to align them with seasonal changes in the weather. In most climates, different annual flowers bloom in spring, summer and fall. By using annuals to help carry out the changing moods of each season, your garden becomes a unique reflection of nature's changing cycles.

For example, you might celebrate the gentle dawning of spring with cool-season flowers in soft, contemplative colors: blue pansies, white sweet alyssum, pink dianthus, pink or yellow snapdragons. Then, in summer, let warm-natured annuals in bright colors take center stage: bright red geraniums, salvias or zinnias accompanied by yellow celosia or blue ageratum. As the season winds down, use late-blooming orange and yellow flowers to reflect

One of the most enjoyable aspects of working with annuals is playing with color. Color sets the mood in the garden. Soft, light colors like pink, lilac, white and lemon yellow will infuse any area with a relaxed mood that soothes the soul. Bright, saturated reds and oranges have the opposite effect. They impart an intensity to the scene that is both forceful and exciting.

A tapestry of bright verbena and blue ageratum is slightly tamed by bands of red salvia, white petunias and white begonias. But the effect is still lively and full of punch!

ALL MIXED UP

Multicolored plantings of a single flower, such as a mixed bed of impatiens or zinnias or petunias, look best when you carry out the kaleidoscope of color on a large scale. Let such plantings be large ones, at least 3 feet square, and frame them with foliage plants or flowers that bloom in neutral colors such as white or soft yellow. If necessary, take the cruel step of pulling out individual plants in colors that don't strike your fancy or that seem to clash with the rest of the group.

Rich red and violet tones from phlox, fuchsia and foxglove create a harmonious picture before a home that is naturally shaded. Softer colors can be used in separate sections of the landscape.

When used as edging plants near shrub beds, annuals such as these wax begonias form a lacy collar of color. Note how different colors are repeated in a pattern so that the planting appears well organized.

the natural tones of autumn. Yellow dahlias, marigolds or multicolored red and orange lantana are but three possibilities for ending the season with a bang.

But what if you feel like celebrating the first warm days of spring and tend to feel oppressed by summer's heat? In this case, you might be happiest using bolder colors as season openers and then switching to soft pastels in an attempt to cool down summer. For example, spring might bring red and yellow pansies, vivid red poppies and deep blue lobelia. Then fade to pastels for the hottest weather: soft pink impatiens or vinca, white or pink lavatera, perhaps laced together with dusty miller, blue sage, or blue fan flower.

Counting Up Colors

During any season of the year, most landscapes can handle at least three concurrent colors. One of those colors is always green, which leaves you with limited choices for the colors you want to feature in your garden. Sometimes it's best to stick with one color, particularly if your yard already includes numerous shrubs and trees. But for most gardeners, restraining ourselves to two dominant colors per season is the difficult challenge.

Yet limiting your color selection to two main colors need not place burdensome limits on growing an exciting assortment of different flowers. Simply use slightly different hues of the same colors, and then add neutral elements in gray and white. See the color wheels on the right to check to see if your color choices are likely to work.

Color Wheel

There are three ways to use the color wheel to see if a color combination you want to try will clash or turn into a breathtaking pocket of beauty:

1 Pick opposites. *Colors that are directly opposite one another on the color wheel are called complementary colors. Although radically different, they match like magic.*

2 Make triangular choices. *Imagine a triangle in the center of the color wheel. The three colors at each point of the triangle, called split complementary colors, can be counted upon to work together well.*

3 Go with a cluster. *Choose two colors that are next to each other on the wheel and use annuals in various hues of those colors. This plan, called analogous harmony, still leaves room for a bit of contrast. You will find your contrasting color directly opposite your cluster on the color wheel.*

A puffy cloud of ageratum is accompanied by sprightly dahlias growing out of a sea of mixed dianthus. The repeating tufts of white dianthus keep this color combination in the safety zone.

Impatiens in pastel pink and white glow in filtered shade. Close spacing of the plants helped create this full display in which the colors appear to flow into one another.

USING ANNUALS TO PROMOTE HARMONY

White goes with everything, especially if that white is an elegant petunia. Keep some plants in pots so you can easily shift them around in the garden.

We gardeners are always curious about new plants, so we eagerly expand our collections. While plant collecting is fun, it can result in a slightly unsettling landscape made up of mismatched pieces, some of which may be long-lived shrubs or trees. If this sounds like your house, put annuals to work unifying your landscape into a more pleasing whole. This is easily done by using annual flowers to implement special design tricks that promote harmony among many different plants.

Repetition

Repeating a single type of flower in a single color in different parts of your landscape is an unbeatable way to give your yard a more cohesive character. Compact annuals sold as bedding plants are ideal for this purpose since they can be popped into the ground in small nooks and corners, with a few more installed in strategically placed containers. Since the idea is to accessorize different parts of your landscape with a common plant, the best flowers for the job are capable of adapting to varying amounts of sun and shade.

Five vigorous, trouble-free annuals make outstanding candidates for repetitive plantings: wax begonia, pansy, petunia, impatiens and dusty miller. All are widely available in cellpacks or flats in individual colors, so it's easy to get the plants you need. Be sure to buy enough! You will need to place at least three plants together in a clump to achieve good visual impact. Count up how many repetitive planting sites you want to fill before heading off to buy plants.

Rhythm

If you're trying to improve harmony in a single flower bed or well-defined section of your yard, use annuals to give the site a strong rhythm. Imagine that the space in question is a piece of music, and conjure in your mind where logical "beats" might fall. Then fill those spaces with a single type of annual, or possibly different annuals that are similar in size and color. Frequently the "beats" are at approximately even spacing, but not always. The prettiest flower gardens are not planted in straight lines, so you may find that rhythmic elements are best placed in diagonal "trills" or curved "chords."

The best rhythmic annual flowers have bright, eye-catching colors and bloom continuously for a long period of time. Top choices include plume celosias, coleus, dianthus, geranium, lantana, French marigolds, phlox, sages and salvia, verbena, vinca, and compact zinnias. Many of these come in numerous colors, which simplifies match-making. For example, you might plan rhythmic accents of soft yellow by making use of yellow

When looking for a versatile color for repetitive use, look at blue, white or pale yellow first. Here flowing drifts of cream and yellow violas are separated by matching strips of blue plumbago.

Wax begonias planted in large drifts are hard to beat for easy-care color. They flatter larger plants nearby, in this case sun-splashed yellow marigolds and shaded pink impatiens.

celosia, marigold and zinnia. Brighter "percussion" points would evolve from rhythmic patterned plantings of red geranium, salvia or verbena—assuming you get a tight match on hard-to-match reds!

You won't have to worry about hues so much if you use foliage plants to carry out a rhythmic planting pattern. Coleus, dusty miller and Persian shield all are worthy of consideration.

Edgings

Dressing the edges of flower beds with naturally neat edging plants gives them a manicured look while helping anchor them to the spot in which they are planted. And, because an edging becomes a ribbon of color and texture that winds through the landscape, it helps tie things together like a ribbon on a nicely wrapped present.

Ideal edging plants have a fine texture, a mounding habit that helps plants grow together into a solid mass, and uniformity of size. Prime annuals for edging include dwarf dianthus, lobelia, dwarf melampodium, nierembergia, pansy, dwarf petunia and sweet alyssum. To establish a flawless edging, set plants a little closer than usual and mulch between them to control weeds.

Tall cosmos dance at the rear of a layered bed. Even small flowerbeds take on a deep, lush appearance when plants of varying heights are used. Put the tallest plants in the back.

Three colors of geraniums form a broad edging for a shrub bed. In this highly uniform edging, the varying shades of green in the foliage are as important as the flower colors.

Backdrops

The same way a mat and frame set off a pretty painting, some sort of backdrop is needed to make your landscape look like a finished scene. Woods, shrub groupings, or wood privacy fences are backdrops, and so are tall annuals, including cleome, hollyhock, Mexican sunflower, regular sunflowers and the tallest varieties of zinnia you can find. Tall trellises planted with annual vines help frame a garden when planted behind other flowers too. Good choices for vining backdrops include hyacinth bean, moonvine and morning glory.

In addition to framing the scene, the height of backdrop plants brings dramatic vertical interest to the garden. Just be sure to plant smaller annuals in front of tall ones so that the bases of the tall flowers are hidden from view. It is also often necessary to stake tall flowers to keep them upright. You can either tie plants to individual stakes, or install stakes between plants and weave jute or string among the stakes and stems to bind them together in a strong upright position.

ANNUALS FOR ACCENTS

Annuals are unbeatable for focusing attention on certain spots. You can use a few plants in a small bed or container to add small dashes of color, or make a bigger splash with a dozen like plants that grow together into a colorful carpet.

It's always smart to use light-colored annuals to accent areas that are dominated by shade or dark green shrubs. Light naturally contrasts with dark, so white petunias, impatiens or browallia have an illuminating effect when placed near evergreens or perhaps in shaded corners of your deck. Light-colored flowers also are easy to see at night, so they are great for edging walkways or planting near patios that are often used after dark.

Enhancing Your House

Also consider the colors of your house when choosing colors to use as accents. Most houses have a primary color (white siding, red brick, brown stucco) plus a second dominant color used for doors and trim. Such houses come alive when a third color is added—a special talent of annual flowers that deserves wider use.

Clear contrast is the best approach to take when using annuals

Pots teeming with pink begonias bring life and color to a small sitting area. Begonias work well near buildings because they readily adapt to both sun and shade.

Heavy colors are easily lightened up by the right companions. Huge fuchsias are the stars of this landscape planting, but they might appear gaudy if not for the presence of a cloud of soft pink impatiens.

to accent the colors of your house. If you have a white house with dark shutters, splashes of red to accent the entryway will bring the house to life in vibrant style. If your house has gray siding, you have an excellent opportunity to try deep blues, pinks, or purples as accent plants. You can use the color wheel to choose accent colors the same way you'd use it to choose several colors for a special flower bed.

Accent colors become an irresistible treat for the eye when they are carried out via differing heights. For example, imagine that you want to accent your front entryway with similar tones of pink. Ankle-

high pink wax begonias, knee-high pink cosmos and a pair of hanging baskets planted with cascading pink petunias would do the trick. In red, the same idea might be carried out with red dianthus, red zinnias and a large pot of red impatiens.

When choosing accent colors for your house, keep in mind that bright reds, oranges and yellows are most effective at drawing attention from a distance—a big plus if your house is set back far from the street. On the other hand, soft blues, pinks and whites have a special way of making small spaces seem larger—a definite boon if you want your house and yard to look bigger.

Matching flower colors to the colors of your house always has a unifying effect. Here a third color makes the planting more interesting and dynamic, but the repetitive planting pattern keeps it under tight control.

Dwarf marigolds in varying sunny shades impart a feeling of warmth to a brick house. Small trees, pruned to remove low branches, make it possible to grow many sun-loving flowers close by.

Containers filled with frothy white sweet alyssum and blue pansies set the stage for this informal patio garden. Annuals can be kept in continuous bloom, offering color long after the perennial shasta daisies are gone.

Even a tiny pocket garden benefits from flowers in varying forms. Tall ageratum, touch-me-not and orange gomphrena frames a small collection of culinary basils.

Using Neutrals

Flowers that bloom in white or pale yellow, as well as those with gray or white variegated foliage, are often called neutrals since they seem to go with everything. Neutral colors help quiet near-clashes, and they also enrich the garden with luminous textures. If you are trying a complicated planting plan with several colorful annuals, it is more likely to work if you prominently feature neutral plants in your design.

It's fine to cheat a little in this endeavor by keeping an emergency supply of neutral plants growing in roomy pots, ready to slip into the garden as the need arises. Dusty miller is endlessly versatile for this purpose since it has a novel texture and color that flatters the appearance of anything else that happens to be growing nearby. Other prime problem-solving neutrals include chartreuse coleus, euphorbia, ornamental sweet potato, Persian shield and any annual that blooms in pale yellow or white.

Variations in Flower Form

There is more to designing with annuals than picking compatible colors. To keep things interesting, also think about varying flower forms. In addition to classic daisy shapes (cosmos, gazania, zinnia), there are upright spikes (plume celosia, foxglove, larkspur), rounded clusters (ammi, trachymene and verbena), and tiny blossoms that appear in such profusion that they look like soft cushions (lobelia, nierembergia, sweet alyssum). If you find yourself on the threshold of overstocking your garden with a single type of flower form, make a change. Plant partnerships that utilize but one flower form are dull compared to the dynamic look you get when your garden includes flowers of varying shapes and sizes.

Vibrant Visions

Of course, it is never required that you limit your fun with annuals to enhancing your landscape. As you will see in the following pages, annual flowers can be put to work in some very special ways—in pots, as cut flowers, as butterfly magnets, and as reseeding wildflowers. Once you get acquainted with the good growing techniques described in Chapter 3, there is no limit to the beauty you can create with these forgiving plants.

Don't wait for a special occasion to bring your garden flowers inside. Tall ageratum and trachymene make fine filler flowers for arrangements, and frequent cutting helps keep the outdoor plants in bloom, too.

The more you grow flowers, the more uses you will find for gray-leafed dusty miller. It cools down any company it keeps, and is always smashing near pink or blue.

ANNUAL GARDEN PLANS

Annuals occupy special places in our hearts, and you can also use them to create special places in your yard. You may already be dreaming of beautiful garden scenes painted with annuals for the special ecological niches your property has to offer—the sunny side of your deck, a neglected side yard or perhaps the cool shadows of a large shade tree. By choosing the best plants and using special techniques to grow them, you can create distinctive garden areas that will become a treasure trove of color and fun.

In the garden and planting plans that follow, we take annual flowers beyond their typical landscaping uses. The emphasis here is on using different groups of annuals to compose highly focused gardens for specific purposes.

Finding Your Focus

How can you use annuals to bring more pleasure to your day-to-day life? Whether you've been gardening for a month or a lifetime, this is a worthy question to ask yourself at the beginning of each new season. In case you need a little help answering such a weighty question, see if you can recognize important parts of yourself in the following descriptions.

Home-Centered

Do you take special delight in decorating your home? Is the appearance of your home an important source of personal pride? If so, you are sure to find special satisfaction in container gardening (pages 30 and 31) and growing cut flowers (pages 32 and 33).

Creative Artist

Do you love to make crafts? Are you an artist at heart? Don't let a season pass without making at least one unique container bouquet

Yellow strawflowers, pale pink acroclinium (a type of strawflower) and blue statice provide color and texture in crafts made with dried flowers. You can wait until winter to turn dried flowers into unique crafts.

(page 31) and planting flowers that can be dried to make indoor arrangements or pressed pictures (pages 36 and 37). And of course you'll need plenty of fresh cut flowers too (pages 32 and 33).

Stressed Out

Do you work long hours and seek peace and tranquillity in your garden? One of the best places to recharge yourself is a shade garden (pages 34 and 35) . Besides the natural allure of a cool oasis of shade, shade gardens often need less watering and weeding than flower gardens in the sun.

Pretty flowers are the perfect accompaniment to big vegetables in this raised-bed garden. Add herbs or even strawberries if you like. Annuals go with everything!

Nature Watcher

Does seeing a flock of goldfinches feeding on bachelor button or sunflower seeds make your day? Are you fascinated by flittering butterflies? If you have enough space, try growing annuals as semi-wildflowers in a natural area (pages 40 and 41). Even a small garden can accommodate a few special annuals that attract butterflies (pages 38 and 39).

Light-textured annuals help mask the foundation of a low house, without impeding easy entry. Here purple and yellow pansies, pink and red schizanthus, and luminous dusty miller work together beautifully.

Sometimes garden visitors are as interesting as the flowers you grow. Butterflies, hummingbirds and numerous types of bees are naturally attracted to colorful annual flowers.

PORTABLE ANNUALS IN POTS

You can add colorful accents to any part of your landscape by growing annual flowers in containers. Whether you use container-grown annuals to accent your entryways or to dramatize your deck, there is much fun to be had with pot-grown summer flowers.

Always choose large containers at least 12 inches in diameter that have drainage holes in the bottom. Bigger is better because large containers hold water longer than small ones. When buying window boxes, look for models that can be fitted with inexpensive plastic liners. As the seasons change, you can create your masterpieces in the liners and then slip them into permanently installed boxes.

To give lightweight pots extra weight (a plus in windy places or when pots are placed near where people and pets come and go), place an inch of small stones in the bottom of the pots. Then fill the containers with a good-quality potting soil, and add your plants. Your containers will look more lush and full if you set plants a little closer together than you would in beds. When you finish planting, drench the containers thoroughly. Wait an hour, and drench them again.

White sweet alyssum, violet blue lobelia and pink geraniums fill an old stone trough. In heavy containers, it's fine to reuse potting soil 2 or 3 times if you refresh it each time you replant.

Creating Container Bouquets

Half barrels and other large containers often can accommodate several different annuals—a great opportunity to explore the interplay of the plants' textures and forms. There are no rules on how many different plants you can add to a "container bouquet," but three is a good plan for beginners. One time-tested strategy is to work with one upright annual (like geranium or lisianthus), another with a soft, mounding form (ageratum, petunia), and a third with a very fine texture and cascading growth habit (bacopa, lobelia, sweet alyssum). Use white flowers or bits of luminous gray dusty miller to infuse your compositions with light and help offset potential color clashes among the other flowers.

Growing annuals in pots is fast and rewarding. It will take only minutes to marry these white nierembergias with variegated ivy—creating a masterpiece that will dazzle all summer long.

Fragrant heliotrope gets a deep drink. Other annuals in this container garden include zinnias with bacopa, ageratum with melampodium, and plenty of rich purple lobelia.

Well-Fed Flowers

As the weather gets warmer and your plants grow larger, they will need lots of water and fertilizer. To gauge their need for water, get into the habit of feeling the weight of your pots and baskets. If they feel very light you can conclude that they are quite dry, while containers that feel heavy can wait longer for water. Check your containers daily in hot weather, especially if you are growing plants with high water requirements, such as coleus and impatiens.

Constant watering leaches nutrients from the soil, so plants in pots need frequent feeding. Add a small amount of organic fertilizer or timed-release fertilizer to the potting soil at planting time, and then top-dress the pots with another light feeding about 6 weeks later. If plants seem to need more nutrients, you can feed them every 2 weeks with a soluble liquid fertilizer. If you have a number of container-grown plants to feed, consider buying a hose-end fertilizer applicator that automatically mixes fertilizer into the water when you turn on the faucet.

Tips for Better Baskets

Planning to accessorize your entryway or outdoor living area with graceful hanging baskets? Besides looking for plants with a cascading growth habit, here are some other things to consider when choosing and using hanging baskets.

- **Get the light right.** If the site is sunny and hot, try fan flower or sanvitalia. Brachychome and bacopa like mostly sun and a slight bit of shade. A half day of sun is perfect for browallia or fuchsia. Coleus and impatiens need only a little sun to thrive.

- **Hang `em low.** Except for fuchsia, which looks good viewed from below, most basket-grown annuals look best when hung just above eye level. Use short sections of chain to adjust the height of your hanging baskets.

Unlikely candidates sometimes make smashing companions in window boxes and other large containers. Here nasturtiums emerge supreme among pink geraniums, blue fan flower, and sprigs of ivy and aster.

- **Watch the wind.** Strong gusts can tear a basket from a hook and leave you with a massive mess. If you live in a windy area, place baskets in sheltered spots against walls or fences.

TWENTY TOP ANNUALS FOR CONTAINERS

Containers restrict the roots of plants, which often causes them to grow smaller than usual. The following annuals seldom have this problem, and often grow as well in containers as they do in the ground.

ageratum	sweet alyssum
bacopa	verbena
brachychome	vinca
browallia	
coleus	
dusty miller	
fan flower	
fuchsia	
geranium	
heliotrope	
impatiens	
lisianthus	
lobelia	
nierembergia	
pansy	
petunia	
sanvitalia	

Want a no-fail flower for containers? Choose petunias in any shade of pink. Routine watering and feeding will keep them in bloom from planting until frost—no green thumb required.

AN ANNUAL CUTTING GARDEN

When you bring flowers indoors to enjoy, you see things that you might never notice in the garden. The details of your favorite flowers become even more beautiful and exciting when you can study them up close, at eye level, whether they are part of an elaborate arrangement on your mantel or stuck in a jelly jar in your kitchen window.

To enjoy your annuals as cut flowers, you can grow them in a special backyard bed, plant them in a row of your vegetable garden, or simply gather them from your front yard flower beds. Most of the best flowers for cutting need plenty of sun to develop long, straight stems and big blooms, but they are no more difficult to please than other annuals.

Choice Cuts

Plan for a long season of bloom by growing annuals that bloom at different times. Besides providing plenty of flowers to cut, growing different flowers helps keep your arrangements seasonal and interesting—sweet peas and bachelor buttons in spring, celosias and sunflowers in summer, and gomphrena and strawflowers in late summer and fall. Choose colors that work

A beautiful arrangement of flowers brings the magic of the garden indoors for days of enjoyment. Use plenty of greenery to give your flower arrangements structure and depth.

Who can sleep when a sunny breakfast nook is ready and waiting, complete with full spikes of celosia? The vibrant colors will hold in containers, or can be cut for larger arrangements.

well with your indoor décor. Include hues that match your interiors and brighter shades that provide riveting contrast. Light and bright colors are often more useful than very dark shades, which often get lost in dim indoor lighting.

Your flower-arranging possibilities will be endless if your cutting garden includes a wide range of flower forms. For example, you might use flowers that produce rounded umbels, such as ammi or trachymene, to frame the large daisy-shaped blossoms of calendula or zinnias. Flowers with a spiking form are valuable for giving arrangements strong structure. Also include soft-textured "filler" flowers such as tall ageratum and statice in your cutting garden. With all flowers grown primarily for cutting, choose tall varieties that have long stems rather than compact dwarf types.

Patience does indeed have its rewards, as you will find with lisianthus. This beautiful cut flower is slow, yet not difficult, to grow. To save time, start with stocky container-grown plants in spring.

Cut flowers need fresh, clean water. To keep the water in your arrangements from being fouled with bacteria, remove all leaves that will be under water in the vase, and change the water often.

25 FINE ANNUALS FOR CUTTING

Almost any annual will last in a vase for a day or two, but these have the best staying power in indoor arrangements. If the water level in a container of cut flowers drops overnight, it's a sign that the stems are still taking up water— the one talent needed by all good cut flowers.

ageratum*	gomphrena	sweet pea
ammi	grasses	trachymene
aster	larkspur	zinnia*
bachelor button	nicotiana	
bells of Ireland	salvia	
black-eyed Susan	scabiosa	
calendula*	snapdragon*	
celosia*	statice	
cobbity daisy	stocks	
euphorbia	strawflowers	
foxglove	sunflower	

*choose tall or long-stemmed varieties

The most willing of all annual flowers for cutting, zinnias produce more blossoms the more you cut them. Blossoms last longest in arrangements when they are gathered when freshly opened.

The Kindest Cuts

Harvesting blossoms is actually good for many annual flowers in that it forces them to develop additional bud-bearing stems instead of expending energy nurturing seeds. Most flowers last longest in a vase if you cut them the day that they open. With flowers that grow on spiking stems, like snapdragons and salvia, cut stems when half of the blossoms along the spike have opened.

Use a sharp knife or pruning shears to cut blossoms early in the morning, when the flowers are well rested from a day in the sun and the petals are full of water. Immediately place the stems in a deep vessel of water and move them to a cool, dark place until you are ready to arrange them. It's important to pinch or strip off all of the leaves that will be below the water level in the vase. If left intact the low leaves will quickly rot and foul the water. Groom and arrange the stems out of strong sunlight, in a place where you can make a mess. Once an arrangement is complete, change the water every day or so to make the blooms last as long as possible.

Collecting Containers

Most of the cut flowers you grow in your yard will have stems only about 10 to 12 inches long, and they will not look right if you put them in tall, narrow bud vases intended for long-stemmed roses. As a general guideline, flower arrangements look best if the container is less than half as high as the length of the tallest stems. So, with homegrown cut flowers, you will probably find that low containers are more useful and versatile than very tall ones.

Collect bottles, jars with narrow mouths, and small pitchers and vases with varying types of finishes. Elegant crystal or clear glass containers are ideal for arrangements of a single type of flower, but with mixed arrangements it's often best to hide the stems in a solid-colored container.

If you're generous by nature (as gardeners tend to be), rescue promising-looking jars or plastic bottles from your recycling bin. When you want to share a bouquet, you can dress up something as plain as a soft drink bottle by wrapping it with tissue paper tied with a piece or raffia or ribbon.

To provide the right scale for homegrown cut flowers, collect containers that are not very tall. Low pitchers and other squat containers are best for flowers with short stems.

ESSENTIAL ANNUALS FOR SHADE

A moss-covered wall includes planting pockets for annuals that thrive under low light. Impatiens and wax begonia (with its eye-catching bronze leaves) work great here.

Give plants elbow room. Crowded plants shade each other from the side, which can make them stretched out and leggy. In shady sites it's better to give plants extra space than to plant them too close together.

Beating the Competition

Large shade trees dominate the sky, and they often rule the soil too. Use a spading fork to find spaces between thick surface roots where you can amend the soil and plant flowers. Tree roots also rob the soil of moisture and nutrients, so you may need to fertilize and water plants in your shade garden frequently. In some sites, you may find that light rain showers barely moisten the soil under trees since the leaves block the rain before it touches the ground. Soaker hoses that slowly weep moisture to the ground below are an easy way to deliver needed moisture to the root zones of your plants.

Most flowers grow best in bright sun, but people gravitate toward comparatively cool pockets of shade. You can use selected annuals to bring color and interest to parts of your landscape that are in shadow provided the site is not darkened by shade at all times.

Annual flowers that grow well in shade bloom best in partial shade. Partial shade means that the site gets 3 to 4 hours of sun each day or that it receives dappled sun as light filters through high tree limbs overhead.

If the shady spot where you want to grow flowers gets less than 3 hours of bright light each day, you may be able to increase available light by pruning low limbs from nearby trees. Raising the canopy of branches so that the site

gets what is called high shade also improves air circulation—an added benefit for the health of your plants. Another smart strategy is to grow some shade-loving flowers in containers, and move them from a bright spot to your shaded area when they are in full bloom so you can better enjoy their company.

Because shady places are naturally dark, they are great places to use flowers that bloom in light colors. When choosing colors, use as much white as you dare, especially near decks or patios that are often used at night. Pale pink or yellow flowers are welcome too, as are plants with light-colored foliage, such as chartreuse green coleus. To make the most of brighter colors, grow them in the company of white or pale pink flowers. For example, you might mix purple torenia with white impatiens or edge a bed of mixed coleus with pink wax begonia.

This robust hanging basket thrives on morning sun, with filtered shade the rest of the day. Plants include geraniums, violas, wax begonias and a few sprigs of pink lantana.

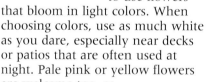

Combining Annuals and Bulbs

When trees shed their leaves in the fall, there is suddenly more sun than there was before. Perennial spring-flowering bulbs that return year after year, such as daffodils, tulips, and hyacinths work well where the sun shines brightly only until late spring.

Place a spreading annual in the middle of a circle of spring-flowering bulbs. While the bulb foliage ripens, the annual flower will help hide it from view.

With a little planning, you can grow annuals among your bulbs during every season of the year. As you plant new bulbs in the fall, set hardy pansies and violas over and between the bulbs. Another trick is to arrange bulbs in circles, leaving a 10- to 12-inch space inside each ring of bulbs. In spring, pop an impatiens or other shade-tolerant annual into the middle of the circle. It will hide the fading bulb foliage, which must be left in place if the bulbs are to bloom well year after year.

FIFTEEN FINE ANNUALS FOR SHADE

asarina	impatiens
bacopa	lobelia
begonia, wax	mimulus
begonia, tuberous	nicotiana
browallia	pansy and viola
coleus	torenia
forget-me-not	touch-me-not
foxglove	

Impatiens need constant water more than they need constant light. Filtered sun, or a few hours of morning or afternoon sun, is plenty enough to please them.

Willing Reseeders

If you are patient by nature and don't mind giving your plants a few extra weeks towards the end of the season to nurture mature seeds, several shade-loving annuals will reseed themselves in hospitable spots. Dainty blue forget-me-nots (*Myosotis*) sprout in late summer and fall and bloom the following spring. Summer-blooming touch-me-not will reseed too, as will nicotiana. You may also see seedlings of pansy and impatiens in your shade garden, but they may be the offspring of hybrid parents. If so, the seedlings may not have the size, color and vigor of the previous generation.

Where plenty of moisture is available in shady spots, use water-lovers such as impatiens or fuchsia. The small blue groundcover plants in this garden are fragrant violets (Viola odorata).

A fine foliage plant for shade, coleus can be found in a rainbow of colors and patterns. Leaf texture varies too, and ranges from flat and refined to extremely frilly or finely cut.

Shade Garden Tips

Especially if your shade garden is small, it's important to add plenty of small details to transform it into a cool oasis of color. Here are three ways to design a spectacular garden in the shade.

- **Think texture.** In addition to the textural combinations of foliage and flowers, enrich your shade garden with other textures. Cover the ground with a bark mulch. Pave walkways with pebbles or stone. Mask the bases of trees with evergreen groundcovers.

- **Add depth.** Use plants of varying heights, and create slight changes in elevation with low stone walls.

- **Get wet.** A small water feature becomes an instant focal point in any shade garden. Add a small fountain or a few fish to make it even more fun.

Fuchsias, impatiens and wax begonias are joined by large-flowered tuberous begonias by a shady waterfall. Constant moisture is needed to maintain a good cover of moss like this one.

EVERLASTING ANNUALS

Strawflowers including acroclinium (left) and helichrysum (right) are among the most beloved of all dried flowers. Protected from extreme humidity, they will keep their good looks indefinitely.

Nigella flowers are pretty in the garden or the vase, and the plants' mature seedheads make good dried material too. You also can gather attractive wild grasses or weeds to use as dried flowers.

One of the easiest ways to surround yourself with beautiful flowers year-round is to include everlasting annuals in your garden. These are flowers that retain their forms and colors after they are dried. Everlastings can do this because their showy petals are not really petals at all. Instead, they are papery bracts, or in some cases, calyxes, which contain much less moisture than true petals. After they are cut and brought indoors to dry in a warm, dark place, many everlasting flowers keep their good looks for years.

In the garden, everlastings are every bit as beautiful as other flowers, so it's fine to feature them in mixed flower beds or a cutting garden. All everlastings are sun lovers, and you will harvest the most blooms if you grow them in fertile soil that has been amended with organic matter. It's a happy coincidence that everlasting annuals often can get by on less water than other annuals. In fact, dry conditions near harvest time often enhance the staying power of the blossoms.

In addition to collecting and drying delicate blossoms, don't over-look decorative seedpods such as those produced by nigella and poppy, or feathery plumes of amaranth or celosia. They will come in handy on the gray winter day when you decide to create a refreshing wreath or arrangement from flowers and seeds gathered months before.

Pretty Pressed Flowers

Numerous small flowers such as pansies and brachychome can be dried via the process called pressing. You can use a flower press, or simply arrange leaves and blossoms between sheets of waxed paper and place them between the pages of a heavy telephone directory for several weeks. When they are completely dried, gently glue them onto greeting cards, arrange them on a piece of mat board and frame them, or use them to decorate homemade candles or decoupage items.

If you have access to a color copy machine, you might enjoy making collages of leaves and small blossoms by a more modern method. Arrange any flat flowers and leaves on the glass bed of the machine, and press go. Photocopied flowers don't have the antique look of those that are pressed to dry, but it's a fast and fun project that fascinates children of all ages.

Months after they are cut, helichrysum blossoms still look fresh from the garden. When dried, the petals are as stiff as straw, hence the common name of strawflowers.

Pansies, ammi and numerous other flowers are simple to dry in a flower press or heavy phone book. After drying, glue the blossoms onto note cards for a lovely personal touch, or imbed them in homemade candles.

Drying Everlastings, Step-by-Step

1 Most everlasting flowers are best picked when the blossoms are about halfway open. With flowers that form spikes and open gradually from the bottom to the top (such as bells of Ireland and blue salvia), wait until at least two-thirds of the flowers are open. Choose perfect blossoms that have not been damaged by wind, water or insects.

2 Harvest when the flowers are completely dry. Late morning, after the dew has dried, is the best time. Cut all flowers with long stems attached, even if you must remove a few buds along with the blossoms (buds often dry well too). Gather more material than you think you will need. Blossoms shrink a little as they dry, and the best dried flower crafts and arrangements are packed with plenty of blossoms.

3 Strip off all of the leaves from each stem; they slow the drying process and can host molds and mildews. Sort your flowers into small bunches of 10 to 12 stems, and secure the ends with rubber bands. Very large stems that tend to bend, such as amaranth and bells of Ireland, are best dried singly. Hang the stems or bunches upside down from nails or pegs (a bent paper clip inserted into the rubber band makes a great hanging hook). To save space, use clothespins to clip three small bunches to a wire clothes hanger.

4 Hang the prepared stems in a warm, well-ventilated place that does not receive strong sunlight. A garage, storage room, or closet is better than a stuffy attic, where conditions may be too hot. Use a small fan if necessary to keep the air circulating freely. Under good conditions, your flowers should be thoroughly dry in 1 to 2 weeks.

5 Store your dried flowers in airtight boxes. To simplify storage, you can use brown florist tape to bind together small bunches of slender flowers such as gomphrena. When you make a wreath or arrangement, use the bundle the same way you'd use a single stem in an arrangement of fresh flowers.

Bells of Ireland are easy to grow and fun to dry. Expect the stems and bracts to become slightly distorted as they dry. You can trim away unsightly parts when you're ready to use the dried stems.

To make your dried flowers smell as good as they look, infuse your homegrown potpourri mixture with a few drops of essential oil. Avoid synthetic scents if you are prone to allergies.

Make Your Own Potpourri

Collect dried blossoms that break or shatter and put them aside in a large jar to use as base for homemade potpourri. Also collect and dry blossoms and petals from other flowers removed during routine deadheading, including calendula, cosmos, marigold, verbena and roses. Transform your collected dried material into potpourri by scenting small batches with essential oils of your choice. After adding the oils, let the mixture infuse in a closed jar for at least a week.

TEN TOP EVERLASTING ANNUALS

amaranth	poppy seedpods
bachelor button	nigella
bells of Ireland	statice
blue salvia	strawflowers
celosia	
gomphrena	

Like most other dried flowers, the "blossoms" of statice aren't flowers at all— they are papery bracts that enclose a tiny flower. The flower is long gone by the time the bracts begin to dry.

ANNUALS FOR BUTTERFLIES

The part of the zinnia that butterflies crave is the fringe of tiny yellow flowers in the center of each blossom.

You can expect to see lots of butterflies in any sunny garden planted with annual flowers, but butterflies like some flowers better than others. The preferred flowers offer two things every butterfly wants—a secure place to stand or perch and a good supply of fresh nectar that the butterfly can reach with its proboscis—a retractable hollow tongue through which it sips nectar, fruit juices, or water.

The best butterfly flowers excel in both ways. Flat flowers make great landing pads for butterflies, so butterflies often visit cosmos, Mexican sunflower and zinnia. The tiny florets in the centers of these flowers hold nectar. Butterflies find it easier to reach the nectar in simple single flowers like these than in frilly blossoms that are packed with petals.

Yet not all great butterfly flowers are flat. Heliotrope, lantana and verbena produce flower clusters in which new florets appear every day, each one with a fresh supply of nectar. Footing on such flowers can be slippery for winged visitors, but butterflies are determined creatures. They will try and try again until they learn how to approach a new flower that's rich with nectar. Once they master the maneuver, they will return to that species repeatedly until the nectar is gone.

All butterflies spend their juvenile stage as plant-eating caterpillars, but they seldom eat garden flowers. Instead, various species prefer weeds, wildflowers, trees and members of the carrot family as host plants for their larvae. Adult butterflies seek out these host plants when they are ready to lay their eggs. So, you can enjoy numerous butterflies in your garden without worrying that their young will nibble your plants down to nubs.

Butterflies can never get enough of lantana. New florets typically offer the best supply of nectar, so they are the ones that get the most attention from monarchs and other winged visitors.

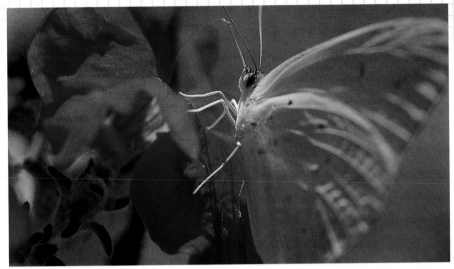

Like a built-in drinking straw, butterflies use their proboscis to sip nectar from flowers with deep throats, such as this petunia.

BEST ANNUALS FOR BUTTERFLIES AND MOTHS

cosmos	Mexican sunflower
four o'clock	moonflower
heliotrope	nicotiana
impatiens	pentas
lantana	verbena
marigold, French	zinnia

Visitors after Dark

Butterflies are most active during warm, sunny days because they rely on the sun's warmth to enable them to fly. Things are different for many moths, which fly at night and hide themselves away during the day. Several annuals are especially attractive to moths, including moonflower, nicotiana and four o'-clocks. It is no accident that these flowers also have fragrances that become more intense after the sun goes down. The flowers' fragrances help attract the moths, which might not otherwise find the flowers under cloak of darkness. Sit quietly near these flowers at dusk to catch the moths in action.

Right at dusk, hawk moths appear to gather nectar from night-blooming moonvine. Also look for them if you grow other night bloomers such as nicotiana or four o'clock.

A Puddle in the Sun

Butterflies need water, but they like to drink in situations where they won't get their wings wet. Male butterflies in particular like to gather in puddles of damp mud in warm, sunny places. You can create a scene for these sipping parties by fashioning a special butterfly puddle near your garden. Excavate 3 inches of soil from a spot about 18 inches wide, and place a sheet of black plastic in the bottom. Refill the basin with a mixture of stones, soil, and sticks, and add water every few days to keep it moist. Arrange flat rocks around the edges. Besides using the puddle for drinking up water rich with dissolved salts and minerals, butterflies may use the rocks for basking in the sun.

Make a Tempting Treat

If you want to identify the butterflies in your garden by species, get a good field guide and whip up this special butterfly smoothie. Butterflies often move too fast for you to study their markings when they're working flowers, but they tend to linger over a low dish of this sweet butterfly treat. Be sure to place sponges or small balls of crumpled chicken wire in the dish so the butterflies will have a place to stand while they sip the mixture.

Play It Safe

To make your garden a highly hospitable place to butterflies, it's important to limit the use of pesticides to absolute emergencies. If you decide that you must use an insecticide or fungicide in your garden, immediately cover the treated plants with an old sheet or piece of rowcover to keep butterflies and other beneficial insects from accidentally poisoning themselves.

The most successful butterfly gardens have flowers in bloom at all times. That way, butterflies always find a satisfying source of flower nectar when they stop.

Butterfly Treat

1 overripe banana, mashed (you can substitute peaches, pears or other soft fruits)
1 T. molasses
1 T. sugar
$\frac{1}{2}$ cup stale beer
$\frac{1}{2}$ cup apple juice
$\frac{1}{2}$ cup water

Mix ingredients together in a blender until smooth. Pour into a shallow pan, and place a clean, damp sponge into the mixture. Place in a sunny spot, preferably on a pedestal or small table so that it is raised up to flower height.

GOING NATURAL WITH ANNUALS

To be successful with wildflowers, you need only find flowers that like your climate and soil. Naturally, vibrant orange California poppies are mainstays in the West, their native home.

A number of annuals have the cast-iron constitutions needed to thrive in half-wild, minimally culti-vated areas. You can use these vigor-ous annuals to paint your property with large swaths of seasonal color, or mix them up to create a magical wildflower meadow.

The challenge in growing annuals in large swaths—or a natural meadow—is finding species that like your soil. The annuals listed here grow in a wide range of soils, but you will probably find that some thrive while others sulk—even if you carefully work fertilizer into the soil prior to planting. Experiment to find species that prosper in the site you have provided.

Compared to popular hybrid an-nuals like petunias and impatiens, most of the annuals suitable for nat-ural areas have short, 4- to 6-week bloom times. Because of this, it is more practical to plant them in concentrated drifts, with like species planted together, than to attempt a mixed meadow. By fol-lowing a drift design, you can mow down indi-vidual species when they pass their prime and possibly replant the area with an-other annual.

If you use an-nuals to turn a natural area into a colorful meadow, pay close atten-tion to proper planting times and sow seeds of different species when they are most likely to germinate and grow. The lists here are sorted into seasonal groups to simplify this process. To add more flowers to a meadow that is already established, use a hoe to scratch open patches of soil, then plant the open spaces with seeds.

Planting Half-Wild Annuals

To grow annuals in a natural area you will need to cultivate the soil be-fore planting seeds, but you need not dig too deeply. Deep cultivation often aggravates problems with weeds. Cultivate primarily to mix in pre-plant fertilizer and to expose a plant-ing surface of roughly crumbled soil. Then broadcast the seed and walk over the area to push the seeds into the soil. If you plant just before rain is expected, the rain will help settle seeds in crevices, so walking over the area may not be necessary.

Weeds will almost certainly sprout in any natural area, and some weeds make acceptable wild-flowers. Still, it's important to sub-due weeds that are so large and numerous that they smother out your flowers. If weeding by hand is impractical and your worst weed problem is crabgrass, you can try using a special postemergence her-bicide called Ornamec™ that kills grasses but not flowers. Do not, however, use a crabgrass preventer when preparing the site for plant-ing. It can stop germination of flower seeds the same way it in-hibits the germination of crabgrass.

Even if you begin with a mixture of different colors, over several seasons many flowers that reseed will revert to a primary color with slight variations in hue. Cosmos will become pink, bachelor buttons blue.

HALF-HARDY ANNUALS

Sow these flowers about 2 weeks before your last expected frost, while the soil is cool.

calendula   gaillardia
cosmos bipinnatus   phlox

If you're not sure that a favorite annual flower will reseed on its own, gather some seeds and store them in an airtight container. Seeds often fare better in storage than in nature.

Stock Up on Seeds

Several excellent mail-order companies sell seeds of these half-wild annuals in bulk. You will need to buy enough seeds for an initial planting, but after that you can easily harvest more than enough seeds for planting the following year. All of the annuals listed here are strong seed producers, and they will reseed themselves when conditions are good. However, reseeding of any annual is never guaranteed, so it's wise to go to the small trouble of gathering ripe seeds. See pages 57-58 for information on harvesting and storing seeds.

When to Mow?

It's time to mow down annuals when they stop blooming and their leaves start to wither. If you're still collecting seeds, use a scythe or machete to cut down whole plants, and pile them in a sunny spot to dry. You can go back in a few days to gather the dried seeds.

Use a mower or string trimmer to cut off remaining vegetation close to the ground, and rake it up. You can now plant more flowers provided there's enough time left in the growing season. Or, switch to a cover crop that will improve the soil and thus benefit your next crop of flowers. Buckwheat is a choice cover crop to sow in summer, when the soil is warm. Various clovers make excellent cover crops for cool weather.

Although it is often not a strong reseeder, cosmos thrives in a wide range of climates and soils. It can be sown in fall where winters are mild, or in spring in other areas.

A strong native wildflower, gaillardia (called blanket flower) is at home in wildflower meadows, small display beds or in a mixed border. It's among the best of all flowers at reseeding itself.

Delicate corn poppies grow from surprisingly tough plants. In many sites corn poppies reseed themselves with ease, but it's always a good idea to gather some seeds for sowing by hand in fall or early spring.

HOT WEATHER ANNUALS

Sow these flowers after danger of frost has passed. In long-season areas, a second planting in mid-summer will provide welcome color in the fall.

coreopsis   Mexican sunflower
cosmos sulphureus   sunflower

❧ CHAPTER 3 ❧
GROWING ANNUALS
The care and feeding of annual flowers from seed to bloom, and back to seed again.

While it's true that annuals are among the simplest and easiest flowers you can grow, you still have to know the individual plants you're dealing with, and give them what they need to promote the blooms and color you desire. From where you plant to how you plant to how you treat your soil, it takes some knowledge to grow annuals effectively and beautifully. Here's that know-how.

Raised beds look good, and they improve drainage, which benefits plants. Like other annuals, cosmos and purple lobelia respond to superior growing conditions well, covering themselves with blossoms.

Do-it-yourself soil test kits give you a good approximate reading of the major nutrients in your soil, as well as its pH.

Few plants are as easy to grow as are annual flowers. They want nothing more than to bloom, often for weeks or even months at a time. Getting the most flower power from your annuals is a small challenge, but it is a challenge just the same. And, as with all garden plants, your long-term success begins with the soil.

Because annuals are planted anew every year, they are fine plants to grow in soil that is in the early stages of improvement. With rare exceptions, most soils need to be dug and amended several times, over several seasons, to bring them into peak condition. But even if you begin with hard compacted clay or featherweight porous sand, gradually adding organic matter to your soil will make it much more hospitable to plants.

Creating high-quality soil for annual flowers is usually a simple matter of digging in a 2-inch layer of compost, leaf mold, peat moss, rotted manure, or inexpensive potting soil each time you renovate a bed. Organic soil amendments like these improve the soil's texture and drainage. They also improve the effectiveness of fertilizers, and the proof is in the growing. Compared to plants grown in poor, unimproved soil, annuals grown in rich, well-aerated soil show such superior vigor that they almost appear to be different plants.

Sweet peas cling to support with curling tendrils, so they are good candidates for a loose-string trellis attached to tall stakes. As the vines become taller, you can gradually add more tiers of string.

With an adequate foundation in the soil, there is no limit to the fun you can have growing annual flowers. In this chapter, you will learn how to grow annuals from seeds, pick up tips on handling bedding plants, and explore the fine points of fertilizing and grooming these heavy-blooming flowers. Armed with this information, you will be ready to embark on new adventures every season as you try new annuals in your garden or invite old favorites to return year after year.

Incorporate organic matter into the soil to improve its drainage and texture, which makes it more hospitable to plant roots. Do this once a year and your soil will become better and better.

Tremendously winter-hardy and always willing to reseed, old-fashioned blue forget-me-nots are ideal annuals to naturalize in partial shade.

GROWING ANNUALS FROM SEED

One of the special pleasures of late winter is getting a head start on spring by starting seeds indoors. Many interesting annuals are hard to find as bedding plants, or you may want to grow a dozen or more plants in a particular color. But seed starting is not limited to spring. In summer and fall, you can gear up for the "second season" by starting ornamental kale, pansies, foxglove, and other hardy plants indoors. On hot summer days, seeded containers kept outdoors can be impossible to keep moist.

Turning a tabletop into a seedling nursery is easily done with the help of suitable containers, growing medium, and supplemental light. For containers, simply clean and reuse the cellpacks commercial growers use to grow bedding plants. Other good seedling containers include peat pots, small plastic cups with drainage holes punched in the bottoms, or deep trays saved from fresh produce or convenience foods. Or, you can sow entire flats with seeds if you want to grow a large number of the same plant. All containers used to grow seedlings should be at least 2 inches deep to accommodate the plants' fast-growing roots. They must have drainage holes too.

What you put in the containers is more important than the containers themselves. Potting soils used for starting seeds are not really soils at all, and are more properly described as soil-less mixes. In place of soil, these products are made up primarily of either milled sphagnum peat moss or vermiculite—both very fine, soft-textured substances that will not form a crust over emerging seeds. Labels vary from one product to another, but most bags of soil-less mix do claim to be great for starting seeds.

Before planting seeds, fill containers to the top with

Make up your own planting mix or use potting soil straight from the bag. Be sure to mix materials together well before filling pots or seedling containers.

soil-less mix and dampen them thoroughly. Prepare markers that will identify the flowers you are planting, and get ready to sow.

Seeds will be more likely to stay at the proper planting depth if you moisten the planting medium before sowing seeds. Lay seeds on the surface and then push them into the mixture with a stick or pencil.

After seeds are planted, use a fine mist of water to keep the soil's surface slightly moist at all times. Avoid a strong stream of water, which may make the seeds float toward the surface.

Annual flower seeds come in many shapes and sizes. Clockwise starting from bottom left, note the differences between impatiens, bachelor button, snapdragon, nasturtium, zinnia, sweet alyssum, and marigold and cosmos in the center. Very small seeds are often coated to make them easier to handle, as has been done here with the snapdragon seeds.

Conditioning Seeds

Most seeds of annual flowers can be planted in moist soil-less mix straight from the packet, but some need special treatment to help them germinate. Some gardeners like to refrigerate all flower seeds for a few days before sowing them. Chilling is most beneficial to cool-season plants that are sown while the weather is warm, such as foxglove, pansy, and ornamental cabbage and kale, but it will not hurt any flower seeds. The logic behind this practice is that chilling gives the seeds the impression that winter has suddenly turned to spring, the season for sprouting.

Large, hard seeds such as abelmoschus, hyacinth bean, sweet peas and nasturtiums will germinate faster if you soak them overnight in warm water before planting them. Place the seeds you want to plant in a clean container, cover with an inch or more of warm water, and allow them to sit at room temperature until the next day.

Some seeds that have very hard seedcoats sprout much faster if you nick the dry seeds with a sharp knife or abrade them with a steel file. The objective of this process, called scarification, is to make deep scratches in the seed-coat. These scratches help the seeds soak up water and make it easier for the seed to break open when the sprout is ready to emerge. Some annual seeds that benefit from scarification include cup and saucer vine, moonvine and morning glory.

Some seeds have such thick coats that they absorb moisture better if they are abraded with a knife, steel file or coarse sandpaper. This is called scarification.

Planting Depth

The standard guideline for seed planting, which is to bury seeds about three times as deep as the seed is wide, will serve you well with most flower seeds that are larger than a pinhead. But the seeds of many annuals are smaller than this, and the smaller the seed, the more likely it is to respond well to surface planting.

Planting tiny seeds by barely pressing them into the surface of containers filled with moist soil-less mix has two advantages. First, the seeds are exposed to light, and light acts as a germination trigger for some species. And later, when the seeds germinate, they are in no danger of being buried so deeply that the sprouts face a difficult struggle making it through a cover of soil to life-giving light.

To keep surface-sown seeds constantly moist, commercial growers use elaborate mist systems that moisten such seeds several times a day. For gardeners it's more practical to enclose planted containers in loose plastic bags until the first green sprouts appear.

Some of the more challenging annual seeds need shallow or surface sowing and dark conditions to germinate well. For these flowers, enclose the planted containers in a brown paper bag or place them in a dark cabinet or closet for a few days. Check them often after the fourth day, because you will need to move them to good light promptly after germination begins.

To keep seeded containers constantly moist, enclosed them loosely in a plastic bag or cover the surface with a piece of plastic. Remove the covers as soon as the first seeds sprout.

Large seeds with hard seedcoats benefit from being soaked in warm water overnight before planting.

If you tend to lose track of time, use an auto-matic timer to turn your plant lights on and off. Stretched out, leggy growth is a sign that seedlings need more light.

When the roots of seedlings are kept warm, they often grow faster and stronger. If you use a heating cable or other heat source for this pur-pose, turn it on during the day and off at night.

Promoting Strong Germination

To simulate the brightness of the sun, buy a fluorescent grow light that can be suspended above the plants and kept on 10 to 12 hours a day. Ideally, the light should be adjustable

so you can keep it about 2 inches higher than the tops of the plants. Special bulbs made for growing plants emit a very intense spectrum of light, but they do cost more than stan-dard bulbs. You can save money by building your own fixture and buying the bulbs separately. An inexpensive automatic timer is also a good investment, especially if you are often away from home.

Besides helping seedlings grow, the light will provide a little supplemental heat. Young seedlings often grow faster if their roots are kept a few degrees warmer than room temper-ature. Special heating cables are

sold to provide bottom heat to seeded flats, or you can rig up your own using a small heating pad set on its lowest setting. But instead of placing damp containers directly on a heating pad, set 2 short wood boards on bricks or books, slide the heating pad into the space below the boards, and place your seedlings on the boards.

Thinning and Transplanting

Frequently more seeds will sprout than should be allowed to grow in a small container. To ease crowding, use tweezers to pull out all but two seedlings in each 2-inch-wide container. You also can use cuticle scissors to clip off un-wanted seedlings at the soil line.

If you have planted a mixture of colors of a certain annual, be care-ful not to thin out only the smallest seedlings. Flower color is often as-sociated with seedling vigor in an-nual flowers, so it's important to thin out an even distribution of small, medium, and large-sized seedlings to make sure you end up with a nice mix of colors.

You also can replant crowded seedlings as soon as they show their first true leaf. This process, called pricking out, calls for pa-tience and steady hands, but it is not difficult to do.

Pricking Out

1 Lifting or squeezing from the bottom, remove the clump of seedlings from their container.

2 Lay the clump on its side and tap the roots gently to nudge the soil from the roots.

3 Pick up a seedling by gently grasping a seedling leaf. Do not touch the main stem or roots except to give them gentle support.

4 Gently replant seedling into a new con-tainer filled with lightly dampened soil-less mix. Water well. Protect the replanted seedlings from strong light for 2 days.

Fertilizing Seedlings

Seeds contain sufficient nutrients to energize newly germinated seedlings, but because soil-less mixes contain little, if any, plant food, it's important to start feeding your seedlings as soon as they show one true leaf. The simplest method is to use a soluble fertilizer mixed with water at half the rate recommended on the label. Many organic gardeners use fish emulsion fertilizer for this purpose, but other water-soluble fertilizers work well too. For best results, mix a small amount of fertilizer with the water each time you moisten the soil. To avoid spilling, use a squeeze bottle to deliver "rich water" to your seedlings. Wait until you set your plants out to switch to a more convenient granular or powdered plant food (see page 53).

After seedlings show shapely true leaves, begin fertilizing with a water soluble fertilizer mixed at half strength. Water the soil rather than the leaves, which are best kept dry.

Hardening Off

Whether you grow your own seedlings or adopt them in six-packs, the process of moving young plants outdoors is best done gradually over a period of about 2 weeks. This process, called hardening off, helps stems to toughen, lets leaves become accustomed to the effects of full-strength sun, and forces roots to adapt to fluctuating day and night temperatures. You do not need to wait until your homegrown seedlings are as large as those sold as bedding plants to harden them off. As indoor growing space becomes crowded, it's fine to start hardening off your most cold hardy seedlings when they have as few as 4 to 6 leaves. After hardening off, you can keep them in a protected place outdoors until you are ready to plant them.

The classic way to harden off seedlings is to use a cold frame, which is basically a wood box with a glass or translucent lid, set on the ground. However, any place where the seedlings will get good light and be protected from strong winds will do, including plastic-covered tunnels, an enclosure made from bales of hay, or near a warm south-facing wall of your house.

The important thing is to harden off seedlings gradually. Leave them outdoors for only an hour or two the first day, then a half day, and finally all day by the end of the first week. The second week, allow seedlings to stay outdoors day and night unless the weather is very cold or windy. By this time the plants should be tough enough to transplant whenever you are ready.

Until weather conditions are right for planting, keep seedlings in a cold frame or other protected place. Remove covers on bright sunny days to let excess heat escape.

Direct Seeding

Annuals with fragile or brittle roots such as poppies and larkspur are so easily damaged that the gentlest of transplanting operations leaves them weak. The solution is to sow the seeds where the plants are to grow. You can also direct-sow bachelor buttons, nasturtiums, sunflowers, zinnias and many other annuals to save time and unnecessary trouble. Among annual flowers, most of the best candidates for direct seedling have medium- to large-sized seeds.

Direct seeding is simple if you have soft, loamy soil, but it can be a challenge if your soil type is clay. Because clay soil often forms a hard crust over germinating seeds, it is best to first blanket the planting site with an inch of compost or peaty potting soil—the next best thing to starting seeds indoors. Plant seeds directly into this medium and keep them constantly moist. For the first 3 to 4 days after planting, you can place an old blanket or boards over the seeded site to help keep the soil damp at all times. Remove the cover at the first sign that green sprouts are trying to push themselves through to the surface.

Until you learn what various seedlings look like, sow seed in a recognizable pattern such as parallel lines, zigzags or overlapping circles. Unless heavy rain rearranges the placement of the seeds, the pattern will make it easy to distinguish between flower seedlings and weeds.

If too many seedlings appear, thin them to proper spacing gradually. Should some seedlings pop up in odd places, you can move them

In loose, porous soil, direct seeding is a simple matter of placing seeds in a shallow furrow and covering them up. Plant twice as many seeds as you really need, and thin them to proper spacing a few weeks later. It's much better to have too many seedlings than too few.

To thin crowded seedlings, pull them out roots and all. Use tweezers if needed to thin closely spaced plants. If the roots of adjoining plants become damaged as you thin, use sharp scissors to cut off the unwanted ones at the soil line.

by using a tablespoon to lift both the seedling and the ball of soil beneath it. Slip the little plant into its new site without shattering the root ball, and water well. As extra insurance, it's a good idea to shade transplanted seedlings with a small box or upside-down flowerpot for a day or two after they are moved.

DIRECT-SEED IN SEASON

Here are the best times to plant annuals that grow well when direct-seeded:

- **Late Winter:** Hardy annuals including bachelor button, larkspur, poppies and sweet peas. In mild winter areas, these flowers can be planted in the fall.

Bachelor button seedlings withstand cold weather, so they can be planted in fall in many areas. They reseed well, too, and the seeds are goldfinch favorites.

Cosmos are such energetic germinators that there is little point in starting them in containers. Simply sow them where you want them to grow from early spring to early summer.

- **Early Spring:** Cool-season annuals such as ammi, bells of Ireland, black-eyed Susan, calendula, cosmos, gaillardia and sweet alyssum.

- **Mid-spring to Early Summer:** Tender annuals like abelmoschus, coreopsis, hyacinth bean, lavatera, marigold, melampodium, Mexican sunflower, morning glory, sunflower, touch-me-not and zinnia.

Direct seed zinnias where you want them to grow, and look for plenty of volunteer plants in subsequent seasons. Should you find yourself with too many seedlings, they are easy to dig and move.

WORKING WITH BEDDING PLANTS

Bedding plants that already show a bloom or two make it easy to choose colors that you find appealing. Select plants that appear young and vigorous, and set them out as promptly as possible.

If seedlings are too tall and leggy, pinch them back after transplanting. Within a few weeks they will develop new stems that are stronger and stockier than the ones you removed.

their root problems right away. To do this, turn the plant upside down, squeeze the roots out of the container, and use your fingers to tease apart the bottom third of the root mass. Frequently you will need to break some roots to spread them, but this is necessary violence. Left in a tight spiral, the roots may never spread out into surrounding soil, which results in skimpy, short-lived plants.

After transplanting to larger pots or to the garden, pinch off any old blossoms as well as stems that may have been twisted or broken. Then thoroughly soak the plants. In very bright sunny weather, it's a good idea to shade plants for a few days after setting them out, especially if they have lost a fair number of roots.

Buying the Big Ones

Flowers that have a spreading habit will sprawl into a tangled mess when confined to cellpacks, so they are typically sold in 4-, 6-, or even 8-inch-wide pots. Although they are more costly, buying a large specimen of fan flower or fuchsia or browallia may be a good move. Many sprawling plants can be propagated from stem cuttings (see page 52), so you can snip off a few tips, root them, and quickly increase your supply of plants. Plants sold in large containers tend to have extensive root systems too.

In gardening, few things are as simple as picking up a cellpack or two of bedding plants and popping them into the ground. The greenhouse growers who raise the plants control temperature, light and fertilizer very closely to produce high-quality plants that grow vigorously once you set them free in your garden.

Should you buy large plants or small ones? Those already in bloom or others just showing their first buds? Although most shoppers choose plants already in flower, bedding plants that have already produced several blooms are less desirable because of their advanced age. Confined to a small cellpack, many annuals are held back by matted, compacted roots if they wait too long on the shelf.

However, bedding plants showing their first one or two blooms are perfectly adoptable if you remedy

Gently loosen the roots of seedlings after you remove them from containers, and spread those roots out as you set the plants in the soil. This helps plants develop the extensive root systems needed to support strong flowering.

Combining bedding plants into a container bouquet is easy and fun. In containers, choose colors and textures the same way you would if you were arranging annuals in an outdoor bed.

PROPAGATING CUTTINGS

Coleus is the easiest annual to propagate from stem cuttings. Cuttings are so willing to develop roots that they will do so when kept in plain water.

Growing new plants by rooting stem cuttings is fun, and it's much easier with some annuals than with others. The best candidates for vegetative propagation include coleus, geranium, impatiens, lantana, Persian shield and ornamental sweet potato. If you are careful (and lucky), you can also root stem cuttings of bacopa, wax begonia, browallia, dusty miller, fan flower, fuchsia, heliotrope and mimulus.

Some of these plants only can be propagated from cuttings, but with others you have a choice between rooting cuttings or starting seeds. The biggest advantage to cuttings over seeds is time. You can grow a new plant from a cutting fast, in only 4 to 6 weeks, which is about half the time it takes to grow a new plant from seed.

Smart Sticking

Stem cuttings root best in a warm, humid environment where there is good light, but out of strong sun. You can "stick" cuttings indoors, or work outdoors in a shady, sheltered spot. The most versatile rooting medium is a half-and-half mixture of peat moss and clean sand, but you can also use perlite, vermiculite, or sterile soil-less mix. Whatever medium you choose must be kept constantly moist.

Use a sharp knife to take 4-inch-long cuttings from stem tips that do not have flowers. Pinch off all of the leaves except the cluster on the tip of the stem, dip the end in rooting powder (sold at nurseries and garden centers), and "stick" the cutting 3 inches deep in a container or bed filled with rooting medium. Cover the cuttings with light-colored cloth if needed to protect them from strong sun. With luck, the cuttings will grow roots and be ready to transplant in about a month. To check to see if a cutting is ready, pull on it gently. Cuttings with roots will resist a moderate tug.

When rooting stem cuttings, keep in mind that not every cutting will "take." To allow for failure, set a few more cuttings to root than you actually plan to use.

To prepare a stem cutting for rooting, clip off blooms and buds along with all but 2 or 3 leaves near the tip. When roots develop, new stems should grow from the topmost nodes on the cutting.

Double Pot Propagation

Here is a tried and true method for rooting stem cuttings indoors in a bright room. Fill a large unglazed clay flowerpot half full of rooting medium. Plug the hole in the bottom of a small unglazed pot, and place it in the center of the larger one. Fill the space between the two pots with rooting medium, and dampen thoroughly. Fill the small pot with water, and set cuttings to root in the space between the pots.

Moisture from the small pot will keep the medium moist. If desired, erect a plastic tent over the cuttings to help maintain high humidity—an easy way to ensure a high rate of rooting success. Once the cuttings have rooted, lift and transplant them the same way you would handle seedlings grown from seed.

FERTILIZING ANNUAL FLOWERS

Coated timed-release fertilizer.

Annual flowers need a moderate supply of all three major plant nutrients to make good growth. These three nutrients are: nitrogen (N), which supports the development of new leaves and stems; phosphorous (P), which stimulates the growth of roots; and potassium (K), the nutrient that promotes flowering and

seed production. All fertilizers bear a 3-number rating on their label, called the guaranteed analysis, which tells you how much of each nutrient the product contains. High numbers, such as 13-13-13, indicate that the fertilizer is highly concentrated, while low numbers reflect a more modest supply of nutrients.

Organic fertilizers made from natural materials such as bone

Organic fertilizer.

Granular fertilizer with coated timed-release granules.

tions. Although it might seem simplest to use liquid fertilizers all along, this can be a time-consuming proposition compared to the ease of using solid fertilizers that provide nutrients over an extended period of time.

Using Fertilizers

1 To get plants off to a strong start, mix either an organic or a timed-release synthetic fertilizer into the soil before planting your flowers, including soil used to fill containers.

2 Six weeks later, you can give plants a little more fertilizer, but only if you think they need it. Always fertilize plants that are sheared back in midseason to stimulate new growth.

3 If plants appear yellowish or grow very slowly, you can check to see if they are starving by feeding them with a soluble liquid fertilizer. If you see darker leaves and eager new growth after three days, follow up with a light topdressing of granular or powdered fertilizer, or continue using a liquid every week to 10 days.

CHECK YOUR pH

Plants cannot make full use of the fertilizer you provide if the soil has an extremely high or low pH, and the only way to know is the take some soil samples and check them out. You can use an inexpensive pH test kit, available at most garden centers, to see if the pH of your soil falls somewhere between 6.0 and 7.0—the very slightly acidic range that's preferred by most flowers. If your soil is too acidic (has a low pH), add lime to set things right. Lower the pH of alkaline soil by adding organic matter and small amounts of soil sulfur.

If you have a large yard with many planting areas, a pH meter with a metal probe is handy and reliable.

meal, fish meal and alfalfa meal often have a low analysis, yet they are tremendously popular among flower growers. As organic fertilizers decompose, they also provide small amounts of trace nutrients that can be taken up by plants. Flowers fed with organic fertilizers usually show steady robust growth, and there is little danger of spoiling them with fertilizer overload.

Overfertilizing can be a problem with synthetic fertilizers. To be on the safe side, choose a coated timed-release fertilizer intended for use on flowers, and follow label directions exactly. You will not need much. With very high analysis timed-release fertilizers such as 17-17-17, 1 pound of fertilizer can meet the needs of up to 50 plants.

Soluble liquid or powdered fertilizers meant to be mixed with water are handy and effective, especially if you are growing lots of annuals in containers. Their drawback is that their nutrients seldom stay in the soil for long; those not taken up by plants may be washed away by the next rain. Keep a soluble fertilizer on hand to use with seedlings, container plants, and for emergency situa-

Soluble fertilizer.

WATERING AND MULCH

Install a drip irrigation hose in your flower beds to save both time and water. For best appearance and maximum efficiency, cover drip lines with mulch.

Wise Watering

Annual flowers grow best in soil that stays lightly moist at all times, and some need more water than others. It's natural for plants to wilt slightly on hot summer days, but plants that remain wilted well into evening definitely need more water.

You can save yourself hours spent hand-watering by installing drip irrigation hoses in your flower beds. Attached to a faucet turned on at very low pressure, these hoses slowly weep water into the soil below.

Whatever your watering method, try to give your plants a deep soaking once a week rather than watering them lightly more often. Water that soaks only into the top 2 or 3 inches of soil encourages the development of surface roots, which dry out much faster than roots that stretch deep into the soil.

Well-Managed Mulch

An organic mulch of old leaves, straw, hay, pine needles or shredded bark will discourage weeds while keeping the soil cool and moist. Where winters are cold, wait until the soil has warmed in late spring to mulch your plants. In warmer climates where you want to keep the soil as cool as possible, mulching year-round is a sound practice. Always apply mulch after the soil below is thoroughly damp.

Beware of slugs setting up housekeeping in your mulch. These slimy creatures hide in mulch during the day and come out at night to eat holes in leaves. You can trap slugs with shallow containers of beer, hand-pick them, or use any of a number of other remedies from copper tape to pesticide baits.

An organic mulch of pine needles, shredded bark, cocoa shells or other natural material looks attractive, discourages weeds and goes a long way toward retaining soil moisture.

SUPPORTING YOUR PLANTS

All annual vines need a trellis on which to grow, and several tall flowers need to be staked or otherwise supported to help them stay upright. Plan ahead when you grow an annual that you know will need support, and install trellises or stakes at planting time if you can. Be as creative as you like when choosing support strategies for your annuals, and tailor your approach to the special needs of the plants.

Vertical Trellises for Vines

Because annual vines are short-lived plants, temporary trellises that can be put up or taken down quickly are best. Whenever it seems practical, see if you can find a way to weave a trellis with jute or lightweight cotton string. At the end of the season, you can cut down the string and the vine in one fell swoop and toss the whole thing in your compost heap. This saves you the tedious job of picking dead stems and tendrils from wire, chainlink fencing, or polyester netting.

When you use an annual vine as a free-standing upright feature in a bed, a teepee made of bamboo or wood is hard to beat. By design, a teepee-shaped trellis stands up well since the weight of the vine pushes in upon itself. Twining vines that twist around their support (asarina, black-eyed Susan vine, hyacinth bean, moonvine, morning glory) will run right up a teepee trellis, but to please the delicate tendrils of sweet peas you'll need to weave string horizontally between the stakes.

Staking Tall Flowers

As tall flowers come into bloom, the briefest of summer showers can cause them to list badly or to fall over entirely. Usually a combination of factors is involved: The flowers become heavy with rainwater, the soil softens, making it easy for roots to slide about, and then a gust of wind comes along and pushes the plant over.

When this happens to foxgloves, hollyhock, Mexican sunflower, and sunflower, the plants continue to bloom as best they can, but not with the grandeur of upright plants. Stake these annuals by pushing thin bamboo stakes into the ground that are as high as you think the plant will grow. Use twist ties to secure the main bud-bearing stems to the stake at 12-inch intervals.

Hollyhocks often need help staying upright, and benefit from being tied to thin stakes. Paint stakes green to better hide them from view.

Morning glories and other twining vines do well on any firm type of trellis made of wood, wire or even chainlink fence.

TIP

Horizontal Support for Lanky Plants

To keep cosmos, dahlia, lisianthus, large-flowered marigold, snapdragon, stocks and tall zinnias upright, let their main stems grow up through a wire arch, wire support hoops or a matrix of string woven between secure stakes. For best results, the horizontal trellis should be about 15 inches above the ground.

Support bushy plants that are prone to toppling over, such as tall snapdragons, with stakes and string. By the time the plants reach full size, foliage and flowers will hide the support structure from view.

GROOMING YOUR FLOWERS

Pinching off dead blossoms, called deadheading, is a crucial step for keeping annuals in bloom for the longest possible time. Pinch off tender stems with your fingers. You may need pruning shears for bigger jobs.

TIP **Handling Reseeders**

What about flowers that you want to reseed? Gather blooms or deadhead them for the first 2 to 3 weeks that the plants are in bloom, then let the flowers grow until they produce mature seeds. See page 57 for tips on how to tell when the seeds from your annual flowers are ripe.

Some annual flowers are called "self cleaning" because they do such a neat job of shedding their spent flowers. Impatiens and vinca are famous for this talent, which makes easy work of keeping the plants looking neat and well groomed. Ammi, larkspur, sunflower, and other annuals that bloom all at once also require little upkeep, but many long-blooming species benefit from deadheading or shearing back.

Deadheading

An annual flower's prime purpose in life is to produce seeds. So, when you come along with a sharp pair of pruning shears and nip off blossoms as soon as they lose their looks, the frustrated plant has no choice but to respond by making more flowers. Because deadheading (garden lingo for trimming off old flowers) stops the seed-making process in its tracks, it's a fundamental way to make annuals bloom as long and strong as possible.

When deadheading, cut stems off just above a place where it looks like a new bud-bearing stem is poised to emerge. These growing points, called nodes, quickly grow into leafy new stems. With plants that bear on spikes, you need not wait until the last blossom on the spike has opened. Instead, cut them off when the bottom half of the spike has begun to wither. If you clean off the spent blossoms, the rest of the spike may still be useful as a cut flower.

Shearing Back

It's not practical to deadhead species that produce hundreds of bud-bearing stems such as lobelia, nierembergia, or sweet alyssum. Instead, use hedge clippers, sheep shears, or a large pair of scissors to cut the plants back by about half their size in mid-summer. This process, called shearing back, is also used to stimulate new growth of tired browallia, fan flower, and petunia being grown in hanging baskets. After shearing back any annual flower, follow up with a fresh application of fertilizer and a deep drench of water.

Just as with most other plants, new stems emerge from growing points along the stems of annual flowers, called nodes. Overgrown annuals will make a quick comeback if you prune stems to just above a healthy node.

To promote the growth of new flowering stems on lobelia and other small-flowered annuals, shear them back by one-third their size in mid-summer, after a very heavy flush of flowers leaves them looking slightly ragged.

SAVING SEEDS

Gather seeds when blossoms are completely withered and begin to fall apart. With bachelor buttons, you will know seeds are ripe when finches and other birds appear to eat them.

27 EASY ANNUALS FOR SEED SAVERS

abelmoschus	celosia	marigold
amaranthus	cleome	melampodium
ammi	convolvulus	morning glory
bachelor button	cosmos	nigella
bells of Ireland	four o'clock	poppy
black-eyed Susan	gaillardia	scabiosa
black-eyed Susan vine	gomphrena	sunflower
calendula	hyacinth bean	sweet pea
coreopsis	larkspur	zinnia

When you save seeds from your favorite flowers, your garden becomes a much more personal place. Saving seeds is also a great way to keep your garden stocked with flowers that have proven that they like your climate, soil, and the level of care you are willing to provide.

Old-fashioned annuals in particular are happy to offer up a fresh crop of seeds each year, free for the small trouble of gathering and storing them. Many of these plants produce medium to large seeds that are easy to recognize, or, in the case of poppies, that are neatly packaged in their own containers.

Don't waste your time saving seeds from hybrid plants. Because of the way hybrids are created, their genetic makeup is so unstable that saving and replanting seeds often gives unpredictable results.

Selecting the Best Seeds

Do you want bachelor buttons in a certain color? Zinnias with flat, open flowers that attract butterflies? These objectives are easily accomplished by tagging individual plants with bits of string or twist ties, and saving seeds from those plants. Allow your selected plants to grow free and uncut until their blooms fade to shriveled tufts. For best seed quality, keep the plants adequately watered and fed to the very end.

Species vary in the time needed for a flower to produce mature seeds, so it may take some experience to learn the best time to gather the seeds. Generally speaking, blooms that are full of ripe seeds become loose and fragile, a necessary prelude to the process of shedding seeds into the ground below.

Harvesting and Storage

Collect seeds by snipping off whole mature flower heads into a shallow pan. Allow them to dry in a warm, well-ventilated place for a week or two, and then pulverize them with your hands. Mature seeds should fall into the bottom of the container; those less mature (and less likely to germinate) will remain attached to the flower. Discard the immature seeds along with the chaff, and pour the seeds into a clean jar or envelope. Store seeds in a cool, dark place until you are ready to plant them.

Where Are the Seeds?

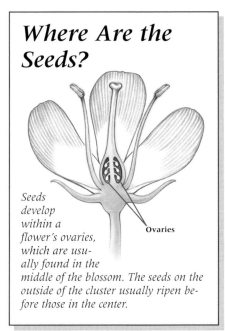

Seeds develop within a flower's ovaries, which are usually found in the middle of the blossom. The seeds on the outside of the cluster usually ripen before those in the center.

To gather thousands of seeds in seconds, collect whole ripe seedheads in a broad container. After a few days of drying, the seeds will knock loose easily, and you can store them in a dry, airtight container.

A willing producer of easily gathered seed, cosmos sulphureus *reseeds itself modestly in most climates. To be on the safe side, save and replant some seeds from year to year instead of depending on Mother Nature.*

RAMPANT RESEEDERS

When conditions are good, these annuals have a high potential for becoming weedy.

amaranth	gaillardia
cleome	melampodium
sulphur cosmos	morning glory
euphorbia	

Working with Reseeding Annuals

As long as you allow some faded flowers to remain in the garden until the seeds become ripe, numerous annual flowers will shed seeds that suddenly come to life when soil temperatures are conducive to germination. As you learn to recognize these seedlings, you may be amazed at how many annuals reseed themselves.

In the garden, the ability of annuals to reseed is both good and bad. The most prolific reseeders are so satisfied with the climate in which they are grown that they flower for a long period of time, producing thousands of seeds in the process. However, when they are too successful, otherwise wonderful annuals can become weeds.

Welcome Reseeders

You can save a lot of time not spent sowing seeds by inviting certain annuals to colonize your garden. Like magic, the seedlings will appear at just the right time in fall, winter or spring. The only special skill required is being able to recognize the seedlings so that you don't accidentally pull them up while weeding. After a few seasons you will come to know these good friends very well, and spotting them will not be a problem.

Don't be surprised if some of the seedlings appear in unexpected places, because wind and birds often scatter tiny flower seeds far from where the parent plants grew. If needed, you can lift and move misplaced seedlings with a large spoon, the same way you would move seedlings that are planted on purpose. As long as the soil around the roots is not disturbed and you water the plants after transplanting, most reseeding annuals easily accept a change of location.

Weedy Reseeders

Some annuals reseed so well that they may become unwelcome weeds! Aggressively pull out these seedlings when you see them to keep them from taking over your garden. When you find that a certain annual reseeds itself to the point of weediness, plant it only near grassy areas that are mowed often, or alongside concrete surfaces. Also make it a habit to clip off faded flowers before they can set seeds.

EASY RESEEDERS

These reseeding annuals are usually welcome in the garden.

abelmoschus	marigold
bachelor button	Mexican sunflower
black-eyed Susan	nicotiana
coreopsis	poppy
celosia	sweet alyssum
forget-me-not	touch-me-not
foxglove	verbena
impatiens	vinca
larkspur	zinnia

Morning glory is such a heavy reseeder (in southern areas) that it can become a serious weed. To keep seedlings from taking over your garden, grow this plant near lawn areas or hard surfaces where it cannot spread and gain a foothold.

WINTER PROTECTION

When planted in the fall, new varieties of hardy annual dianthus do not bloom during the winter. But they survive the cold easily and bloom heavily in the spring.

Depending on your climate, you may be able to grow at least some hardy annuals in your garden. But except in the very mild winter areas of Zones 9 and 10, hardy annuals need special care to ensure strong winter survival.

Where winters are cold, it's important to grow hardy annuals in well-drained sites that offer some protection from frigid winds, such as near south- or west-facing walls. South or west exposures also get more sun, which results in significantly warmer soil temperatures during the winter months.

The ability of hardy flowers such as forget-me-nots, hollyhocks, pansies and snapdragons to survive cold weather is strongly influenced by

how well-rooted they are when winter begins. So, setting plants out as early as possible (usually in late summer or early fall) can make a big difference with these plants.

Preventing Winter Damage

In all climates where freezes occur, the biggest enemy of hardy annual flowers is frost heaving. As the ground freezes and thaws, the expansion and contraction of the soil pushes plants up out of the ground. You can push the plants back down, but their roots are left damaged nonetheless. A mulch that moderates soil temperature will limit winter heaving. Any organic mulch is better than none, but light-textured pine needles or hay are the best materials for this job.

When applying winter mulch, avoid smothering the crown of the plant. If deprived of fresh air, larkspur and foxglove are particularly prone to rotting in winter. If an ice storm threatens, place a loose evergreen bough over these and

other minimally mulched plants. Remove the bough when open weather returns.

If you don't mind looking at a garden studded with plastic milk cartons all winter, by all means try nursing some hardy annuals through winter under milk carton cloches. Place them over young plants just before frosty weather commences, and mulch around the cloches to provide further insulation from cold. You also can put milk carton cloches to work in late winter. Protected under cloches, many hardy annuals can be set out a full month before the last expected frost.

Use evergreen boughs to create a loose mulch that will protect foxgloves and other hardy annuals from winter's heavy loads of ice and snow.

Tuck in pansies and other hardy annuals with a pine straw mulch after the soil turns cold. Use just enough to almost cover the plants.

HOW COLD WILL THEY GO?

Tolerance of cold winter weather is often difficult to predict, but the following hardy annuals are good candidates for growing from fall to spring.

Sometimes hardy to Zone 4:

English daisy
forget-me-not (*Myosotis*)
foxglove
pansy
poppy
snapdragon

Many pansies are hardy as far north as Zone 4. For maximum cold hardiness, plant them in early fall so they can grow plenty of roots before soil temperatures drop below 45°F.

Often hardy to Zone 7:

all listed above, and:
bachelor button
black-eyed Susan
dianthus
dusty miller

hollyhock
larkspur
nicotiana
nierembergia

PESTS AND DISEASES

Grasshoppers are often the most voracious eaters of annual flowers in the summer garden. Grasshoppers weaken plants and mar their beauty, but seldom stop them from blooming altogether.

Like all garden plants, annual flowers sometimes have problems with pests and diseases. The problems described here are the most common ones that affect annuals, and you will notice that they tend to occur within botanical family groups. This is because insects and disease microorganisms prefer specific host plants and their close relatives that share similar chemistry. The positive aspect of this situation is that a problem that strikes one type of flower is not likely to bother other, unrelated species. So, when you grow annuals, you can always have a successful garden by planting a diversity of species and emphasizing those that show superior health and vigor when grown in your garden.

Problems with Seedlings

Damping Off
Damping off is the name given to the disease process that causes seedlings to suddenly shrivel up and die. Several soil-borne fungi cause damping off by attacking tender roots and stems, causing them to rot. Using a sterile soil-less mix for starting seeds drastically reduces problems with damping off.

Salt Intolerance
Salt intolerance is a common reason why seedlings fail to thrive despite perfect care. Bells of Ireland, forget-me-not, salvia, and several other annuals respond to very low levels of salt in soil as though it were toxic. They stay alive, but show extremely slow growth. Set such seedlings out in the garden at the earliest possible time, because salt buildup is fast and continuous when plants are grown in containers.

Aphids are tiny sucking insects that weaken plants and may transmit diseases. Aphids are commonly seen on sweet peas, ornamental kale and cabbage, nicotiana, and a few other annual flowers.

Problems with Plants

Root Rot
Root rots are the most common reason why plants unexpectedly collapse and die. If you pull on a shriveled plant and it comes right up, it has succumbed to root rot. Several types of fungi that live in the soil cause root rot by attacking the roots and crowns of annual flowers, especially aster, larkspur, lobelia, pansy and vinca. Damage may be limited to individual plants, or might affect a large planting. Pull out affected plants, dig some good compost into the soil, and start over with a different flower.

Aphids
Aphids are tiny sucking insects that congregate on new stems and leaves in large numbers. First try spraying them with insecticidal soap (available at most garden centers).

If the aphids persist, move on to an all-purpose insecticide labeled for use on annual flowers.

Leaf-Eating Insects
Leaf-eating insects often chomp on annual flowers after the weather turns warm in early summer. You can hand-pick many of them, or simply tolerate light damage. If you decide to treat badly infested plants with an all-purpose insecticide, cover them with an old sheet or

piece of floating rowcover for 2 to 3 days after application to keep bees and butterflies from entering the treated area. Be especially alert to the following insects, which often appear in large numbers on their preferred host plants.

- **Japanese beetles** are strongly attracted to four o'clocks, hollyhock and lavatera, and often cause light to moderate damage on members of the morning glory family.

- **Blister beetles** feed in large groups, eating leaves of amaranth, calendula, statice and many other plants.

- **Grasshoppers** rarely meet a flower they don't like, and they often do like the very plants that other insects leave alone, such as marigolds. In a bad grasshopper year, pesticide baits are your best hope.

- **Slugs and snails** feed at night and hide in mulch and soil during the day. They make holes in leaves, and can seriously weaken plants if feeding is heavy. Mulch only when needed if you live in an area that is heavily infested. The easiest way to reduce slug populations is to trap them in shallow containers of beer set into the soil up to their rims. Attracted by the beer, slugs crawl inside and drown.

Leaf diseases

Leaf diseases are usually caused by fungi that manage to establish themselves in leaf tissues. Infection occurs when fungal spores land on damp leaves, germinate, and then proceed to kill growing cells. Humidity and heat often contribute to the problem, which is why many flowers "melt out" when hot, humid weather prevails. The meltdown is usually a result of one or more obscure leaf diseases, often in combination with various root rots.

Two specific leaf diseases affect specific annual flowers:

- **Powdery mildew** causes the leaves of black-eyed Susan, verbena, zinnia and a few other annuals to look as though they have been dusted with fine white powder. Older plants are at highest risk, and it's usually best to simply pull them out. Making use of resistant varieties minimizes problems with powdery mildew.

- **Rust** can be a devastating disease of hollyhocks. Leaf undersides show fuzzy deposits of cinnamon to orange deposits. If you catch the disease early, snip off affected leaves and dispose of them in the garbage. It is often useless to spray a seriously infected planting with a fungicide, but you can try. Or, pull out badly diseased plants and start over the next season with a resistant variety.

Nematodes

Nematodes are microscopic worms that live in the soil and parasitize plant roots. Affected plants look sick, grow very slowly, and stay thirsty all the time. It is not unusual for one bed to become infected, while others flower beds in different parts of your yard remain nematode free. The most common type, rootknot nematodes, are most prolific in sandy soils in warm climates with abundant rainfall. They are rare in cold climates where the ground freezes hard in winter. The most commonly affected annuals include dusty miller, pansies and zinnias, but numerous others are also at risk. You can confirm the presence of rootknot nematodes through a soil test or by checking the roots of plants for small knotlike nodules, or knots. For a flower gardener, the most practical way to control nematodes is to starve them out by planting lots of French marigolds, which nematodes abhor. They do a wonderful job when planted close together for 3 months or more.

Problems with Flowers

Blossoms that are misshapen are usually caused by stressful weather conditions. You may also notice that flower size tends to shrink the longer flowers are in bloom—a common sign that the plants are nearing exhaustion. When blossoms have many dark wet spots or shrivel into a damp mess, they may be infected with botrytis fungi. This disease comes and goes with damp weather, and often affects pansies, petunias and other flowers that grow close to the ground. Dry growing conditions usually cure the problem.

Japanese beetles eat numerous flowers, especially roses. Among annuals, you are most likely to see them on hollyhocks and four o'clocks.

‹ CHAPTER 4 ›

ANNUALS A TO Z

Old classics, new beauties and everything in between.

*T*he full power of annual flowers becomes crystal clear when you consider the almost endless variety of colors and shapes available, as well as the seasonal preferences, soil needs, moisture requirements and sun tolerances that various plants prefer. These 100 annuals should be more than enough to get you started or expand your repertoire … and even whet your appetite to search for more.

Viewed from above, dwarf cockscomb celosias make interesting garden subjects.

'Hopi Red Dye', a prince's feather type amaranth, produces good material for drying and dying.

There are good reasons why the 100 annuals listed here are also the ones you are most likely to grow in your garden. This group represents a balance of cool-season, warm-season and transitional annuals that can be used to fill any garden with color for the longest possible time. With few exceptions, either plants or seeds are easily obtained at garden centers or through mail-order companies. And, because there is no such thing as a perfect climate for flower gardening, we have included several selections that adapt to high heat, such as abelmoschus and ornamental sweet potato, along with cool climate favorites like fuchsia and schizanthus.

Some of these flowers are quite new to American gardens, but they are so remarkable that they deserve much wider use. If you live where summers are typically mild, you won't want to miss trying bacopa and cobbity

Morning glory.

Nasturtium.

'Snowflake' bacopa.

for decades, but there are many more annuals to explore should you ever run short of interesting possibilities. Because many of the newest, most heavy-flowering annuals are propagated from cuttings rather than from seed, you are more likely to find a good selection at a large garden center than in a seed catalog. But don't let those seed catalogs gather dust, either. One thing an annual gardener must never do is lose track of the wondrous fun of growing flowers from seeds.

daisies. In warmer climes, angelonia is simply astounding, and the same can be said of pentas and Persian shield.

Variety names are so important that each flower listed includes a discussion of remarkable or outstanding varieties, as well as varying species or types of particularly popular flowers like celosias, marigolds

and zinnias. You will also find plenty of planting ideas for all of these infinitely appealing annuals.

Growing the flowers described here will probably keep you busy

Touch-me-nots.

Fan flower.

ABELMOSCHUS

Abelmoschus moschatus, A. manihot

One glance at the blossoms of abelmoschus and you know you are looking at a member of the hibiscus family. A close cousin to okra and to perennial hibiscus, abelmoschus is a beautiful summer annual in climates that provide sufficient heat to satisfy its tropical nature. The plants produce a constant parade of flattened trumpet-shaped blossoms in red or pink from mid-summer onward, and they often reseed. Some other common names for this outstanding hot weather performer include sunset muskmallow and silk flower.

In the Garden

Because it can be planted in early summer, after conditions are too hot for many flowers, abelmoschus makes a fine successor to pansies, annual phlox, and other flowers that quickly melt away under hot, humid conditions. Abelmoschus needs full sun but is not picky about soil. If you use abelmoschus to replace heat-weary pansies or dianthus, you need only add a little fertilizer to the bed to make the sunset muskmallows happy. Plants normally grow about 18 inches tall and wide, but under excellent conditions they may grow a little larger.

How to Grow

Start seeds indoors in late spring, at about the time of your last frost, when most other seedlings have already been moved outside. Use cellpacks, peat pots or individual containers rather than flats. As soon as seedlings appear, move them outdoors to a warm, sunny spot, and make sure they don't dry out. Transplant to the garden as soon as a spot becomes available. Be careful with the roots, which are quite delicate. Space plants 14 inches apart, and mulch between them to retain soil moisture and deter weeds.

Expect slow growth at first. Abelmoschus plants need about 8 weeks after transplanting before they will begin blooming, but once they get started the show never stops. Individual flowers last only a day, and plants are quick to form green seedpods. Pinching the seedpods off every week or so keeps the plants intent on producing new flowers.

Abelmoschus blossom.

Selecting Varieties

Species names can be confusing and may include either of those listed above. Good variety names to look for include 'Pacific Scarlet' and 'Oriental Red' (both red with white centers), and 'Oriental Pink' and 'Mischief' (light shell pink with white centers).

Colorful Companions

You will find plenty of possibilities among other hot-natured annuals that share bloom time with abelmoschus. Mix or match pentas or lantana with the abelmoschus color you have chosen. Joseph's coat amaranth makes an arresting backdrop for abelmoschus.

Abelmoschus is a fine annual hibiscus for warm summer areas.

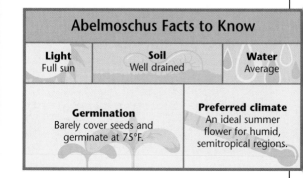

Abelmoschus Facts to Know

Light Full sun	**Soil** Well drained	**Water** Average
Germination Barely cover seeds and germinate at 75°F.		**Preferred climate** An ideal summer flower for humid, semitropical regions.

AGERATUM
Ageratum houstonianum

'Blue Horizon', a tall ageratum variety.

One of the few blue flowers that bloom well in hot weather, ageratum is deservedly popular in all areas where summers are long and warm. It also can be grown in more moderate climates, where it is often used to add a puff of blue to container bouquets and window boxes. Although blue is the most popular color, ageratums are also available in shades of pink and white.

In the Garden
Compact mounds of ageratum can be used to create two special effects in the garden or in containers. When grown with white or pink flowers, or with gray foliage plants like dusty miller, ageratum creates a cool oasis of soft-textured blue. When part-nered with bright orange or red flowers such as sulphur cosmos or zinnias, ageratum provides high contrast color in just the right measure. Ageratum usually grows best in full sun, but in hot summer climates the plants welcome a few hours of shade.

How to Grow
Ageratum seeds are tiny and grow slowly, so it is seldom worth the time and trouble to start your own seeds unless you are growing tall ageratum for cutting, which can be hard to find as bedding plants. Stocky plants of dwarf varieties are widely available in the spring.

Set plants out, 8 to 10 inches apart, at least 2 weeks after the last frost has passed, when the soil is warm. Mix a timed-release fertilizer into the soil around the plants, and water well. Add a light mulch to discourage weeds. Ageratum can take more crowded quarters in containers, but be sure to feed container-grown plants regularly with a soluble fertilizer.

For the remainder of the season the plants should need no additional care be-yond occasional watering during dry spells. Ageratum plants gradually gain size and usually do not become large mounds until quite late in the summer.

Selecting Varieties
At 30 inches, 'Blue Horizon' is much taller than varieties grown for bedding and makes an excellent cut flower. 'Blue Lagoon' is the classic marine blue of the species in compact dwarf form. 'Hawaii' hybrids are available in two shades of blue and white. Be careful with white ageratums, however, because the flowers turn an unsightly brown color as they pass their prime.

Colorful Companions
Thanks to its cool blue color and the unusual texture of the blooms, ageratum is a rare goes-with-everything annual. Use it to unify beds planted with several different flowers by placing puddles of ageratum near the front of the bed in a repetitive pattern.

Dwarf ageratum.

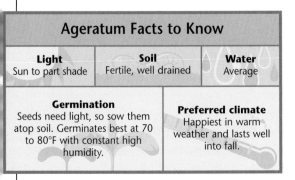
Ageratum Facts to Know

Light	Soil	Water
Sun to part shade	Fertile, well drained	Average

Germination	Preferred climate
Seeds need light, so sow them atop soil. Germinates best at 70 to 80°F with constant high humidity.	Happiest in warm weather and lasts well into fall.

AMARANTH

Amaranthus tricolor, A. caudatus, A. cruentus

Love-lies-bleeding, also called chenille plant.

The huge amaranth family includes ancient grain-producing plants, dreaded weeds and at least three treasured old flowers. The most widely grown one is *Amaranthus tricolor*, commonly known as Joseph's coat, fountain plant and summer poinsettia. This species is grown for the colorful leaves that appear on the tops of the plants just as they reach maturity. Like a fountain, the arching, curved-back leaves provide technicolor contrast with the ones below, and persist through the hottest part of summer.

If you don't care for the rather morose name of love-lies-bleeding, you can call *Amaranthus caudatus* by one of its other names: tassel flower, chenille plant or pendant amaranth. This is a tall, open plant with lackluster green leaves that give way to drooping fuzzy red seed clusters up to a foot long. The chenille "cords" can be used in flower arrangements both fresh and dried.

A third species sometimes grown in the rear of summer gardens is prince's feather (*A. cruentus*). This species grows very tall, to 6 feet or more, and produces large pointed plumes in red, tan or a mixture of colors. The plumes hold within them tens of thousands of edible seeds. You will be wise to gather the plumes for flower arrangements before the plants can shed seeds in the garden. This species has a high potential for becoming weedy just like its close cousin, redroot pigweed.

'Joseph's Coat' amaranth.

Amaranth Facts to Know		
Light Full sun to slight shade	**Soil** Well drained	**Water** Below average
Germination Start seeds indoors and germinate at 70°F or sow outside after frost danger has passed.		**Preferred climate** Tolerates extreme summer heat very well. Dies back after producing seeds.

'Hot Biscuits' amaranth.

How to Grow

All types of amaranth are very easy to grow. You can start seeds indoors 3 weeks before your last frost date and transplant them outdoors a month later, or simply sow the shiny seeds where you want them to grow as soon as the soil has warmed to about 60°F.

Germination rates are high. Selections that develop colorful foliage usually show some color in their stems, too, which makes them easy to differentiate from weeds.

Use only modest amounts of fertilizer when growing ornamental amaranth. As long as the plants get plenty of warm sun, the effect of a little nutritional stress is to deepen dark leaf colors. Plants respond to regular water by growing extra large and bushy, but they are also tremendously tolerant of drought.

Expect to see random holes in the leaves of your amaranth. June beetles and other night-flying beetles feed casually on amaranth leaves, and a number of other insects are likely to stop in for snacks as well. However, this damage is usually slight and does not affect the ultimate performance of the plants.

Stake plants to keep them upright if you live in a windy area. Install stakes when the plants are about 18 inches tall. With Joseph's coat, pinching off the little seed bundles when they form along the main stem will help the plants channel energy to the leaves.

In the Garden

Joseph's coat is sure to get attention wherever it is planted, and makes a good shrub substitute in underdeveloped landscapes. It is also useful grown here and there in the rose garden to provide color in mid-summer, when many roses take a break from blooming.

Love-lies-bleeding fits in well in an old-fashioned garden setting that can accommodate its 4-foot height. Plant two or three love-lies-bleeding plants together so they will grow into a shrubby mass at the edge or rear of the garden.

Prince's feather is best relegated to the back of a cutting garden or summer border, perhaps to fill in among tall sunflowers or Mexican sunflowers. These plants are so large and heavy of texture that they can knock a garden completely out of scale if not planted in just the right spot.

Grown in a pot, love-lies-bleeding makes an interesting accent plant. Place it where you can admire its strange form and rich color.

Selecting Varieties

You can choose your color scheme in *A. tricolor*. Selections sold by species name are highly variable, and may show red, yellow, cream or unique combinations of these colors in the "color" leaves at the tops of the plants. 'Aurora' has a creamy yellow crown atop green foliage, while 'Illumination' develops a dazzling sunburst of yellow and fuchsia over red-bronze lower leaves. 'Early Splendor' most closely resembles poinsettia, with bold red leaves covering the tops of mature green plants.

Variety names are rare for love-lies-bleeding. In recent years, a variety of prince's feather called 'Hot Biscuits' has gained popularity for its giant buff-brown seed spikes.

Colorful Companions

Many summer gardens are built around the hot colors of *A. tricolor*, a scene stealer in the warm months when it is at its prime. Lantana or plume celosia are excellent annuals that share amaranth's zeal for warm humid weather.

Sunflowers make great partners for most types of amaranth. Prince's feather in particular is so huge and ungainly that it must be accompanied by giant sunflowers, tithonia or other plants that play down its somewhat coarse presence. Try more refined, bushy types of sunflowers as companion plants for love-lies-bleeding, or bring in big pink or yellow zinnias. Love-lies-bleeding also can be placed at the rear of a bed with smaller yellow flowers such as melampodium or marigolds at its feet.

AMMI

Ammi majus

Also known as white lace flower, bishop's weed and white dill, ammi is an essential annual for flower arrangers. The blossoms also can be pressed or hung upside down to dry. Ammi's white rounded umbels resemble those of Queen Anne's lace, but the plants are much more refined, the flowers are pure snow white, and they shed much less pollen than Queen Anne's lace when used in a vase. Originally from South Africa, ammi prefers cool weather and will reseed in hospitable climates.

Ammi.

In the Garden

In full bloom, only three plants spaced 8 inches apart will form an airy cloud of white 3 to 4 feet tall and equally wide. You can also use individual plants, planted repetitively at even spacing, to bring unity to a complex border. Because of their size, color and light texture, ammi plants are excellent accents for the middle of a flower bed.

How to Grow

Start seeds indoors about a month before your last freeze, and set them out under cloches around the time of your last frost. Ammi plants grow slowly at first, and do not take off until they have more than a dozen celery-like leaves. Keep the plants mulched and watered until they burst into bloom in early summer. Ammi usually blooms for 4 to 6 weeks about 3 months after the plants are set out. Frequent cutting will prolong the blooming period.

Where nights stay cool through early summer, make a second sowing directly in the garden in late spring. Lengthening spring days encourage heavy flowering.

Ammi's rounded umbels enrich the garden with their texture, and they are great for cutting.

Selecting Varieties

Mail-order catalogs that emphasize good annuals for cutting usually sell ammi seeds. The 'Queen of Africa' variety has very long, stiff stems preferred by cut-flower growers. However, ammi seeds sold by species name are well worth planting and have a more relaxed presence in the garden.

Colorful Companions

Ammi softens the appearance of all flowers grown near it, and because of its size it is often planted near large perennials and shrubs. In many climates, spring-sown seedlings bloom at the same time as lilies and roses.

Clouds of airy ammi team up with larkspur.

Ammi Facts to Know		
Light Sun or light shade	**Soil** Well drained	**Water** Average
Germination Plant seeds 1/8 inch deep and germinate at 60°F. Move to strong light as soon as the seeds sprout.		**Preferred climate** Seedlings tolerate frosty nights if covered with cloches.

ANGELONIA

Angelonia angustifolia

Angelonia has been grown in American gardens only since 1995, but it has quickly become popular for its beauty and tolerance of persistent heat. A tropical snapdragon cousin from Central America, angelonia bears delicate purple, pink or white blossoms on upright spikes. It blooms continuously through the hottest part of summer, and is especially useful in warm climates where many other flowers suffer in mid-summer's heat.

In the Garden

Enjoy this tough flower as a feature plant in any sunny, well-drained spot. A few hours of shade are beneficial in very hot climates. Angelonia is actually a perennial, but it is reliably winter hardy only to Zone 8. Mature height is usually slightly more than 2 feet, but no staking is needed to keep the plants upright.

Angelonia in its ancestral purple color.

'Pandiana Pink' angelonia.

How to Grow

In mid to late spring, look for plants sold in 4- to 6-inch pots. These plants are grown from stem cuttings, so there is usually but one plant per pot. Set plants out at the same depth they grew in their containers, and water well. Continue to keep the soil constantly moist for 2 weeks. After that, the plants should be well established and able to tolerate high heat with routine watering.

Mix a small amount of balanced fertilizer into the soil prior to planting. Six weeks later, trim off old bloom spikes and give the plants a second light feeding. After trimming back, the plants often produce a number of bushy new stems. If desired, you can snip off 3- to 4-inch-long stem tips that have not yet produced flower buds and root them

indoors. Dip the cut end in rooting powder. Your new plants should be ready to harden off and transplant in about a month.

Selecting Varieties

Angelonia is a light purple flower that horticulturists insist on calling blue, hence variety names such as 'Blue Pacific' and 'Blue Angel'. Cultivars that bloom pink or white are not quite as vigorous or heavy flowering as those that bloom bluish-purple.

Colorful Companions

The best way to feature angelonia in a cool color scheme is to flank it with dusty miller or any white flower, such as white nierembergia or white narrow-leaf zinnias. Purple angelonia also pairs well with yellow French marigolds, yellow lantana or dwarf yellow zinnias.

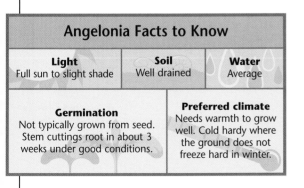

Angelonia Facts to Know		
Light Full sun to slight shade	**Soil** Well drained	**Water** Average
Germination Not typically grown from seed. Stem cuttings root in about 3 weeks under good conditions.	**Preferred climate** Needs warmth to grow well. Cold hardy where the ground does not freeze hard in winter.	

ASARINA

Asarina scandens

The velvety blossoms of asarina vine fit the dainty demeanor of its foliage. This vine can take some heat if it gets a good head start in cool spring weather.

This petite annual vine deserves much wider use. Also known as chickabiddy and climbing snapdragon, asarina features small snapdragon-type blooms in soft shades of pink and purple, with lighter contrasting throats. Asarina plants are willing growers yet less exuberant than other annual vines, so they are easy to fit into small spaces.

In the Garden

A loose climber of a vine, asarina does best on a woven trellis. You can make one using string or polyester netting, or simply let the vines scramble up a chainlink fence. To get good coverage of a chainlink fence, space plants no more than 10 inches apart. When grown in cool, fertile soil, asarina vines grow about 6 feet long. Hot weather has a dwarfing effect.

This vine also makes a wonderful addition to container bouquets planted in large containers. If allowed to do so, pot-grown plants will cascade over the side of large pots and then form a small skirt of greenery on the ground.

How to Grow

Start seeds indoors 8 to 10 weeks before your last spring frost. The seeds and seedlings are small, so it takes them several weeks to get going. Go ahead and set seedlings out when they are about 6 weeks old, even if they are still small. The seedlings are surprisingly hardy and will easily stand through light freezes provided they are protected with milk carton cloches.

Amend the soil with organic matter prior to planting, and mix in a standard application of any complete fertilizer. Add an organic mulch after the plants show vigorous new growth. Asarina likes cool, moist soil, so chopped weathered leaves or other mulches that lower soil temperatures are ideal.

To encourage the plants to bloom for the longest time possible, pinch off old flowers every two weeks.

Selecting Varieties

Several large mail-order companies sell asarina seeds. Mixtures such as

'Bright Jewel Mix' include purple, pink and white flowers. Individual colors are available in 'Mystic Pink' (light pink with pale yellow throats) and 'Joan Loraine' (purple with white throats). A closely related species commonly known as creeping gloxinia (*A. erubescens*) produces large lavender blossoms up to 3 inches long.

Colorful Companions

If you need a vertical accent plant for a cool color scheme, asarina is it. Asarina's colors blend especially well with those of torenia. White or pink wax begonias are a good choice for masking the base of this vine.

Asarina entwined on a chainlink fence.

Asarina Facts to Know		
Light Full sun to part shade	**Soil** Fertile, well drained	**Water** Average
Germination Press seeds into top of sterile soil-less mix and germinate at 65 to 70°F.		**Preferred climate** Grows vigorously in spring. Often survives winter in Zones 8 and 9.

ASTER, CHINA

Callistephus chinensis

Like their perennial cousins, annual asters bear outstanding cut flowers. When grown in soil that pleases them, asters grow into bushy plants that produce dozens of blooms. Asters bloom best during the second half of summer, when days are slowly becoming shorter. Cool fall weather further enhances this flower's staying power in the garden.

In the Garden

Grow asters in any sunny, well-drained spot, or enjoy the company of dwarf asters in pots. Color mixtures usually include soft shades of pink and purple that are fun to mix and match with other annuals. Asters grow best in cool weather, so you can set them out quite early in the season in most areas.

Double-flowered China asters make fine cut flowers.

How to Grow

Bedding plants are widely available in spring, or you can start your own seeds indoors of varieties you find especially appealing. Seedlings are ready to set out after 8 to 10 weeks. Whether purchased or home grown, asters will not bloom heavily until they are at least 4 months old.

If your soil is naturally deep and rich, do not add fertilizer before setting out asters. In poor soil, use only enough fertilizer to get plants off to a good start. Besides lean soil, asters need a near-neutral soil pH around 7.0. Mulch lightly between plants to maintain soil moisture and discourage weeds. Once

asters come into bloom, gather blossoms freely and snip off dead flowers. Asters respond to cutting by producing more blooms.

Should your plants become spindly and refuse to grow, the problem is likely to be fusarium wilt, a soil-borne disease that cannot be cured once infection has occurred. However, you may have better luck with a more resistant variety planted in a different place.

Selecting Varieties

Dwarf varieties grow to only 10 inches tall, but most full-sized annual asters grow 2 to 3 feet tall. Flower form also varies between flat daisies and big frilly pompoms. If you are willing to grow your own seedlings, check mail-order seed catalogs for seed mixtures that include a range of colors and flower types. If great cut flowers are your goal, 'Matsumono' is outstanding because of its long, stiff stems.

Colorful Companions

Because the bloom time of annual asters varies with climate, you may need to experiment with this flower to find suitable partners. Pink is always the strongest color in annual asters, so they are excellent anchor plants in a pink and yellow garden.

China aster.

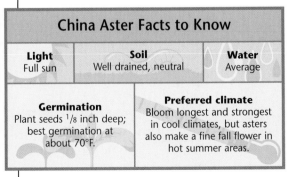

China Aster Facts to Know

Light	Soil	Water
Full sun	Well drained, neutral	Average

Germination	Preferred climate
Plant seeds 1/8 inch deep; best germination at about 70°F.	Bloom longest and strongest in cool climates, but asters also make a fine fall flower in hot summer areas.

BACHELOR BUTTON

Centaurea cyanus

Whether you call them bachelor buttons, cornflowers, or use the Scottish name of bluebonnets, you will love this easy annual. Bachelor buttons bloom for a long time, tolerate all kinds of weather, and can even be dried for winter arrangements. An ancient flower that has been planted in home gardens since Chaucer's time, bachelor buttons in their ancestral blue color were once used as a source of dye.

In the Garden

Bachelor buttons are 2- to 3-foot-tall upright plants that make a good backdrop for smaller dwarf flowers. Grow them in good sun, in soil that is not too rich or fertile. In Zones 6 through 9, sow seeds in fall for bloom from mid-spring to early summer. In northern gardens, plant bachelor buttons first thing in the spring and again in mid-summer for a repeat performance in the fall.

How to Grow

Bachelor buttons are energetic sprouters. Simply plant the seeds where you want them to grow, and go back a few weeks later and thin the seedlings to 10 inches apart. For heaviest flowering, bachelor buttons benefit from a period of cool weather while they are young.

To prolong the bloom period of your plants, either gather blossoms for indoor display or deadhead the plants weekly while they are in bloom. If you want your bachelor buttons to reseed, allow a few plants to stand in the garden until seeds are hard and ripe. Birds like the seeds too, but bachelor buttons reseed so well that even if you share the seeds with birds, you can expect to see numerous gray-green seedlings in future seasons. You can move volunteers that pop up in awkward places if you dig them with a clump of soil firmly packed around their roots.

Selecting Varieties

Blue is the strongest cornflower color, or you can plant mixtures that include pink, red, white and dark maroon. Expect unique hues and some bicolors if you let your

Bachelor buttons in mixed colors.

plants reseed. Dwarf varieties including 'Polka Dot' and 'Florence' grow only 18 inches tall. A slightly different species, sweet sultan (*Centaurea moschata*) is not as cold tolerant or heavy flowering as bachelor button, but sweet sultan blooms offer excellent fragrance.

Colorful Companions

Bachelor buttons are fine partners for poppies, calendulas, larkspur or sweet peas. For dramatic contrast, pair either dark maroon or deep blue bachelor buttons with dusty miller. Sow bachelor buttons freely in wildflower meadows. You can also plant them with cool-season cover crops such as crimson clover, Austrian winter pea or purple vetch.

True blue bachelor buttons.

Bachelor Button Facts to Know		
Light Full sun	**Soil** Adaptable	**Water** Average
Germination Refrigerate seeds for 2 days before planting ¼ inch deep. Germinates best at 65°F.		**Preferred climate** Seedlings are cold hardy to about 10°F.

BACOPA

Sutera cordata

'Lavender Showers' bacopa.

Bacopa is a fine new flower for little niches in the garden where you want to add something with fine texture but not a lot of color. The blossoms look like tiny white or almost-white snowflakes, but when combined with the small-leafed, spreading green foliage the effect is quite charming in both containers and beds.

In the Garden

Bacopa grows only 4 inches tall but can spread more than 12 inches wide. You can use bacopa as a flowering summer groundcover, as a broad edging for beds, or plant it in containers and window boxes. Well-drained soil with a gritty texture is ideal. Bacopa can adapt to both cool and warm weather, and it will grow in sun or half-day shade. The warmer your climate, the more the plants are likely to need shade. Too much sun and heat will cause bacopa to stop flowering, but it won't kill the plants.

How to Grow

Start with new purchased plants each spring. At garden centers you will find bacopa in 4-inch pots and pre-planted in hanging baskets. Although propagation of bacopa is subject to patent restrictions, you can make the most of your purchase by encouraging plants to multiply themselves, which they are quite willing to do. To help them along, set a plant in a sandy bed or broad container, weight a few leggy stems with stones to keep them in contact with the soil, and they will strike new roots immediately. Gently sever and dig the new plantlets as you need them elsewhere in your yard.

Drench plants with a complete liquid fertilizer about once a month, and water as needed to keep them from wilting. If plants become ragged, you can restore their good looks by trimming them back by half, fertilizing them and perhaps refreshing the soil a bit if they are growing in containers. Keep renovated plants in shade for at least a week to allow them their best opportunity at recovery.

Selecting Varieties

'Snowstorm' produces white flowers, and other varieties with 'Snow' names present slightly different color twists. This flower is constantly being improved for color and heavy flowering. Garden centers always offer the most up-to-date varieties.

Colorful Companions

Once you get to know bacopa, you will constantly find new ways to use it. Pair it with red geraniums in a window box. Combine it with blue fan flower in a hanging basket. Use it as a groundcover between widely spaced torenias in half-shaded beds. Especially in its neutral white color, bacopa goes with everything.

Bacopa is one of the few annuals you can use as a blooming groundcover.

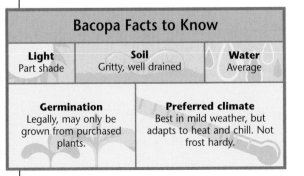

Bacopa Facts to Know		
Light Part shade	**Soil** Gritty, well drained	**Water** Average
Germination Legally, may only be grown from purchased plants.		**Preferred climate** Best in mild weather, but adapts to heat and chill. Not frost hardy.

BEGONIA, WAX

Begonia semperflorens

Adaptable and trouble free, wax begonias are outstanding in both beds and containers. They are at their best in partial shade, but can tolerate full sun provided they receive regular water. Small clusters of white, pink or red flowers with delicate yellow centers come on continuously all summer. Leaf color also varies with variety, and ranges from apple green to dark reddish bronze. Originally from Brazil, wax begonias tolerate hot weather well once they are established.

In the Garden

Wax begonia's strong natural uniformity makes it a fine choice for edging or for planting in beds where you want a neat, formal look. Most varieties grow into upright mounds only 6 to 10 inches tall. The rich hues of red-flowering varieties can easily be seen from a distance, while pink or white varieties have a quieter presence in the garden.

How to Grow

Buy bedding plants in spring from the extensive selection offered at most garden centers. Seeds started indoors in late winter take 3 months to grow into blooming plants. Transplant seedlings to the garden after the last frost has passed.

Before planting, enrich the soil with organic matter to improve its drainage and texture. If your soil is alkaline, use peat moss to nudge it toward a slightly acidic pH. Also work in a timed-release fertilizer or a rich soil amendment such as rotted manure. Wax begonias bloom best when they have a modest yet continuous supply of the major plant nutrients. Water as needed to keep the soil lightly moist. When growing wax begonias in containers, feed them with a liquid fertilizer. This is also a good annual to pot up and bring indoors in late fall, where they will continue to bloom for several weeks.

In beds, baskets or pots, wax begonias are non-stop bloomers.

Selecting Varieties

Choose plants with flower and leaf colors you like. For containers that will be seen up close, consider wax begonias with picotee coloring in which the white flower petals are edged with pink or red. Varieties with very large flowers do not have the strong uniformity of more common dwarf varieties, but they are fine choices for containers.

Colorful Companions

Pair bronze-leafed varieties with dusty miller or grow them near plants with yellow flowers or chartreuse foliage. Pink varieties fit easily into any color scheme that accents cool pastel colors. Regard white varieties with green leaves as neutrals, and use them to fill in bare spots in beds or containers.

Bronze-leafed wax begonias form a handsome edge.

Wax Begonia Facts to Know		
Light Full sun to half shade	**Soil** Well drained	**Water** Average
Germination Lightly press seeds into top of soil-less mix. Germination best in good light at 75°F.		**Preferred climate** Likes warm weather. Growth comes to a standstill when temperatures dip below 50°F.

BEGONIA, TUBEROUS
Begonia tuberhybrida

Tuberous begonias are fine flowers for baskets grown in moderate shade.

Tuberous begonias are among the most colorful summer flowers to grow in shade. Originally from Brazil, the plants are actual tender perennials that regrow anew from lens-shaped tubers. You can save and replant these tubers from year to year, or start with fresh tubers or seedlings each spring. Tuberous begonias are warm-season plants that cannot tolerate frost.

In the Garden

Tuberous begonias are most often grown in pots, baskets or window boxes, but you can also plant them in well-drained beds beneath trees. If tree roots prevent extensive digging, set the plants in 10-inch plastic nursery liners, set the pots in the ground up to their rims, and mulch to hide the pots.

How to Grow

To grow tuberous begonias from seed, plant the dust-sized seeds indoors in winter, and grow the plants on an east-facing windowsill until late spring. It is much faster to buy dormant roots or plants in spring than to handle seedlings.

To plant tubers, look for a small raised bud on one side and plant the tuber 1 inch deep with the bud side facing up. Use a peat-based potting mix amended with a little sand to aid in drainage for container-grown plants. Prepare beds by working in

Tuberous begonias grow from round, flattened, dormant roots.

plenty of peat moss or compost along with a timed-release fertilizer. Tuberous begonias like a slow, steady supply of fertilizer. Feed pot-grown plants weekly with a dilute liquid fertilizer, but be careful not to overwater the plants. Ideally, the soil should become almost dry between waterings.

Pinch back old flowering stems every few weeks to keep plants in bloom continuously. Let plants die down in late fall and harvest the flat, round tubers before the first freeze. Clip off stems and roots and allow them to dry at room temperature for a week. Store the tubers through winter packed in dry peat moss in a cool place where they will not freeze.

Selecting Varieties

Choose varieties based on flower color, which may be red, orange, yellow or white. A few new varieties have interesting reddish bronze leaves veined with green. For hanging baskets, look for naturally long-limbed varieties such as 'Hanging Sensations' or 'Illumination'.

Colorful Companions

A mixed planting of tuberous begonias under a shade tree needs no further embellishment beyond an attractive mulch of bark or pine needles. Dress up potted tuberous begonias planted in plain clay or plastic containers by slipping them into attractive brass planters.

Tuberous begonias.

Tuberous Begonia Facts to Know

Light	Soil	Water
Shade	Rich, moist	Above average

Germination	Preferred climate
Barely press seeds into top of soil-less mix. Germinates best at 70°F. Plant dormant tubers after nighttime temperatures average above 50°F.	Thrives in mild weather and may be stressed by high heat. Cannot tolerate frost.

BELLS OF IRELAND

Moluccella laevis

A cool-season annual from the eastern Mediterranean region, bells of Ireland gets its common name from the green bell-shaped bracts that surround its tiny white flowers. The bracts turn buff brown when dried and will last for years as everlastings. You can use stems in fresh flower arrangements too, or simply enjoy their unusual form and light fragrance in the garden.

In the Garden

Bells of Ireland is best grown in a sunny spot in the spring garden. Its apple green color and unusual form make it a fine foliage plant to work into a complex bed or border. The bushy plants produce long spiky stems up to 2 feet long studded with shell-shaped bells all at once in early summer. After the stems are harvested, the plants should be pulled up and replaced with something new.

How to Grow

Chill seeds in the refrigerator for a few days before sowing in containers 6 weeks before your last frost. Germination is often erratic, but the seedlings are easy to grow. They transplant best at a young age and easily survive light frosts when protected with milk carton cloches. Set seedlings at least 15 inches apart, and mulch to suppress weeds and keep the soil cool and moist. This is a fast-growing flower that benefits from rich, well-drained soil that has been amended with an organic or slow-release fertilizer.

Stems destined for use in fresh arrangements can be cut any time, but wait until the topmost bracts on a stem open to gather it for drying. Snip off all of the leaves, and hang the stems singly in a dry, airy place. Should the tips of the stems shrivel and curl, simply cut them off after the stems are dry.

Selecting Varieties

Seeds are sold exclusively by species or common name. You can save seeds from outstanding plants to develop a strain that is especially well suited to your garden.

Colorful Companions

The bushy growth habit and light green color of bells of Ireland make it a fine plant to combine with spring-blooming perennials or bulbs. Among annuals, group this flower with other cool-season flowers that bloom in early summer, such as ammi, dianthus, poppies and larkspur.

Bells of Ireland.

Bells of Ireland Facts to Know		
Light Full sun	**Soil** Rich, well drained	**Water** Average
Germination Barely cover seeds with soil-less mix and germinate at 60°F.		**Preferred climate** Prefers cool spring weather. Seedlings tolerate light frosts.

BLACK-EYED SUSAN

Rudbeckia hirta

This native wildflower comes into its glory when grown in a garden. As with many native plants, there are numerous strains of black-eyed Susan, which vary in appearance and cold hardiness. All of them reseed. Depending on your climate, you may find that black-eyed Susan is a short-lived perennial, a biennial that reseeds itself each fall, or a hardy annual that appears first thing in spring. Once you learn to recognize the hairy seedlings and become familiar with how this flower likes to grow in your climate, it will stay with you forever.

The "eyes" of black-eyed Susans are typically a rich chocolate brown.

Black-eyed Susan.

In the Garden

A resolute sun lover, black-eyed Susan will grow in any well-drained soil. The soil's quality will be clearly reflected in the size and vigor of the plants. Space plants at least 12 inches apart when planting them in spring. Allow 18 inches between plants when planting them in the fall, because overwintered black-eyed Susans grow into very large plants that require extra space.

How to Grow

Direct-seed in fall to establish a resident population. You also can start seeds indoors in late winter and set the seedlings out under cloches a few weeks before your last frost. You can prolong the bloom time of this species by planting more seeds in spring, at about the time of your last frost. Spring-sown plants bloom in late summer, and are not as large as those grown from seed planted in fall. Water plants when young and during periods of severe drought.

Deadhead as needed to keep your plants looking neat, but always allow some blossoms to mature and shed seeds. From fall to spring, look for the hairy seedlings in odd places in the garden. Lift them from beneath with soil packed around their roots, and transplant them to where you want them to grow.

Selecting Varieties

This varied species includes named cultivars that are strongly perennial (such as large-flowered 'Indian Summer') and strains that bear flowers tinged with mahogany, often called gloriosa daisies. If you plant several packets of inexpensive seed sold by species name, you will likely see interesting variations in both flowers and plants. Save seeds from the plants you like best.

Colorful Companions

When in full bloom, black-eyed Susan steals the stage. Let large fall-sown plants fill corners or grow into a mound near a fence. The rather rough texture of the flowers and plants combines beautifully with delicate white ammi or lavender angelonia.

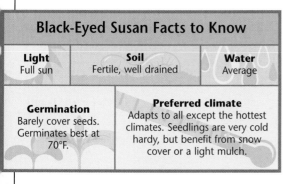

Black-Eyed Susan Facts to Know

Light	Soil	Water
Full sun	Fertile, well drained	Average

Germination	Preferred climate
Barely cover seeds. Germinates best at 70°F.	Adapts to all except the hottest climates. Seedlings are very cold hardy, but benefit from snow cover or a light mulch.

BLACK-EYED SUSAN VINE

Thunbergia alata

In addition to sunny orange, black-eyed Susan vines flowers can be white or yellow.

Long flowering and heat tolerant, this vine is actually a tropical perennial from Africa that is easily grown as an annual and often reseeds. The short, tubular flowers have dark brownish-purple throats. Combined with the yellow-orange petal color that dominates the species, the blooms vaguely resemble those of black-eyed Susans. Another old name, clock flower, refers to the way the blooms open during the day and close up at night.

In the Garden

This twining vine will grow to 10 feet when planted in a fertile spot that receives full morning sun and a few hours of afternoon shade. Its growth is more restrained in cooler climates or when it is grown in containers. If you have a low stone wall, this is an excellent vine to plant at the top so that the vines gently cascade to the ground. It is also unsurpassed as a summer cover plant for a chainlink fence, or for training onto a string trellis attached to a mailbox post or lamppost.

How to Grow

Start seeds indoors 6 weeks before your last frost, but wait until the last frost has passed to move them to the garden. Black-eyed Susan vine will not grow well unless night temperatures are above 55°F.

Before planting, amend the soil with organic matter so that it holds moisture well, and mix in a light application of timed-release or organic fertilizer. After watering in the seedlings, follow up with a mulch of bark, weathered leaves or straw piled at least 2 inches thick. Vines usually have no trouble finding a trellis, but you may need to guide them along their way at first. If needed, trim back secondary stems that reach out laterally and form a spreading tangle of foliage at the base of the plants.

Selecting Varieties

This flower is most often sold by common or species name, or you may run across one named variety, 'Susie Mix'. Mixtures include some plants that bloom white or yellow, but the lighter colors are usually not as numerous as those from plants that bloom yellow-orange.

Colorful Companions

The rich orange tones of black-eyed Susan vine work best when paired with purple to blue flowers such as ageratum, angelonia, blue convolvulus, heliotrope, blue salvia or verbena. Experiment with this vine in container bouquets, too. It works especially well with purple and white petunias.

Black-eyed Susan vine.

Black-Eyed Susan Vine Facts to Know		
Light Sun to partial shade	**Soil** Fertile, moist	**Water** Average
Germination Plant seeds 1/4 inch deep in sterile soil-less mix and germinate at 75°F.		**Preferred climate** Tolerates high heat and benefits from warm humidity. Dies back soon after frost.

BRACHYCHOME

Brachychome iberidifolia

Brachychome features pretty flowers and feathery, fine-textured foliage.

Commonly known as Swan River daisy, this petite beauty from Australia produces hundreds of faintly fragrant blooms in various shades between lilac and white, always with contrasting eyes. Flowers are less than 1 inch across, but their small size is made up for by their profusion. Brachychome's ferny foliage is pretty, too, though you will hardly see the leaves when the plants are in full bloom. This flower will bloom all summer in the North, and it often reseeds. In the South it is most useful in the spring to early summer garden.

In the Garden

Brachychomes are small plants that grow to less than 1 foot tall, so they are best used to accent small spaces, as an edging, or they make fine container plants. Provide rich, well-drained soil in a site that gets full morning sun and a little afternoon shade. Brachychome prefers weather that is not extremely hot or humid. In hot climates, brachychome planted in spring will bloom heavily in early summer and then fade away.

How to Grow

Buy bedding plants as soon as they become available in spring, or start seeds 6 weeks before your last frost. Enrich the planting site with compost or other organic soil amendment along with an organic or timed-release fertilizer. Keep soil lightly moist continuously until the plants are well established. When growing brachychome in containers, fertilize plants every 2 weeks with a soluble liquid fertilizer.

Where nights stay cool all summer, make a second sowing in early summer. Also look for volunteer seedlings near places where you grew brachychome in previous seasons, and trans-

plant them to where you want them to grow. Keep some soil packed around the roots during transplanting, and cover the plants with a pot or box to protect them from strong sun for a few days after the transplant operation.

Selecting Varieties

Blue varieties are usually the best flower producers. However, mixtures that include various shades of lilac have an icy-cool look unmatched by other flowers. The vigorous 'Splendor' variety can be had in a mixture or individual colors. 'Blue Star' blossoms have unusual quilled petals that make them look like tiny stars.

Colorful Companions

Blue brachychome shines in the company of white flowers or those with gray-green foliage. Soft yellows work well with brachychome color mixtures. Grow a few plants in large pots that can be moved to different places in the garden for temporary pairing with other annuals and perennials.

Brachychome blossoms.

Brachychome Facts to Know		
Light Sun to part shade	**Soil** Rich, well drained	**Water** Average
Germination Press small seeds into top of soil-less mix, and barely cover. Germinate at 70°F.	**Preferred climate** Very hot weather reduces flowering. Likes cool nights, but cannot tolerate frost.	

BROWALLIA

Browallia speciosa

Native to Colombia, the starry blossoms of browallia have earned it two jewel-like common names, sapphire flower and amethyst flower. Best known as a blue bloomer for hanging baskets, browallia is also available in pure white. One of the few annuals that blooms well in shade, browallia has slightly sticky leaves like those of its distant nightshade cousins, tomatoes and petunias.

In the Garden

Browallia is a fine choice for pots, hanging baskets or well-drained beds. Plants grow into relaxed mounds from 8 to 18 inches tall and wide, depending on variety. Ideally, they should receive a few hours of morning sun and filtered shade the rest of the day. Browallia is not difficult to grow and deserves much wider use, particularly as a change of pace from impatiens.

How to Grow

Bedding plants are widely available in the spring, or you can start seeds indoors 8 weeks before your last frost. Where frost lingers well into late spring, be prepared to cover plants with milk carton cloches. Pinch back the main stems to help induce branching when the plants are about 5 inches tall. Be patient as long as the weather is cool, because browallia plants often start out slowly in spring.

Browallia foliage is naturally a medium shade of green. Don't fertilize too much in an attempt to

'Jingle Bells' browallia.

make it darker, because overfertilization (and overwatering) will reduce flowering. Should blooming subside in mid-summer, shear back the plants by half their size and feed well with a liquid fertilizer. A new flush of flowers should appear within 3 weeks. If you feel lucky, you can try rooting stem cuttings to increase your supply of plants. Also, container-grown plants brought indoors in fall often continue to bloom for several weeks.

Selecting Varieties

Full-sized varieties that grow to 18 inches such as the 'Bells' series come in blue, white or a mixture of both colors, and are excellent for large containers or baskets where you want some of the stems to cascade over the edges. For accenting or edging beds, look for dwarf

'Troll' browallias, which grow to only about 10 inches tall and wide.

Colorful Companions

A lush mound of either blue or white browallia, or a mixture of both colors, stands well on its own. In container bouquets, combine blue browallia with gray dusty miller and white impatiens. White browallia makes a fine companion plant for torenia.

'Sapphire' browallia with 'Snowflake' bacopa.

Browallia Facts to Know		
Light Partial sun to shade	**Soil** Well drained	**Water** Average
Germination Barely cover seeds with sterile soil-less mix. Germinate at 70 to 75°F.	**Preferred climate** As long as they are not scorched by excessive sun, plants often bloom all summer in a wide range of climates.	

CALENDULA

Calendula officinalis

'Calypso Orange' calendula.

Dependable and easy to grow, calendula has long been called pot marigold because of its edible petals. Pull petals from well rinsed blossoms and use them as a saffron substitute to color foods yellow, or as a sunny garnish. A favorite of medieval herbalists, calendula is also a lasting cut flower that reseeds itself well in cool climates. Very hot summer weather cuts the bloom time short and limits calendula's garden presence to spring or fall in Zones 7 to 9.

In the Garden

Calendula is at its best in sunny flower beds where it can grow quickly in sync with the lengthening days of spring. Fertile soil results in bigger, more heavy-flowering plants. Space tall varieties 12 inches apart. Dwarf varieties can be used as an edging, or you can put them to work masking the bases of taller flowers.

How to Grow

You can buy bedding plants in the spring and in the fall in mild winter areas where they are often grown during "the second season." In either season seed starting is fast and sure, and it may be the only way to grow exactly the colors you want. Start seeds 6 weeks before your last frost in spring or 12 weeks before the first frost is expected in the fall. In cool climates where calendulas bloom intermittently all summer, simply cutting the plants back severely will usually push out a new fall crop of flowers.

Work a little starter fertilizer into the soil before planting, but avoid over-feeding calendulas. Should the plants appear malnourished, give them a booster feeding with a liquid plant food. It's also important to deadhead calendulas often to keep new flowers coming on.

Selecting Varieties

If you love cut flowers, look for tall, long-stemmed varieties such as 'Pacific Beauty', 'Kablouna' or 'Indian Prince'. 'Touch of Red' produces double bicolored flowers with red middles and petal tips. Some other varieties feature shaggy cactus-type petals. Dwarf varieties sold as bedding plants are numerous. Many dwarf mixtures include bicolored flowers with dark mahogany centers.

Colorful Companions

In spring, calendula works well with several other cool-season flowers that share its bloom period, including white ammi, blue bachelor buttons, purple larkspur and red poppies. Calendula's rich orange tones are natural accents in the fall garden too.

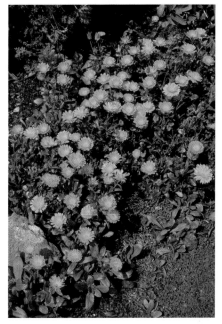

Calendula.

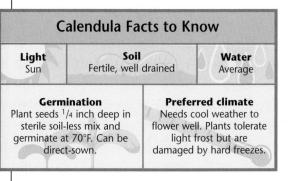

Calendula Facts to Know		
Light Sun	**Soil** Fertile, well drained	**Water** Average
Germination Plant seeds ¹/₄ inch deep in sterile soil-less mix and germinate at 70°F. Can be direct-sown.		**Preferred climate** Needs cool weather to flower well. Plants tolerate light frost but are damaged by hard freezes.

CANDYTUFT
Iberis umbellata, I. amara

Candytuft.

feed with a liquid fertilizer when the plants are 4 inches tall.

Where cool nights last well into summer, so does candytuft. Globe candytuft will re-bloom if sheared back in early summer, and rocket candytuft responds well to frequent cutting or deadheading. If you live where summers are hot, expect either type of candytuft to disappear after hot weather arrives. However, you may be surprised to discover volunteer seedlings the following spring.

Candytuft requires that you learn the art of handling seeds, but that does not mean that this flower is difficult to grow. Any enterprising gardener can enjoy annual candytuft in two equally delightful forms: Globe candytuft (*Iberis umbellata*) bears rounded umbels of flowers in shades of pink, while rocket candytuft (*I. amara*) is sometimes called hyacinth candytuft because of its fragrant flower clusters.

Candytuft blossoms cheer small corners in the garden.

In the Garden

Globe candytuft has a naturally dwarf growth habit that makes it suitable for edging. Because it is a reasonably good reseeder, globe candytuft is often used for spring color in wildflower meadows. You also can mass globe candytuft in beds so that the blooming plants form a blanket of color. Rocket candytuft grows taller, to about 18 inches, and is best grown in small groups in the cutting garden or mixed border.

Both types of candytuft have a strong preference for cool weather and neutral to slightly alkaline soil.

How to Grow

Either direct-sow seeds 2 weeks before your last spring frost, or start seeds indoors 6 weeks before your last frost. Seedlings are fast growers and are ready to set out under cloches after about a month. Work rotted manure or compost into the soil before planting either type of candytuft. Space plants about 6 inches apart, and

Selecting Varieties

For edging or beds, try the 'Flash' or 'Fairy' varieties of globe candytuft. If you want a good rocket candytuft for cutting, grow 'Giant White Hyacinth'.

Colorful Companions

Globe candytuft makes an excellent companion for spring-flowering bulbs such as tulips, daffodils and hyacinth. It also works well with cool-season annuals including larkspur, poppies and sweet alyssum. White rocket candytuft is a natural partner for white stock, which is equally fragrant and suitable for cutting.

Candytuft Facts to Know		
Light Sun to partial shade	**Soil** Fertile, well drained	**Water** Average
Germination Sow seeds 1/4 inch deep in soil-less mix. Best germination at about 65°F, but cooler temperatures preferred after the sprouts appear.		**Preferred climate** Grows best when temperatures are between 50 and 80°F.

CELOSIA
Celosia argentea

The celosias are a varied group of annuals to grow during the warmest part of summer. There are three types. Cockscombs are old favorites in country gardens, treasured for their convoluted flowers that resemble intensely colored, velvet-covered cauliflower. Modern landscape designers make heavy use of plume celosia because of its vibrant colors and upright, spiking form. A third type, wheat celosia, has a more refined texture and slightly different cultural requirements. All types of celosia can be used as cut flowers, both fresh and dried.

In the Garden
In any form, celosia is a bold presence in the garden. Its upright spikes make plume celosia a natural for vertical accents in mixed beds or for using as a frame for other types of annuals or small trees. Cockscomb types always command attention as feature flowers. Grow either type celosia in full sun, in fertile soil that drains well.

Yellow plume celosia paired with coleus.

How to Grow
Buy bedding plants in spring, or start seeds indoors at about the time of your last spring frost. There is little point in starting earlier, because celosias need warm soil in which to grow. Set plants out 2 weeks or more after the last frost has passed. Because of their heat tolerance, celosias make great summer replacements for cool-season flowers.

Whether you adopt seedlings or grow your own, never allow them to become chilled or dried out, and repot as needed to keep the roots from becoming overly cramped. Any of these stress factors can lead to premature flowering, which results in weaker, less resilient plants. Fertilize the plants as needed to support strong, steady growth. After celosias commence blooming, deadhead them periodically to force out new flowers.

Cockscomb.

light colors are most versatile in the landscape, while reds are better for drying. Dwarf varieties of both types are widely available as bedding plants. All celosias will reseed, with new seedlings appearing in early summer, after the soil has warmed.

Colorful Companions
With celosias, form is as important as color. The upright spikes of plume types contrast beautifully with flowers that have flat, daisy-shaped blossoms. Use the cockscomb types near flowers with more refined textures such as melampodium, marigolds or cosmos sulphureus.

Selecting Varieties
Time-tested tall plume types include 'Castle', 'Century' and 'Pampas Plume', which has an unusual loose, feathery texture. 'New Look' is especially colorful, with red-bronze leaves and bright red spikes. 'Big Chief' and 'Prestige' are long-stemmed cockscomb types for cutting. With both types, yellows and other

'New Look' plume celosia.

Celosia Facts to Know

Light	Soil	Water
Full sun	Rich, fertile	Average

Germination	Preferred climate
Plant seeds 1/4 inch deep and germinate at 75°F. Germination rate is very high under warm conditions.	A warm-natured flower that thrives in humid heat.

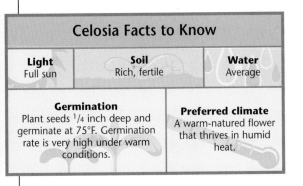

CELOSIA, WHEAT
Celosia argentea spicata

A relative newcomer to American gardens, wheat celosias are tall upright plants that bear long-lasting flower spikes at each stem tip. When planted in masses they create a windswept look and are particularly effective when grown near water features. Wheat celosia is an excellent candidate for the cutting garden, and the flowers also hold up well when dried.

Wheat celosia makes a beautiful addition to any garden because of its unique form and muted color.

In the Garden

Wheat celosia usually grows taller than 3 feet, so it makes a fine background plant for large flower beds. Its soft pink colors qualify it as a neutral in color schemes that make heavy use of pink or purple. Tremendously tolerant of heat, wheat celosia planted in early summer often stays in bloom continuously until fall. This flower is very easy to grow and deserves much wider use.

How to Grow

Bedding plants are increasingly available, but if you want a large number of plants for a mass planting you can start the seeds in containers or flats a week or two before your first frost. To help trigger germination, soak seeds in warm water overnight before planting.

Set plants out 12 inches apart when they are at least 4 inches tall. Plants will naturally develop numerous bearing branches, but you can speed up this process by pinching off the topmost growing tip a few weeks after transplanting, when vigorous new growth is well under way.

If you work an organic or timed-release fertilizer into the soil before planting, you should not need to feed wheat celosia again for the remainder of the season. However, it is important to mulch between plants, because wheat celosia's thin leaves do a poor job of shading out weeds. Established plants grown in good-quality soil are surprisingly tolerant of drought.

Selecting Varieties

'Flamingo Feather' is light shell pink, fading to almost white as the flowers age. 'Pink Candle' and 'Purple Flamingo' are darker pink, almost mauve. As flower spikes of any variety become older, they tend to lighten in color beginning at the bottom, which creates a muted bicolor effect.

Colorful Companions

The soft color of wheat celosia makes it easy to add to beds that contain other shades of pink such as those from cosmos, cleome, lavatera or petunia. Because of its height, wheat celosia is also great for softening the appearance of tall zinnias or for combining with tall ornamental grasses.

Wheat Celosia Facts to Know		
Light Sun	**Soil** Fertile, well drained	**Water** Average
Germination Plant seeds 1/8 inch deep, and germinate in warm temperatures between 75 and 80°F.		**Preferred climate** Strong need for warm growing conditions.

CLEOME
Cleome hassleriana

Originally from tropical America, cleome is among the best tall, heat-tolerant plants for the summer garden. Its common name, spider flower, aptly describes the large fragrant pink, white or bicolored flower clusters that top lanky stems up to 6 feet long. Where summers are long and warm, cleome grows into a huge shrub-like plant that reseeds itself year after year.

In the Garden

Cleome thrives in either sun or partial shade. Because of its height, it makes a fine plant for the back of a border or bed. Plants spaced 18 inches apart rapidly grow into a large shrubby mass. Any reasonably fertile soil will satisfy cleome.

Cleome, also known as spider flower.

'Violet Queen' cleome.

Cleome Facts to Know

Light	Soil	Water
Sun to part shade	Adaptable	Below average

Germination	Preferred climate
Chill seeds in refrigerator for 3 days before sowing. Plant seeds 1/4 inch deep and germinate at 75°F.	Outstanding in the South, where they are unfazed by high heat and humidity.

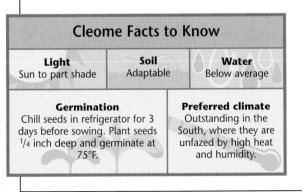

How to Grow

Bedding plants are increasingly available in spring, or you can start seedlings indoors a few weeks before your last frost. In warm climates, it's simplest to direct-seed cleome in mid-spring, after the soil has warmed. In subsequent springs, you will probably find plenty of volunteer seedlings, which are easily dug and moved to where you want them to grow and flower.

Be careful not to spoil cleome with too much fertilizer. Fertilize lightly or not at all if your soil is naturally deep and rich. In poor soil, work a balanced fertilizer into the site before planting, or top-dress self-sown plants with a timed-release fertilizer when they are about 8 inches tall. Water plants regularly for the first 6 weeks, and then taper off. Established plants tolerate high heat better than most other flowers, but they do need ample water.

In mid to late summer, top back stems that are heavy with dangling seed pods to help the plants redirect their energy toward the development of new flowering branches.

Selecting Varieties

No matter what variety you start with, self-sown plants will eventually revert to cleome's ancestral medium-pink color. To have pure white or deep-pink cleomes, set out some plants of named varieties every year. 'Cherry Queen' is bright pink, while 'Violet Queen' is a shade darker. Both look smashing when mixed with sparkling white 'White Queen' or 'Helen Campbell'.

Colorful Companions

Cleomes work well with tall pink cosmos, tall ageratum or by themselves when grown near a fence or a grouping of evergreen shrubs. Use them as central features in freestanding beds, and flank them with blue salvia or white geraniums.

COBBITY DAISY
Argyranthemum frutescens

Cobbity daisies.

Recent advances in breeding have brought cobbity daisies to the forefront of stylishly updated flower gardens. Originally from the Canary Islands and long called marguerite daisies, many of today's cobbity daisies have the tailored "decorative" flower form typical of dahlias and chrysanthemums. Most improved cultivars can bloom nonstop for weeks or even months provided they have proper weather conditions. For cobbity daisies, good conditions are days in the 70s and low 80s and nights in the 50s and 60s. Warmer weather leads to fewer, lower-quality blossoms. However, plants kept fed and watered through short spurts of hot summer weather usually regain their flower power when the weather cools down in the fall.

In the Garden

The compact growth habit of cobbity daisy makes it an outstanding daisy-type flower for containers. You also can grow it in well-drained beds in sun or partial shade. Space individual plants at least 12 inches apart in beds. Crowd them slightly in containers to make sure you get a lush, full look.

How to Grow

You must begin with purchased plants each spring. All of the best cobbity daisy cultivars are patented, which means you are not supposed to propagate your own plants. Before planting, put some energy into preparing the site, amending the soil with both organic matter and a balanced organic or timed-release fertilizer. After planting, mulch between plants to keep the soil moist and deter weeds.

Gather cut blossoms or deadhead cobbity daisies regularly, and drench the plants with a liquid fertilizer monthly during the second half of summer. Where summers are long, it is often best to shear back tired plants about halfway to force out a fresh crop of blossoms for fall. In mild winter areas, try keeping container-grown plants in a cool (but not freezing) place through winter and let them become almost dry, to the point of semidormancy. The following spring you may have great success coaxing them back to life with warmth and water.

Selecting Varieties

Cultivar names are multiplying fast among cobbity daisies. 'Sugar Buttons' bears single white flowers with yellow centers, while the double pink blossoms of 'Sun Star Summer Melody' look like little mums. Many more colors and forms will be available in coming years.

Colorful Companions

Cobbity daisies have a gentle yet elegant demeanor that works beautifully with numerous other long-blooming flowers including petunias, geraniums, salvias, verbenas and vincas.

Cobbity daisies are similar to single mums, but they bloom for a much longer time.

Cobbity Daisy Facts to Know		
Light Sun to part shade	**Soil** Rich, fertile	**Water** Average
Germination Propagation of patented varieties is illegal. The best ones are propagated exclusively by high-tech vegetative methods.		**Preferred climate** Not too hot, not too cold.

COLEUS
Solenostemon scutellarioides

The colorful variegated leaves of coleus make it the most ornamental member of the mint family. Native to Java, coleus has a tropical temperament and a definite penchant for shade. Although some new varieties have been specially developed to grow in bright sun, the deep leaf colors of most varieties are best when the plants receive at least a half day of shade.

In the Garden

Coleus will grow in any situation where the roots can be kept moist at all times, including well-mulched beds and large containers that retain moisture well. Coleus is ideal for bringing spots of color to shady decks and patios.

How to Grow

Start the small seeds indoors 6 weeks before your last spring frost, or buy bedding plants and set them out in late spring, after the soil has warmed. Begin fertilizing seedlings regularly early on, and don't be afraid to give them plenty of nitrogen. In containers, use a peaty potting soil that holds moisture well. Also avoid using small clay pots, which dry out too quickly for coleus. Amend the soil in beds with compost or peat moss prior to planting. Coleus likes a near neutral pH and may struggle to grow in very acidic soil that has not been modified with lime.

Pinch back the growing tips of coleus monthly, or as often as needed to keep plants bushy and to delay flowering. When the blue flower spikes do appear, promptly pinch them off. At any time, you can take 4-inch-long stem cuttings and root them in moist potting soil or water. They will strike roots and be ready to transplant within a month. Vigorous new plants grown from cuttings taken in mid-summer make interesting winter houseplants provided you can place them where indoor humidity is relatively high.

Chartreuse tones always work well with blue.

Selecting Varieties

Good seed-sown varieties include 'Rainbow', which grows to 18 inches, 'Wizard', which grows 10 inches tall, and more compact 'Seven Dwarfs'. These and other series come in mixtures or individual colors. Also check local nurseries for plants with leaf markings you find especially pleasing. Because coleus stem cuttings are so easy to root, you can grow a large number of distinctively colored plants from one large purchased specimen.

Colorful Companions

Color-coordinate coleus with very colorful leaves with blooming flowers. Varieties with chartreuse leaves contrast well with purple or blue flowers including ageratum and torenia. Pair coleus with pink leaf markings with pink wax begonia. Also try mixing dark-leafed coleus with dusty miller or ferns in a half-shaded spot.

Splashed with color, coleus patterns offer endless variations.

Pinch flowers from coleus to encourage the growth of healthy new leaves.

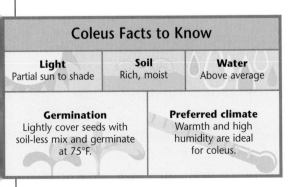

Coleus Facts to Know		
Light Partial sun to shade	**Soil** Rich, moist	**Water** Above average
Germination Lightly cover seeds with soil-less mix and germinate at 75°F.		**Preferred climate** Warmth and high humidity are ideal for coleus.

CONVOLVULUS
Convolvulus tricolor

Convolvulus makes it possible to enjoy the daily drama of morning glories without the burden of supporting vigorous vines. Also called bush morning glory, this native of southern Europe produces vibrant fluted blue or pink blossoms that open each morning and close by afternoon on sunny days. Each blossom features a starburst of white that sets off a lovely yellow throat.

'Royal Ensign' convolvulus.

Convolvulus is sometimes called bush morning glory.

In the Garden

Convolvulus are low, slightly spreading plants less than 1 foot high and up to 18 inches wide. They are perfect for planting atop a stone wall or in hanging baskets, or you can use them as a blooming groundcover in front of taller flowers. Because convolvulus is showy only during the morning hours, locate plants where you can see them first thing in the day. Convolvulus needs good sun and well-drained soil, but is otherwise easy to please.

How to Grow

The easiest way to grow convolvulus is to plant the seeds where you want them to grow in late spring, after the soil has warmed. You can start seeds indoors in roomy containers 2 weeks before your last frost, but they must be transplanted carefully because the roots are thick and brittle. Either way, it helps to nick the hard seeds with a knife or file prior to planting. Alternatively, soak the seeds in warm water overnight. Thin seedlings to at least 10 inches apart when they have at least four leaves.

Fertilize plants monthly with a balanced liquid fertilizer, or more often if the plants appear weak and have yellowish foliage. Every few days, pinch off the fuzzy seed pods to help prolong the flowering period. If the seeds are allowed to mature, the plants usually stop flowering and die soon thereafter.

Selecting Varieties

Two different flower color patterns are available in this species. The 'Ensign' series features the richly colored starburst pattern consisting of blue or pink petals with white and yellow contrasting throats. 'Dwarf Pictoee' has dark pink or blue flowers with white edges and foliage faintly variegated with white.

Colorful Companions

Accentuate the bright contrast of convolvulus flowers by pairing them with white petunias or white lavatera. Yellow marigolds provide a nice counterpoint, or you can use convolvulus to mask the bases of tall sunflowers, Mexican sunflowers or annual vines. In hanging baskets, this flower often makes the most striking statement when grown alone.

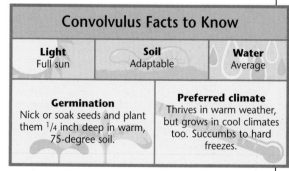

Convolvulus Facts to Know

Light Full sun	Soil Adaptable	Water Average
Germination Nick or soak seeds and plant them 1/4 inch deep in warm, 75-degree soil.		**Preferred climate** Thrives in warm weather, but grows in cool climates too. Succumbs to hard freezes.

COREOPSIS, PLAINS
Coreopsis tinctoria

Plains coreopsis.

Native to the central and southern Great Plains, this is the best-known annual in the large coreopsis family. The common name of calliopsis translates as "beautiful eye," a fitting description for the perky yellow-and-red flowers that dance atop thin, wiry stems. Plains coreopsis is widely regarded as a wildflower, but it such a pretty one that it deserves a spot in the flower garden as well.

In the Garden
Plains coreopsis seeds sprout very early in the spring in most places, so that the plants are in bloom by early summer. In an annual wildflower meadow, annual coreopsis blooms

after bachelor buttons and poppies, at about the same time as black-eyed Susans. Plains coreopsis will flower despite dry conditions, but it really prefers wet spots that offer constant moisture. Plants grown in moist, fertile soil often grow to 3 feet or more, while stressed plants in dry spots may never reach 2 feet tall. Moisture is also the wild card that determines how long plains coreopsis will stay in bloom. With plenty of rain, the plants bloom nonstop for over a month.

How to Grow
For a large planting, order bulk seeds from a wildflower seed supplier. One ounce of seed will cover 1,000 square feet, especially if the site hosts other annual wildflowers. Barely cover seeds with soil, and be patient. Plains coreopsis plants sit as small seedlings for several weeks, and then produce a profusion of thin, threadlike leaves.

Gently dig a few plants, move them to a cultivated bed, and grow them as you would tall zinnias. Plains

coreopsis is naturally upright and will often grow through adjacent flowers. It is also a strong reseeder that can be counted upon to return year after year.

Selecting Varieties
Flowers typical of the species are yellow with a central mahogany-red band. A slightly different form called dwarf red plains coreopsis grows to less than 2 feet tall and bears mahogany-red flowers. The blossoms of dwarf red coreopsis yield a bold red dye when infused in boiling water.

Colorful Companions
The rustic colors of plains coreopsis pair well with sulphur cosmos, Mexican sunflower, sunflower, zinnia and other summer flowers that bloom yellow or red. Like many other wildflowers, plains coreopsis looks better in the company of lowly bred "country" flowers than with very neat, compact hybrids.

Plains coreopsis with orange California poppies and red corn poppies.

Plains Coreopsis Facts to Know

Light	Soil	Water
Full sun to light shade	Adaptable	Average

Germination	Preferred climate
Direct-seed in fall in Zones 7 to 9. In colder regions, sow first thing in spring. Best germination around 65°F.	Adapts to any area and virtually any soil.

COSMOS

Cosmos bipinnatus, C. sulphureus

Cosmos bipinnatus.

Two remarkably different species go under the common name of cosmos. The pink, white or red flowers with ferny foliage familiar to most gardeners as common cosmos are *C. bipinnatus*. This species is best categorized as a cool-season annual, particularly in warm southern climates where it is often planted in fall for bloom the following spring. In the North, common cosmos behaves differently because it does not sprout until spring and tends to flower poorly when days are very long. As a result, cosmos planted in spring in northern latitudes often blooms most heavily from late summer to fall, when days are getting shorter.

Sulphur cosmos blooms in bright orange, yellow or red, and its foliage is less finely cut than that of its pastel cousin. This is a great plant to give a summer color boost to wildflower areas, or for growing in beds in hot climates. It is a rea-sonably strong reseeder, but easy to control with routine weeding.

Both types of cosmos serve as nectar plants for butterflies and have long stems that make them useful cut flowers.

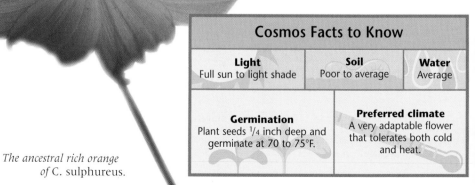

The ancestral rich orange of C. sulphureus.

In the Garden

Varieties vary greatly in height, between 1 and 4 feet, and it's important to pay close attention to this when placing cosmos in the garden. Tall common cosmos are lanky plants suitable for the back of the border, and they benefit greatly from staking or protection from wind. However, more compact varieties have no trouble staying upright and are very versatile in beds and even containers. Sulphur cosmos is a stiff, open plant that holds itself up well. It is most effective when planted in groups or masses.

Cosmos Facts to Know		
Light Full sun to light shade	**Soil** Poor to average	**Water** Average
Germination Plant seeds ¼ inch deep and germinate at 70 to 75°F.		**Preferred climate** A very adaptable flower that tolerates both cold and heat.

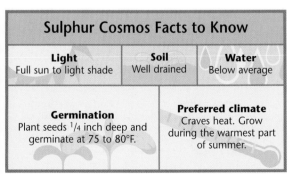

A rare butter yellow selection of C. sulphureus.

The size of either cosmos species is influenced by variety and the quality of the soil. For example, if you plant cosmos in a wildflower area that has been minimally improved, you can expect thrifty plants that bloom well enough yet branch very little. Plant exactly the same seed in a bed that has been improved with deep cultivation and the addition of organic matter, and you will get taller, bushier plants that flower for a longer period of time. But don't try to make up for poor soil quality with excessive fertilizer. Use a modest amount of fertilizer when growing cosmos in very poor soil; use little or none when growing either species in soil of good quality.

How to Grow

Direct-seed cosmos where you want the plants to grow. Plant common cosmos in the fall in Zones 8 and 9, or in early spring elsewhere. Young seedlings usually survive light frosts with ease. Thin plants to 8 inches apart, and mulch to control weeds. Stake tall varieties as needed to keep them upright. Gather cut flowers or deadhead often to prolong the blooming time, but allow some plants to develop mature seeds. Cosmos seeds are

Pink and white cosmos.

very easy to harvest for replanting the following year.

Wait until the last frost has passed to seed sulphur cosmos. If you live in a warm climate where summer lasts a long time, hold back some seed to plant in early to mid-summer. Sulphur cosmos blooms heavily for about a month, so you will get a much longer color display if you make successive sowings every 5 to 6 weeks. Be sure to gather some seeds for replanting in future seasons.

Selecting Varieties

Choose common cosmos varieties based on size and flower color. For containers and formal beds, the semi-dwarf 'Sonata' series is tremendously popular. 'Versailles' has very long, stiff stems favored for cut flowers, or you can opt for unusual bicolored blossoms found in 'Candy Stripe' or early-blooming 'Hinomaru'. There are many more from which to choose.

Selections among sulphur cosmos are becoming more numerous. Expect seed sold under the species name to produce only bright yellow-orange flowers. 'Bright Lights' and 'Ladybird' are available in yellow, orange and red, while 'Cosmic Orange' is just what the name says. The newest color in this species is lemon yellow, represented by the 'Lemon Twist' variety.

Colorful Companions

Follow each species' natural color scheme and you can't go wrong with cosmos. Plant common cosmos near other flowers that bloom in cool shades of pink or blue, or play it safe with white. In the South, where common cosmos blooms in late spring, it works well with bachelor button, dianthus and verbena. In northern areas where the heaviest bloom comes in the fall, cosmos offers a refreshing counterpoint to the yellow tones of the season.

The fiery tones of sulphur cosmos work best with other hot-colored flowers like marigolds, melampodium and zinnia, or you can introduce contrasting blue with heat-tolerant ageratum or blue salvia.

'Ladybird Scarlet' Cosmos sulphureus.

Sulphur Cosmos Facts to Know		
Light Full sun to light shade	**Soil** Well drained	**Water** Below average
Germination Plant seeds ¼ inch deep and germinate at 75 to 80°F.		**Preferred climate** Craves heat. Grow during the warmest part of summer.

CUP AND SAUCER VINE
Cobaea scandens

Native to Mexico, cup and saucer vine is the largest, most shrub-like annual vine you can grow. Also known as cathedral bells or cobaea, the plants produce big cup-shaped blossoms that turn from pale green to purple over a period of several days. This plant is not a prolific bloomer—you may get only a dozen blossoms from a 20-foot vine. However, the lightly fragrant flowers are well worth waiting for, and the vines are excellent foliage plants for shading hot walls or porches. New growth and tendrils are heavily tinged with dark red.

In the Garden

Cup and saucer vine thrives on sun and warmth, and requires little in the way of extra fertilizer or water. Its strong, wiry tendrils will do a good job of attaching themselves to a string trellis, chainlink fencing, or even rough wall surfaces. This is a wonderful vine to train around a south- or west-facing window that gets too much hot summer sun.

How to Grow

Start seeds indoors about 2 weeks before your last frost or outdoors after the soil has warmed. Set out seedlings promptly, when the seedling leaves are fully open but the first true leaves have not yet appeared. Allow about 2 feet between plants. If needed, protect transplanted seedlings from cold winds with milk carton cloches.

Should the vines wander too far, you can clip them back at any time. Where summers are short, you can speed up flowering by clipping back the main stem tips when they are 6 to 8 feet long. Flowering typically begins in mid- to late summer. Expect slight reseeding from especially vigorous plants.

In Zones 8 to 10 (and occasionally in Zone 7 with a thick mulch)

The blooms of cup and saucer vine gradually change from pale green to deep purple.

cup and saucer vine will survive winter and grow as a perennial. In these areas, cut back the plants almost to the ground in winter.

Selecting Varieties

Seed is sold labeled with its species name only. In addition to the predominant purple-flowered variety, specialty seed catalogs occasionally list a second selection, 'Alba', which has pale green flowers that mature to white rather than purple.

Colorful Companions

Because of its size, cup and saucer vine needs large companions such as cleome, Mexican sunflower or bronze-leafed varieties of amaranth. In partially shaded sites, white-flowered nicotiana (*N. alata* or *N. sylvestris*) makes a fine foreground plant.

Cup and Saucer Vine Facts to Know		
Light Full sun to light shade	**Soil** Fertile, well drained	**Water** Average
Germination Scarify seeds with a file before planting edgewise in containers or warm soil. Germinates best at 75 to 80°F.		**Preferred climate** Has a definite tropical temperament, but grows fast enough to be used as an annual.

DAHLIA

Dahlia hortensis, D. **hybrids**

Dwarf dahlia.

Gardeners who grow dahlias for large, exhibition-quality blossoms begin by planting dormant tubers each spring, but you also can grow more petite plants from seed. Either way, growing dahlias is an annual adventure that begins after the last spring frost has passed, reaches its peak when the plants bloom heavily in late summer and early fall, and ends after the plants are killed back by frost. Native to Mexico, dahlias produce richly colored symmetrical blossoms much valued as cut flowers.

In the Garden

Grow dahlias in a fertile, well-drained soil, in a spot that gets full sun until mid-afternoon. Tall plants grown from fleshy tubers always need sturdy stakes, but more compact seed-sown plants grow into lush mounds that remain upright with little or no support.

How to Grow

Start seeds indoors 6 weeks before your last frost. Should you need to thin the seedlings, retain some of the smallest ones, which often produce the showiest flowers. When the soil is warm, set out seedlings or sprouting tubers in deeply dug beds that have been generously amended with organic matter and fertilized with a balanced, slow-release fertilizer. Install stakes soon after planting, and tie the plants to the stakes as they grow. Water as needed to keep the soil lightly moist at all times.

For the biggest blooms, pinch off half of the round flower buds when they are the size of large peas. Skip this step when growing compact, seed-sown varieties. In most climates, August and September are the prime flowering season for dahlias, though established plants will bloom briefly in early summer, too.

Dig dahlia tubers (including those formed by first-season seedlings) after the first killing frost, dry them at room temperature for a few days, and then pack them in sand or peat moss and store them in a cool place until the following spring. When well mulched, tubers can be left in the ground through winter in Zones 7 to 9.

Selecting Varieties

There are hundreds of dahlia cultivars to grow from dormant tubers. Good seed-sown varieties that bloom reliably their first year include 'Figaro' and 'Diablo' (both 15 inches tall) and slightly smaller 'Piccolo'. Taller single-flowered varieties like 'Dandy' will often bloom their first year too.

Colorful Companions

Flank dahlias with dense, bushy annuals that bloom heavily late into the season such as French marigolds, melampodium or narrow-leaf zinnias.

Dahlia Facts to Know		
Light Full sun to light shade	**Soil** Rich, well drained	**Water** Average
Germination Plant seeds ¼ inch deep and germinate at 75°F.	**Preferred climate** Widely adaptable, dahlias flower best when days become shorter in the fall.	

Dahlia.

DIANTHUS
Dianthus chinensis and hybrids

The large dianthus family includes carnations and other perennial species in addition to the lightly scented annuals. Often called China pinks or just plain pinks (because of the fringed or "pinked" edges of the petals), annual dianthus are cool-season flowers that often bloom for more than 2 months, or for however long cool weather lasts. Hardy to at least 15°F, dianthus can be set out in the fall for blooms from late winter to early summer in Zones 7 to 9.

In the Garden

Dianthus plants form low mounds of stiff, narrow leaves that are almost completely hidden by the flowers when the plants are in full bloom. Locate this flower in full sun, in soil where the drainage is nothing short of excellent. If you luck into a fragrant selection, by all means place a few plants in large pots near an entryway or on your deck or patio.

How to Grow

Sow seeds indoors in late summer in Zones 8 to 9, or late winter

Dianthus.

elsewhere. You can save time by starting with bedding plants. Set out dianthus before the last frost, but do protect them from hard freezes with cloches or cardboard boxes. In Zones 8 and 9 (and warm sections of Zone 7), set out dianthus in the fall. The plants may bloom briefly after planting, but will stop blooming during winter's coldest weeks.

Before setting out the plants, work organic matter into the soil to improve its texture and drainage. Also mix in a timed-release or organic fertilizer. Dianthus roots benefit from drying out between rains. When growing dianthus in containers, be watchful for too-dry conditions that develop when the fibrous roots completely fill the containers.

Every 6 weeks while the plants are in bloom, shear back old stems to encourage the development of new ones. In mild winter climates, year-old dianthus often survive winter and bloom well the following spring, but they seldom survive a second summer in good condition.

'Telstar Mix', one of the most cold hardy varieties of annual dianthus.

Selecting Varieties

Hybrids including 'Ideal', 'Festival', and 'Telstar' have improved heat and cold tolerance. Numerous varieties sold as bedding plants have unusual picoteed edges or frilly double flowers. Fragrance is elusive with annual dianthus, but it can happen.

Colorful Companions

Shades of pink dominate this species, but unusual white markings and hues ranging from baby pink to salmon to dark burgundy pink bring plenty of versatility to annual dianthus. Mix them with larger plants that bloom yellow, white or blue, or plant them near dusty miller or other plants with gray foliage. Dianthus are ideal for edging beds of bearded iris, or for growing in the foreground of tall hollyhocks or zinnias.

Dianthus Facts to Know		
Light Full sun to light shade	**Soil** Fertile, near neutral (pH 6.8 to 7.5)	**Water** Below average
Germination Sow seeds 1/8 inch deep and germinate at 70°F. Grow seedlings at 50 to 60°F.		**Preferred climate** Dianthus blooms best in cool weather.

DUSTY MILLER
Senecio cineraria

A frosty hedge of dusty miller.

Any garden can be improved by the luminous gray presence of dusty miller. Pair this gray-leafed foilage plant with a brighter flower and magic happens. Originally from the Mediterranean, dusty miller thrives in a wide range of climates and often survives winter to Zone 7. However, elderly plants are not as pretty or vigorous as young ones, so you should plan to replace them each spring.

In the Garden

Use dusty miller to edge beds in partial shade, to frame other flowers, or to harmonize very diverse flower plantings. It makes a beautiful addition to container bouquets and window boxes. Dusty miller will accept all types of weather except prolonged wet conditions in summer or extended freezes in winter. Because the fuzzy felted leaves dry slowly, morning sun is required in climates where humidity tends to be high.

How to Grow

You can start seeds indoors 6 weeks before the last spring frost or simply buy inexpensive bedding plants. Set them out anytime after your last frost date. Cultivate the soil deeply to promote fast drainage, and add a small amount of organic or timed-release fertilizer. Also mulch lightly to keep rain from splashing mud on the leaves. Except for picking off damaged leaves occasionally, dusty miller often needs no special attention. Should the main rosette of leaves become tattered, cut it off about 2 inches above the soil. New leaf clusters should appear within a few weeks. Small basal rosettes also can be cut away and set to root in a sandy potting mix, but they often are not as vigorous as healthy new seedlings.

Plants that survive winter promptly produce clusters of small yellow flowers in spring. Cut back the flowers to keep the plants in good condition a little longer.

Selecting Varieties

At 12 inches tall, 'Silverdust' has lacy, deeply cut lobed leaves. 'Cirrus' has smoother, spoon-shaped leaves that accentuate its

Felted leaves of dusty miller.

texture and color, and its petite 8-inch height makes it useful for edging. Cold-hardy 'Silver Lace' is actually a pyrethrum species, easily propagated from basal rosettes but slower to start from seed. Its leaves have a slight bluish cast and are very ferny in appearance.

Colorful Companions

Dusty miller is astounding paired with blue pansies or ageratum or hot pink dianthus or petunia. It works well with hot colors too, particularly red geranium or salvia. Also try dusty miller as a partner to annuals with red-bronze foliage such as 'New Look' celosia or red-leafed wax begonia.

Dusty miller with dwarf marigolds.

Dusty Miller Facts to Know

Light	Soil	Water
Sun to partial shade	Fertile, well drained	Below average

Germination	Preferred climate
Press seeds into top of soil-less mix so they are barely covered. Germinate at 72 to 75°F.	Extremely adaptable. Mature plants can survive several hard freezes.

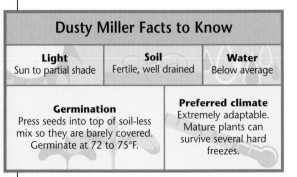

ENGLISH DAISY
Bellis perennis

The availability of pansies and violas that can survive winter to Zone 4 has left gardeners badly in need of companion flowers of comparable hardiness. Enter English daisies, which are actually cool-season perennials. However, as newcomers to the lineup of autumn bedding plants, these dainty flowers are unsurpassed as perky partners for winter pansies. In all climates English daisies produce numerous little aster-like blossoms first thing in spring. In mild winter climates they often bloom intermittently all winter.

In the Garden

Plant English daisies alongside pastel-colored pansies or violas in sunny or partially shaded beds. The petite 6-inch-tall plants are also perfect for planting over spring-flowering bulbs or for adding to rock gardens for early spring color. English daisies thrive in cool weather and perish completely by early summer south of Zone 6. Farther north, they may naturalize in flower beds or lawn areas. When this happens, opinions differ on whether they are welcome flowers or weeds.

How to Grow

Bedding plants are increasingly available in the fall, or you can start seeds indoors about 10 weeks before your first fall freeze. Set plants out in mid fall, after the soil has cooled down, at the same time you plant pansies and violas. In heavy clay, amend the soil with compost or other organic soil amendment to lighten the soil's texture and promote fast drainage.

Pinch off old blossoms to promote the development of new buds. As with pansies, it is helpful to feed English daisies in early spring, soon after new growth and the first flush of flowers appear.

In northern areas, you can pot up a few plants in late spring and keep them in a cool, shady spot until fall. Divide and replant them in September. As long as they have a few weeks to develop new roots, divisions set out in fall have no trouble surviving winter.

Selecting Varieties

'Galaxy' bears flat daisy-type flowers with yellow centers in varying shades of pink. 'Habanera' has

English daisies.

distinctive pink and white blooms that are mostly doubles, while the blossoms of 'Pompomette' are tightly rounded pompoms in deep red, pink and white. 'Super Enorma' bears very large flowers similar to those of 'Pompomette'.

Colorful Companions

Try planting English daisies in flowing ribbons to separate different colors of pansies and violas, or put them to work as edging plants around clumps of pink tulips or white daffodils.

English daisies combine well with pansies. You can plant both in the fall.

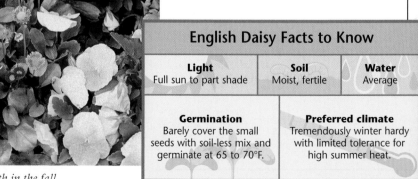

English Daisy Facts to Know

Light	Soil	Water
Full sun to part shade	Moist, fertile	Average

Germination	Preferred climate
Barely cover the small seeds with soil-less mix and germinate at 65 to 70°F.	Tremendously winter hardy with limited tolerance for high summer heat.

EUPHORBIA
Euphorbia marginata

The huge spurge family includes dozens of plants both naughty and nice, and one of the nicest is annual euphorbia. Commonly known as snow-on-the-mountain, euphorbia is native from the Great Plains southward to Mexico. As the plants mature and begin to show tiny white flowers, the topmost leaves become heavily variegated with white, like snow on high peaks. You can use euphorbia to light up the late summer garden, or cut the stems, sear the tips to seal in the milky latex, and use them in cut flower arrangements.

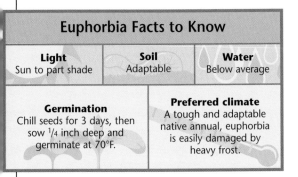

Euphorbia.

In the Garden

Depending on the site and soil, euphorbia grows from 2 to 4 feet tall, and it is always a narrow, upright plant. Most vigorous in full sun and fertile soil, euphorbia is also willing to grow in dry, infertile spots where few other plants will grow. Euphorbia is useful as a central element in container bouquets, and it is a long-time favorite in country cutting gardens.

How to Grow

Start seeds indoors a month before your last frost, or simply sow the seeds where you want plants to grow after the last frost has passed.

The hard-shelled seeds are large enough to handle easily, and the big seedlings grow faster than most weeds. Space plants 12 inches apart, or slightly more if the soil is of good quality.

The seedlings have broad green leaves without a hint of white. Leaf markings appear much later, in conjunction with clusters of white flower bracts. In most climates, plants reach their glory in August. Once established, euphorbia tolerates extreme heat and drought, much like its milkweed cousins. Euphorbia is a strong reseeder in hospitable climates, but unwanted seedlings are easily pulled out. Pinching off the stem tips when plants are about 14 inches tall will help induce early branching.

Should you pinch back your plants or gather stems as cut flowers, wash your hands promptly to avoid possible skin irritation from the latex sap. The leaves are poisonous if eaten, but far from lethal.

Selecting Varieties

A few named varieties are available that have been selected for the extent of their white variegation, including 'Snow Top' and 'Kilimanjaro'.

Colorful Companions

Euphorbia glows in the light of the moon, so it is a welcome addition to white gardens that are often visited at night. Try combining them with white nicotiana. In more colorful spots, the plants make fine partners for late-blooming cosmos or Mexican sunflowers.

Euphorbia Facts to Know

Light	Soil	Water
Sun to part shade	Adaptable	Below average

Germination	Preferred climate
Chill seeds for 3 days, then sow ¼ inch deep and germinate at 70°F.	A tough and adaptable native annual, euphorbia is easily damaged by heavy frost.

FAN FLOWER
Scaevola aemula

Scaevola 'Mauve Clusters'.

From its humble origins as an Australian wildflower, scaevola has quickly become a favorite summer annual in warm, humid climates, where many other flowers die out by mid-summer. Scaevola thrives in muggy heat whether it's planted in baskets, window boxes or the corners of sunny flower beds. Each little bloom resembles a fan, hence this plant's common name.

In the Garden

You can plant fan flower in beds, but the plants are most often used in large containers placed in full sun or lightly dappled shade. Fan flower plants grow into loose mounds about 10 inches tall with numerous trailing stems more than a foot long, each one studded with dozens of flat blue blooms that re-

Try growing fan flower in large containers in any hot, sunny spot.

semble a fan or open hand. As long as it gets plenty of warm sunshine, fan flower is a very tough plant that thrives with little care.

How to Grow

Fan flower is not grown from seeds, but from stem cuttings propagated from plants kept through the winter in heated greenhouses. These are sold in individual containers in mid- to late spring. You will need 3 plants to fill a 12-inch basket. In beds, space plants 8 inches apart. Before planting, mix a small amount of timed-release fertilizer into the soil. Feed and water plants regularly if you grow them in containers. In beds, fan flower is surprisingly tolerant of drought and needs only an occasional drink of liquid fertilizer.

Pruning of the stems is not necessary, but a light trim from time to time improves the appearance of the plants. Stem tips about 4 inches long root readily when set in a half-and-half mixture of damp sand and peat moss, kept in humid shade.

Selecting Varieties

The best-known name in fan flower, 'New Wonder' has won awards for its outstanding performance in field trials in several southeastern states. Other varieties include 'Fancy'. Sometimes fan flower is simply labeled as scaevola. The strongest color in fan flower is a deep violet blue, but some nurseries sell plants that bloom pink or white.

Colorful Companions

Blue fan flowers have faint yellow "eyes" in the center of each bloom, which helps them marry well with yellow flowers. Some good yellows that thrive under the same conditions as fan flower include melampodium, yellow marigolds and yellow portulaca. Chartreuse sweet potato vine also makes a good neighbor. Also try fan flower with multicolored lantana or dusty miller.

Self-cleaning fan flowers require very little maintenance.

Fan Flower Facts to Know		
Light Sun to partial shade	**Soil** Fertile, well drained	**Water** Average
Germination Not propagated from seed, only from stem cuttings.	**Preferred climate** Blooms best in warm weather. Cannot tolerate frost.	

FORGET-ME-NOT

Myosotis sylvestris

Two blue flowers go by the common name of forget-me-not. This one, *Myosotis*, is the mound-forming blue bloomer brought from Europe by the colonists that has become a fixture of spring along the eastern seaboard. Botanically, forget-me-not is a hardy biennial, meaning that new plants that start life one year, bloom heavily the following spring, and then die. However, in cool climates with good winter snow cover, myosotis will persist as a short-lived perennial. Where summers are very hot and humid, it is most definitely a hardy annual to grow on the same schedule with pansies.

Forget-me-not.

In the Garden

Use these small clump-forming plants in a half-shaded rock garden, entryway bed, as an underplanting for daffodils or tulips, or to edge a stone walkway. Plants grow to less than 10 inches tall and reseed themselves if allowed to do so. They can take full sun in cool climates, but in most areas they benefit from partial shade.

How to Grow

You may need to experiment to find the best planting time for this flower in your area. As a starting point, prepare a small "nursery" row in late spring in a place that gets morning sun and afternoon shade. Amend the soil with compost or peat moss and fertilizer so that it is rich, slightly acidic and holds moisture well. Sow seeds while nights are still cool, in the

50s. Thin plants to 4 inches apart. In the South, wait until August to start seeds indoors in an air-conditioned place.

In all areas, move plants to the garden in mid-fall, after nights become cool. Expect little growth during the winter. If needed, use evergreen boughs to protect plants from harsh winds or ice accumulations. Fertilize the plants in early spring, after new growth appears.

Selecting Varieties

Lovely blues include 'Victoria Blue', 'Blue Cloud', and more compact 'Blue Ball'. A new patented variety, 'Gold 'n Sapphires', has chartreuse leaves and is grown from purchased plants (they often reseed true). Varieties that bloom pink are not as showy but certainly of interest, including 'Rosylva', 'Victoria Rose' and 'Rosie'.

Colorful Companions

Forget-me-not is ideal for growing with yellow daffodils or a mixture of red and yellow tulips. It also works very well with the bright orange tones of California poppy or calendula. Pansies are natural partners, especially white ones, which help showcase these true blue flowers.

Old fashioned forget-me-not.

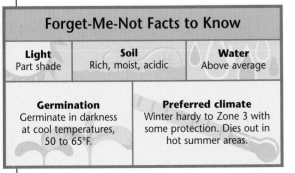

Forget-Me-Not Facts to Know		
Light Part shade	**Soil** Rich, moist, acidic	**Water** Above average
Germination Germinate in darkness at cool temperatures, 50 to 65°F.		**Preferred climate** Winter hardy to Zone 3 with some protection. Dies out in hot summer areas.

CHINESE FORGET-ME-NOT
Cynoglossum amabile

Chinese forget-me-not blossoms offer the same endearing color of blue as myosotis, but on a larger plant that is faster to grow and less challenging to schedule. The flower stems are less than 12 inches long, but they are still useful in small flower arrangements. Native to eastern Asia, Chinese forget-me-not has graceful green foliage with a grayish cast. Because it can withstand light frosts, it is sometimes used as a winter annual in Zones 8 and 9. In other areas, Chinese forget-me-not planted first thing in spring comes into bloom in early summer. Blooming continues for a month or more, usually for as long as cool weather lasts.

In the Garden

With a mature height of 18 inches, Chinese forget-me-not is just the right size to mix with other cool-season annuals in fertile, well-drained beds. Pick a spot that receives at least 6 hours of sun each day. Although the plants need plenty of sun to make strong growth, they are prettiest when viewed in dappled shade, which accentuates the natural contrast between foliage and flower. Locate plants in groups of 3 or more for maximum visual impact.

How to Grow

Start seeds indoors 6 weeks before your last spring frost. Seeds need a few days of darkness to germinate well, but dark treatment is not mandatory. Thin or prick out so that only one seedling remains in a 2-inch container. Harden off for a few days before setting plants out under cloches about a week before the last frost is likely. Exposure to cool weather contributes to strong blooming later on. Transplant the seedlings carefully because the roots are somewhat brittle. Work a balanced organic or timed-release fertilizer into the site prior to planting.

Except for routine weeding, Chinese forget-me-not should need no extra care until the blossoms appear. This flower will reseed itself in cool climates if you let the plants stand until the seeds ripen.

Selecting Varieties

The 'Firmament' variety has been popular since its introduction in 1939. Occasionally strains are offered that produce pink flowers, but they are not as showy as selections that bloom blue.

Colorful Companions

The clear blue color of Chinese forget-me-not is the

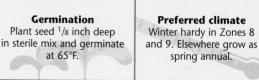

Chinese forget-me-not.

perfect shade to complement rich orange calendulas, California poppies or nasturtiums. In cool color schemes, combine it with white dianthus or stocks. Other good companions include white sweet alyssum and dusty miller.

Cynoglossum, Chinese forget-me-not.

Chinese Forget-Me-Not Facts to Know		
Light Sun to part shade	**Soil** Fertile, well drained	**Water** Average
Germination Plant seed 1/8 inch deep in sterile mix and germinate at 65°F.		**Preferred climate** Winter hardy in Zones 8 and 9. Elsewhere grow as spring annual.

FOUR O'CLOCK
Mirabilis jalapa

Four o'clock blossoms.

used at night, such as beds adjoining patios or decks. The lightly fragrant flowers attract night-flying moths. Japanese beetles also like four o'clocks, so they are not a good plant for areas where this pest is out of control. Plan ahead to give four o'clocks plenty of room during the second half of summer, for they respond to warm weather by growing into robust bushes up to 3 feet tall.

velopment of new bud-bearing branches. If allowed to set ripe seed in the fall, you may find volunteer seedlings nearby the following spring. However, the best way to increase your supply of four o'clocks is to start more plants from seed on purpose.

Selecting Varieties

Depending on variety, four o'clock flowers may be solid in color or vibrantly splashed with streaks of yellow, fuchsia, pink, red and white. 'Broken Colors' is one such blend of bicolored flowers. 'Tea Time' plants grow smaller and more compact, and the mixture includes red, rose, yellow and whites. To grow single colors, the best strategy is to start with a mixture and pull out the plants you don't like. You can also gather seed from plants found in other people's gardens.

Affectionately known to some as Marvel-of-Peru, four o'clocks have the peculiar habit of closing their flowers during the middle of the day. The tubular blossoms reopen each afternoon, and remain that way until the morning sun shines brightly again. These vigorous plants can be grown as annuals anywhere, and make dependable, low-maintenance perennials in Zones 7 to 10.

In the Garden

Four o'clocks are great plants for sunny areas that are frequently

How to Grow

The hard seeds of four o'clocks are as large as beans, so they are a cinch to start indoors in containers. You also may buy young plants in spring. Look for plants in 4-inch pots, because seedlings forced to grow in too-small containers may be stunted.

Enrich the soil with a 2-inch layer of organic matter before setting out seedlings, and cover them with a cloche during spells of cold, windy weather. After the soil has warmed, mulch around plants to control weeds and retain soil moisture.

If blooming slows in late summer, trim the plants back to encourage the de-

Colorful Companions

Because four o'clocks show little color during the day, they need companions that show a bit of color but don't attract a lot of attention. Narrowleaf zinnia, melampodium and lantana are promising candidates, as are pink or white wax begonia.

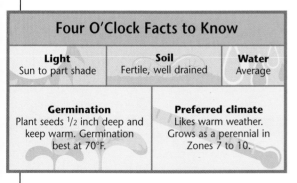

Four o'clocks withstand extreme summer heat and humidity, and persist as perennials in many areas. Easy to grow from seed, these lightly fragrant flowers open in late afternoon and close the following morning.

Four O'Clock Facts to Know		
Light Sun to part shade	**Soil** Fertile, well drained	**Water** Average
Germination Plant seeds 1/2 inch deep and keep warm. Germination best at 70°F.		**Preferred climate** Likes warm weather. Grows as a perennial in Zones 7 to 10.

FOXGLOVE
Digitalis purpurea

Tall spires of foxglove make a dramatic backdrop in partially shaded sections of the garden.

Colorful Companions

Bloom time varies with climate, so the best starting point for finding landscape buddies for foxglove is to work primarily within their planting niche. Pansies, violas, dianthus and English daisies are good winter annuals for framing your foxglove bed. These can be replaced by impatiens, torenia, dusty miller or coleus in early summer.

Are regal foxgloves annuals, perennials or something in between? It depends on where you live, but in all areas they can be grown as annuals. Winter chilling enhances the plants' enthusiasm for flowering, so it's always best to try to grow them as winter annuals or perennials. Well-rooted foxgloves are hardy to Zone 4.

Although it may be difficult to part with the blooms in the garden, foxgloves make excellent cut flowers. A European native with a long history of medicinal use, foxglove leaves contains a potent heart stimulant and should never be ingested for any reason.

In the Garden

Foxgloves thrive in moist, fertile, well-drained soil in partial shade. In most climates, fall is the best time to set out new plants, divide established ones, or dig and transplant volunteers found making a home for themselves in lawns or shrub beds.

How to Grow

The easiest way to begin is to buy some seedlings in late summer or early fall and set them out in a well-prepared bed. If you are growing your own seedlings, start them indoors anytime from spring to mid-summer, and set them out in September. Amend the soil with compost, peat moss or another form of organic matter, and mulch after planting to help keep the soil constantly moist.

Harvest spikes as cut flowers, or deadhead your plants unless you want them to reseed. Should you notice serious yellowing of older leaves, top-dress the bed with a timed-release fertilizer. Also fertilize new or old plantings in early spring, soon after new leaves appear.

Propagate vigorous hybrids every fall by digging and dividing the plants. Cut clumps apart with a sharp knife and immediately re-plant the best ones that have a few roots attached. In winter, use evergreen boughs to protect plants from ice and cold, drying winds.

Selecting Varieties

'Foxy' is a great garden variety because of its vigor, color range, 3-foot size, and long blooming time. 'Excelsior' hybrids are taller, to 5 feet, and may need staking. For cutting, the snow-white 'Alba' cultivar is one of the best spike-forming flowers you can grow.

When grown in partial shade, foxgloves are a breathtaking sight.

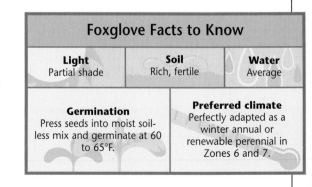

Foxglove Facts to Know		
Light Partial shade	**Soil** Rich, fertile	**Water** Average
Germination Press seeds into moist soil-less mix and germinate at 60 to 65°F.		**Preferred climate** Perfectly adapted as a winter annual or renewable perennial in Zones 6 and 7.

FUCHSIA
Fuchsia hybrida

The common name of ladies' eardrops is easily understood once you admire fuchsia's pendulous flowers hanging from the stems like exotic jewels. Actually tender perennials, fuchsias are grown as perennial shrubs in cool, foggy areas along the West Coast. Elsewhere gardeners use them as summer annuals for baskets and containers. Not long ago all fuchsias were propagated vegetatively, from stem cuttings, but a few new hybrid varieties make it possible for patient gardeners to grow them from seed.

In the Garden

Grow fuchsias in containers or hanging baskets placed in cool partial shade. Morning sun and afternoon shade is best. Place fuchsias where they are easy to reach, because they will need almost daily watering along with frequent grooming. If you have a greenhouse, you can also grow fuchsias as staked standards, which have bushy foliage and flowers atop a slender, treelike trunk.

How to Grow

The simplest way to start with fuchsias is to buy healthy plants in late spring, but you can start seeds indoors in late winter if you prefer. Pinch back young plants to induce branching. Move plants outdoors when nighttime temperatures rise into the mid-50s.

Allow fuchsias to become almost dry between waterings, but

'Display' fuchsia.

never let them dry out completely. During warm summer weather, when the plants are heavy with lush foliage, you may need to water them twice a day. Every week to 10 days, feed your fuchsias with a soluble liquid fertilizer that contains nitrogen, potassium and a little iron. Pinch off spent flowers and seedpods at least once a week.

To keep a fuchsia from one year to the next, prune it back hard in fall, to about 6 inches, and keep it indoors through winter. Water the plant lightly but regularly, and mist the foliage frequently.

Selecting Varieties

Among varieties that can be grown from seed, 'Florabelle' has red flowers with purple centers. 'Swing' has a lighter look, with red flowers with white centers.

Colorful Companions

Fuchsias are typically grown alone in large baskets,

but you can add contrast by combining them with dusty miller, trailing petunias or cascading white lobelia. In large container bouquets, one or two small fuchsias make wonderful dark accents when placed just inside the edge of the pot.

'Personality' fuchsia.

Fuchsia Facts to Know

Light	Soil	Water
Moderate shade	Gritty potting soil	Above average

Germination	Preferred climate
Press seeds into damp soil-less mix, cover with plastic. Germinate at 65 to 70°F.	Best temperature range for fuchsias is 55 to 70°F. At warmer temperatures, high humidity is crucial to their survival.

GAILLARDIA
Gaillardia pulchella

A foundation flower for wild gardens and meadows, gaillardia or Indian blanket has a bushy, uniform growth habit that helps it fit in well even when grown among more refined flowers in beds. Native to the Central Plains and the state flower of Oklahoma, gaillardia grows beautifully in almost any soil and makes a fine cut flower too. Once established, it needs very little water, and it always reseeds itself year after year. Because of its drought tolerance, gaillardia is one of the few annuals that will grow well in sandy beachside situations.

In the Garden

Plant gaillardia in masses in beds, fields, roadsides and ditches. Plant it once, and you can look forward to a fresh stand appearing like magic each spring. Gaillardia prefers full sun but will tolerate partial afternoon shade in hot summer climates.

How to Grow

Sow seeds where you want them to grow in fall or first thing in spring. Seeds planted too late in the spring may not germinate until the following year. Gaillardia blooms in early summer in hot climates, where the seeds typically germinate sporadically from fall to spring. In cold climates, seeds germinate in spring and the plants are in bloom by late summer. Mature plant size varies with climate, between 18 and 24 inches.

Provide water if needed to get plants off to a good start. In dry, arid climates, it is helpful to water gaillardia two or three times during May and June, or every 2 weeks for as long as the plants are showing strong bloom.

If you want your gaillardia to reseed, let the plants stand until very few new blooms appear. By this time numerous older blooms will have borne and shed their seeds, and you can mow the plants down or pull them up. Or, gather whole dried flower heads and crush them to harvest your own seed crop.

Selecting Varieties

Selections sold by species name are inexpensive to buy in bulk. A few unusual varieties have been

Gaillardia.

developed, including 'Red Plume', which has very dark red double blossoms. For cutting, 'Lorenziana Mix' includes many double flowers in a range of unusual colors, including yellow, orange, purplish-maroon and occasional light pinks.

Colorful Companions

Because the texture of gaillardia is somewhat coarse, it is flattered by close association with more fine-textured plants, such as ammi or nierembergia. In wildflower meadows, sow as a follow-up behind bachelor buttons and poppies. Gaillardia also blends beautifully with sulphur cosmos.

'Yellow Sun' gaillardia.

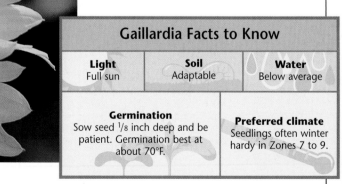

Gaillardia Facts to Know

Light	**Soil**	**Water**
Full sun	Adaptable	Below average

Germination	**Preferred climate**
Sow seed ⅛ inch deep and be patient. Germination best at about 70°F.	Seedlings often winter hardy in Zones 7 to 9.

GAZANIA
Gazania spp.

'Sun Burst' and 'Sun Gold' gazania.

If the sunflower name had not already been taken, it would have been perfect for gazania, sometimes called treasure flower. Every day soon after dawn, the big starry blossoms burst open for a dramatic show of yellow or orange flowers with darker centers. Then they close up by nightfall. Gazania is a South American beauty that is at home in any climate that gets several weeks of hot summer weather. It sometimes grows as a perennial groundcover in Zones 9 and 10.

In the Garden

Gazania asks for little more than full sun and excellent drainage for good performance. The plants are small, only 10 inches tall when in full bloom, so they are best for planting in front of taller flowers. Gazanias are also great to scatter on dry or rocky slopes in small groups of 3 to 5 plants. However, do keep the plants accessible, because you will need to get to them to pinch off the spent blossoms. Low, wide containers are ideal for a miniature gazania garden to grow on a sunny deck or patio.

How to Grow

Bedding plants are increasingly available in spring, or you can start your own plants from seed if you want a particular color. Gazanias in cellpacks quickly become root bound, so it's important to break or loosen matted roots as you set out the plants. Especially when growing gazanias in very sandy soil, work in a balanced organic or timed-release fertilizer before setting out the plants.

Keep mulches pulled at least an inch away from the base of the plants. If the crowns are kept too damp they are prone to rot. Gazania leaves are thick and leathery, and do an excellent job of hoarding limited moisture. Still, you should water plants once a week during prolonged periods of dry weather. Deadheading is crucial if you expect your plants to continue blossoming for a long time.

Selecting Varieties

New colors are showing up in gazania, such as almost-white 'Cream Beauty'. However, flowering is always strong with traditional gazania colors, which can be had individually or in mixtures. The 'Daybreak' series includes every shade from cream yellow to deep bronze red along with 'Daybreak Red Stripe', which has bright red stripes down each gold petal.

Colorful Companions

Gazanias are great fillers for the dahlia bed, where they provide vibrant color during the summer while dahlias are gathering strength for fall. Other good companions include French marigolds, dwarf sulphur cosmos and gaillardia.

'Aztec Queen' gazania.

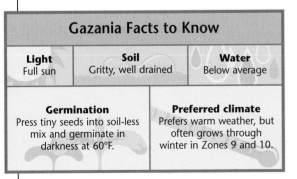

Gazania Facts to Know

Light	Soil	Water
Full sun	Gritty, well drained	Below average

Germination	Preferred climate
Press tiny seeds into soil-less mix and germinate in darkness at 60°F.	Prefers warm weather, but often grows through winter in Zones 9 and 10.

GERANIUM
Pelargonium hortorum, P. peltatum

Zonal geraniums dance in the company of yellow marigolds, tall ageratum and blue salvia.

The summer flowers that we call geraniums are but two representatives from a genus that includes over 200 species. The most popular types, called zonal geraniums, are the ones that produce loose balls of red, white, pink or lavender blossoms on upright plants. When given proper care, zonal geraniums will bloom almost continuously. Some cultivars can be coaxed into bloom in winter when grown indoors in a sunny window. These old "windowsill" zonals are as famous for their leaf color as for their flowers. All zonal geraniums develop dark rings or zones in their leaves in response to cool weather.

Where summer heat is not too intense or long-lived, a second type of geranium, called ivy geranium, is outstanding when used to fill large containers and window boxes.

In the Garden

For every garden and gardener, there is a perfect geranium to grow in just the right spot. Although widely regarded as full-sun plants, all geraniums benefit from partial shade. Zonal geraniums need 6 hours of bright sun in the Far North, 4 hours in the country's midsection, and only 3 hours in the South. Ivy geraniums, which are grown only in the North, need slightly less sun than the zonal types.

Geraniums are naturals for containers, or you can grow them in well-drained beds. Unlike many flowers, which need constant moisture, geraniums grow best if their roots dry out between waterings. To accommodate this need, grow geraniums in light-textured beds that have been amended with peat moss or compost and a dash of sand. In containers, use high-quality potting soil that contains peat, vermiculite or perlite along with a little sand to make it gritty.

How to Grow

Some varieties of zonal geranium can be started from seed, but most gardeners save time by buying them as bedding plants. At the garden center, you will find inexpensive geraniums in cellpacks that have been grown from seed as well as larger, more costly plants

Zonal Geranium Facts to Know

Light	Soil	Water
Partial shade	Light textured, fertile	Average

Germination	Preferred climate
Plant seed ⅛ inch deep in sterile soil-less mix, dampen, cover with plastic and germinate at 75°F.	Adaptable, but shows best growth when temperatures range between 60°F at night and 80°F during the day.

that have been grown from cuttings. Use seed-sown varieties for planting in large display beds. Although the flowers of most seed-sown varieties are single, they are also self-cleaning so little dead-heading is needed. Choose the bigger plants propagated from cuttings for containers or beds that will be viewed up close. Geraniums grown from cuttings usually have bigger double flowers and grow into larger plants compared to those grown from seed. Almost all of the better ivy geraniums are grown from cuttings.

Both zonal and ivy geraniums need a constant supply of fertilizer. You can mix a complete soluble fertilizer into the water every third time you water plants grown in containers, but this can be cumbersome when growing plants in beds. A better approach is to mix a timed-release fertilizer into the soil

To keep geraniums looking good and heavy with blooms, snip off old flower clusters promptly.

before planting, and then to begin light applications of liquid fertilizer after about 6 weeks. Plants that have yellow leaves and show little new growth need more fertilizer.

Trim plants as needed to keep them nicely balanced. Deadhead vegetatively propagated zonal geraniums weekly. In late summer, trim back ivy geraniums if needed to encourage new growth.

To keep geraniums through winter, pot up plants in early fall and then cut them back by half their size. Bring plants indoors before the first frost. You can keep them in a semidormant state by limiting water and light, or grow them through winter on a windowsill as blooming houseplants. In early spring, soon after new stems grow, propagate stem cuttings to multiply your favorite plants.

Selecting Varieties

For top performance in outdoor beds, local garden centers usually do a fine job of stock-

ing varieties known to grow well in your area. Vegetatively propagated zonal geraniums and ivy geraniums usually show a blossom or two by the time they leave the greenhouse, so it's easy to choose plants based on color. Geranium cultivars suitable for windowsill culture are mostly in the hands of collectors, and include names such as 'Dolly Varden', 'Just William' and 'Mr. Everaarts'.

To grow your own zonal geraniums from seed, you will find large color ranges in all of the leading series, including 'Elite', 'Multibloom', 'Orbit' and 'Pinto'. Ivy geraniums that can be grown from seed include 'Summer Showers' and 'Tornado'.

Colorful Companions

Because zonal geraniums bloom for such a long time, they need companion plants that stay in flower for a long time, too. Zonal geraniums and white petunias always look good together. Other lovely partners include ageratum, white browallia, compact yellow marigolds or blue salvia. Ivy geraniums usually look best planted alone in window boxes, hanging baskets or large containers.

Geraniums.

Showy double-flowered geraniums like 'Appleblossom' make wonderful container plants.

Ivy Geranium Facts to Know

Light	Soil	Water
Partial shade	Light textured, fertile	Average

Germination	Preferred climate
Barely cover seeds with soil, dampen well and germinate at 75°F.	Cannot tolerate prolonged temperatures above 85°F. Best in partial shade in cool climates.

GOMPHRENA

Gomphrena globosa

'Strawberry Fields' gomphrena.

Selecting Varieties

'Buddy' and 'Gnome'are dwarf varieties that grow only to about 6 inches tall and come in purple, pink and white. Among full-sized varieties, 'Bicolor Rose' is a beautiful rich pink haloed with white. Gomphrena in red-orange include 'Strawberry Fields' and newer 'Qis Carmine', a stunning red with lighter highlights.

Colorful Companions

Varieties that produce dark purple blooms look great with dusty miller at their sides. Pink selections are easy to combine with big zinnias, pink pentas or white lavatera. Use red-orange varieties in combination with bright yellow marigolds, dwarf sunflowers, or Mexican sunflower.

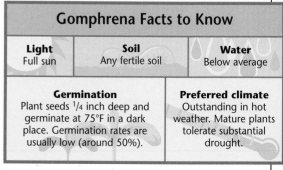

Gomphrena.

Whether your garden is large or small, you can create little pockets of excitement by using the unique flower form available in gomphrena, also called globe amaranth. The blossoms are small balls of papery bracts that provide welcome contrast when grown among flowers with flat or tubular blossoms or when used in flower arrangements. When dried, gomphrena blossoms hold their colors for many months.

In the Garden

Many varieties grow to 18 inches tall, the perfect size for planting in small drifts among other flowers. Gomphrena will also grow in containers, and it mixes easily with other summer annuals in container bouquets. Full sun is needed in all but the hottest climates, but any well-drained soil will do. Gomphrena is very drought tolerant once established, so it's a fine flower to grow in midsummer, when many other flowers suffer from chronic thirst.

How to Grow

Bedding plants of popular dwarf varieties are widely available, but you may need to start seeds of unusual selections in special colors. Start seeds indoors 4 to 6 weeks before your last frost is expected, and grow them in a warm place. Gomphrena is a warm-natured plant that grows very little when exposed to temperatures below 55°F.

Mix a timed-release fertilizer into the soil before setting out the plants, and water regularly to help them become established. Be patient, because gomphrena will grow very little as long as cool spring weather prevails. When summer heats up, the plants will quickly take off and fill in completely when planted 8 to 12 inches apart.

Harvest the flowers as needed for cut arrangements, but don't worry about deadheading gomphrena. After the plants load up with flowers they can hold them for many weeks, often all the way to frost.

Gomphrena Facts to Know		
Light Full sun	**Soil** Any fertile soil	**Water** Below average
Germination Plant seeds ¼ inch deep and germinate at 75°F in a dark place. Germination rates are usually low (around 50%).		**Preferred climate** Outstanding in hot weather. Mature plants tolerate substantial drought.

HELIOTROPE
Heliotropium arborescens

This delightful old flower has been rediscovered in keeping with gardeners' renewed interest in fragrant plants. Once affectionately known as cherry pie plant, lavender to purple heliotrope blossoms give off a fruity vanilla fragrance that's most noticeable at dusk or dawn. The potency of the fragrance often varies between plants and can be intensified by exposing them to slight drought stress while they are in flower. Originally from Peru, heliotrope grows as a perennial in tropical areas.

Fragrant heliotrope.

In the Garden

Heliotrope grows into a 2-foot-tall shrub-like plant with leathery green leaves. Use a pair of closely spaced plants as a specimen in a half-shaded spot in a mixed border, or grow heliotrope in large containers. To make the most of heliotrope's fragrance, locate it near a low wall or other windbreak that will help retain its fragrance. In outdoor living areas, place potted heliotrope at nose level while the plants are in bloom.

How to Grow

Small heliotrope seeds germinate erratically and benefit from a good head start in spring. Plant them 8 weeks before your last spring frost, or buy plants around your last frost date. Heliotrope stem cuttings root easily when kept in a cool place, usually within 3 weeks, so you may want to buy a greenhouse-grown plant and cut it into plantable pieces.

Work compost or another rich soil amendment into the site before setting out the plants. Add a little organic or timed-release fertilizer too, because heliotrope is a heavy feeder. Mulch between plants to keep the soil moist and to deter weeds. A month after planting, pinch back plants to encourage bushy growth. Do not allow plants to dry out until they are in full flower, and then only for short periods of time.

Deadhead plants unless you want them to reseed. Despite the difficulty of starting the seeds on purpose, the plants often reseed themselves very well.

plants you can find and save seeds from your healthiest, most fragrant plants.

Colorful Companions

The traditional bed partner for heliotrope is fragrant sweet alyssum. The two plants make an unbeatable team, especially when white sweet alyssum is combined with dark purple selections of heliotrope. Cascading white petunias are another fine companion plant for heliotrope.

Selecting Varieties

Named varieties include 'Marine', dark purple 'Midnight' and 'Fragrant Delight', which is potentially a dependable source of pure heliotrope perfume. If you are in pursuit of fragrance, another smart strategy is to start with any seeds or

Heliotrope Facts to Know		
Light Full sun to part shade	**Soil** Rich, well drained	**Water** Average
Germination Barely cover seeds with soil-less mix and germinate at 70°F.	**Preferred climate** Grows best in areas with moderately warm summers; does not tolerate frost.	

Heliotrope with dwarf ageratum.

HOLLYHOCK

Alcea rosea

Hollyhocks.

A true antique flower, hollyhocks have charmed gardeners for centuries. Most strains are hardy perennials, but because of problems with a foliar disease called rust, they are often grown as biennials (planted in summer for bloom the following spring) or as late-blooming annuals.

In the Garden

All gardens benefit from the strong vertical lines hollyhocks bring to the landscape. Because of their height, hollyhocks make excellent accents for fences and gates, or you can use them as a blooming backdrop for the back of the border. Plan to stake double-flowered varieties, which often fall over just as they reach peak bloom. Hollyhocks need plenty of sun and deep, rich soil. Japanese beetles eat both the flowers and the foliage, so hollyhocks are not good flowers for areas where this pest is a problem.

How to Grow

To grow hollyhocks as annuals, start the seeds indoors in late winter. Move the seedlings to 4-inch pots when they have at least one large true leaf. About a month before your last frost, put the seedlings outside in an unheated cold frame. Set them out in the garden 2 weeks later, in soil that has been enriched with compost or rotted manure. An early start and exposure to chilly weather helps assure strong blooming the first year.

You can prolong the blooming period of your hollyhocks by cutting off old flower spikes as soon as the topmost flowers lose their looks. Cut plants back to the ground in early winter. Where winters are mild, a few basal leaves may persist year-round.

Selecting Varieties

Many hollyhock strains are biennial or perennial, so they won't bloom the first year following spring plant-ing. 'Summer Carnival' is a notable exception, with a strong track record of blooming about 4 months after seeds are planted. The plants grow to more than 4 feet tall and produce double flowers in red, rose, yellow or pink. Established plants become perennials, hardy to Zone 3. Planted in late summer, it will bloom the following spring and often reseeds before dying back to the ground.

Colorful Companions

The lowest leaves on hollyhock plants often appear tattered, so it's a good idea to hide them from view with smaller annuals, such as candytuft, nierembergia, verbena or dwarf zinnias.

Old-fashioned single hollyhocks edged with signet marigolds, white oxeye daisies (a perennial), and pink English daisies.

Hollyhock Facts to Know

Light Sun	Soil Rich, well drained	Water Average
Germination Plant seeds ¼ inch deep and germinate at 60°F. Exposure to cold weather benefits the seedlings.		**Preferred climate** Established plants are hardy short-lived perennials.

HYACINTH BEAN

Dolichos lablab

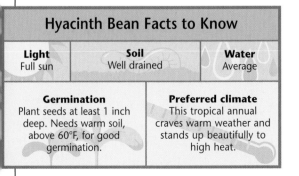

Hyacinth bean.

The trusses of purple pea-like hyacinth bean flowers were first seen by English-speaking gardeners in the early 1800s. Originally from Egypt, this exuberant, fast-growing annual vine resembles an ornamental pole-type lima bean. The immature peas are often said to be edible, but they are unacceptably bitter to most palates.

In the Garden

Hyacinth bean will twine on anything, from string to bamboo teepees to a chainlink fence. The vines will also scramble over a pillar or large stump if you provide a few strings for them to hang onto until they are big enough to twine back upon themselves. In hot summer weather, vines often grow more than 15 feet long, so they can easily cascade over the top of a pergola or overhead arch. Because of their size, hyacinth bean vines make fine plants to grow as a screen to shade hot porches, patios or south-facing walls.

Hyacinth beans can handle hot sun that might make other vines wilt. They usually grow continuously until frost, blooming all the while.

How to Grow

Soak the large seeds in water overnight before planting them where you want them to grow. You can start seeds indoors if desired, but be sure to set out the seedlings promptly, within 2 weeks of germination. Before planting, work a little fertilizer into the soil to as-sure the plants of a fast start. In cool climates, cover the soil with black plastic to help warm it up a little. Hyacinth beans do not grow well in cold soil.

You can snip off errant vines that wander too far, but hyacinth beans do not require regular grooming. However, cutting off maturing seedpods encourages new flowers to develop and prolongs the longevity of the plants. Water the vines deeply once a week during long periods of dry weather.

Selecting Varieties

Most varieties, including 'Ruby Moon', produce lavender blossoms and glossy purple pods, and the stems and leaves also show pronounced purple pigmentation. There is also a white-flowered form that has brighter green foliage and pure white flowers. When both colors are grown together, they both complement and contrast with one another.

Colorful Companions

Purple-flowered hyacinth bean is a dark presence in the garden that intensifies the glow of white or yellow flowers. Because of the sheer size of these plants, use other large flowers such as cleome or sunflower to bring balance to the landscape.

Dolichos lablab, *Hyacinth bean.*

Hyacinth Bean Facts to Know		
Light Full sun	**Soil** Well drained	**Water** Average
Germination Plant seeds at least 1 inch deep. Needs warm soil, above 60°F, for good germination.		**Preferred climate** This tropical annual craves warm weather and stands up beautifully to high heat.

IMPATIENS
Impatiens wallerana, I. hawkeri

Mass planting of impatiens beneath a large shade tree. Impatiens is the perfect solution to many shady challenges!

The most popular annual in America is the impatiens, and deservedly so. Since they are available in almost every color and a number of pretty swirl patterns and bicolors, you are sure to find a selection that's perfect for the spot you have in mind. Originally from Africa and New Guinea, today's hybrid impatiens are actually tropical perennials

Use double-flowered impatiens in containers that are seen up close.

bred to grow as annuals. Breeding work on impatiens has been so successful that plants now produce flowers in as little as 8 weeks from seed, but they have not lost their ability to be propagated from stem cuttings, a throwback to their perennial days.

There are two major types of impatiens—the familiar garden impatiens and taller New Guinea impatiens, which often have variegated leaves and include the color orange. Most New Guinea impatiens plants are grown from stem cuttings, and they usually cost more than garden impatiens grown from seed.

In the Garden

Each type of impatiens has its place in the landscape. Garden impatiens are unsurpassed for bringing light and color to shady areas, whether they are grown in beds or containers. Depending on variety, light and growing conditions, impatiens grow to

between 8 and 15 inches tall. Close spacing and very warm humid conditions tend to increase plant height. So, if you take a variety that tends to grow into a low mound (such as 'Super Elfin') and set plants at least 12 inches apart, you will get a semi-groundcover effect. To fill a bed with a knee-deep blanket of color, plant a tall variety (such as 'Pride') at 10-inch spacing. Grow fancy double-flowered varieties in containers that can be viewed up close.

New Guinea impatiens are larger plants that grow to 2 feet tall. Most of the better varieties have a strong branching habit, yet they still tend

Impatiens Facts to Know		
Light Shade to part sun	**Soil** Rich, moist	**Water** Above average
Germination Barely cover seeds with sterile soil-less mix and germinate at 70°F.		**Preferred climate** Warm growing conditions support heavy flowering from early summer to frost.

A hollowed-out stump makes a surprising planter for rich red impatiens.

Yellowing leaves are the most common sign that plants need additional nutrients, which can be supplied by top-dressing the bed with more organic or timed-release fertilizer, or by feeding them a liquid plant food every week to 10 days.

Older plants often become leggy, showing long bare stems with only a few leaves and flowers at the tips. Use pruning shears to cut back leggy plants by one-third, and follow up with a dose of fertilizer. New blooming stems should emerge within 3 weeks.

Impatiens often reseed in warm weather areas, but the offspring from hybrid parents may not be as pretty or vigorous as the plants that produced them. Still, most gardeners welcome volunteer impatiens, which typically appear late in spring, after the soil is warm.

Selecting Varieties

You can get a good look at state-of-the-art varieties at any good garden center. Leading variety series include 'Accent', 'Super

Window boxes typically receive a half day of shade—the perfect exposure for impatiens.

Elfin' and 'Tempo', among others. Fancy doubles for containers include 'Carousel', 'Confection' and 'Victoria Rose'. Choose New Guinea impatiens with flower and leaf colors you like. 'Tango' is bright orange, while 'Harmony', 'Paradise' and other series include a range of interesting colors.

Colorful Companions

Coleus and impatiens go together like bread and butter. Pair various shades of impatiens with very dark red-leafed coleus or with varieties with lime-green leaves. Wax leaf begonias with green leaves make a fine edging plant to use around big beds of impatiens. Tuck a few bacopa plants just inside the edges of the pots planted with impatiens. It will provide a lovely cascade of greenery to spill over the edge of the pot.

to have a stiff upright silhouette. You can grow New Guineas in beds, but they are most often used as specimen plants in containers. New Guinea impatiens can handle a little more sun than garden impatiens, but otherwise the two species have similar cultural needs.

How to Grow

Most people buy impatiens as bedding plants, but it is not difficult to start your own plants from seed. Plant seeds indoors 4 weeks before your last frost. Impatiens need warm soil, so a late start suits them. Use a high-quality professional soilless mix. Do not fertilize very young seedlings, which are easily damaged by soluble salts.

Set plants out after nighttime temperatures are above 55°F. Work compost or peat moss into the soil to increase its ability to hold moisture. Also add an organic or timed-release fertilizer to the soil. With impatiens, use mulches that dry quickly, such as pine needles, or do not mulch the plants at all. When the base of a plant is exposed to prolonged sogginess, it tends to rot.

Impatiens need increasing amounts of water and fertilizer as they gain size. In warm summer weather, plants in containers may need water twice a day. In beds, plants that appear wilted first thing in the morning are severely short of water.

New Guinea impatiens have extra large flowers, and the plants are taller than other impatiens.

KALE AND CABBAGE
Brassica oleracea

For three centuries Japanese plant breeders have been tinkering with special varieties of kale and cabbage that develop striking leaf colors in cool fall weather. Leaf colors range from white to red, with frilled or fringed edges that make them even more unusual. Generally speaking, varieties with deeply cut, fringed leaves are kales, while those with rounded leaves are cabbages. Either are valuable plants for bringing color to the garden in late fall and early winter, when few flowers are in bloom.

Ornamental cabbage.

In the Garden

Structured mass plantings in which 5 or more plants are planted at even spacing have the strongest visual impact in the garden. Or, you might use a single plant as the central element in a large container, with pansies or violas around the edges. The plants grow best in sunny spots where the soil is deep and rich.

How to Grow

Proper timing will limit pest problems and result in vigorous, well-colored plants. Start seeds indoors in containers 80 days before your first fall frost date. Shift seedlings to 4-inch pots when they have several leaves, and place them in a sunny spot covered with floating rowcover. Uncovered plants are often damaged by leaf-eating caterpillars in early fall. Because the plants do not develop good leaf colors until nighttime temperatures drop below 55°F for 2 weeks, they are safest in protected containers until insect pressure subsides in mid-fall. Feed plants with a liquid fertilizer every 2 weeks until they are transplanted to the garden.

A few weeks before your first frost, set plants out in the garden, 10 to 15 inches apart, as replacements for tired summer annuals. They will stand through winter in areas that rarely have hard freezes. Plants that survive winter bolt into flower as soon as days become longer in early spring. Flowers of all varieties are yellow.

Selecting Varieties

All varieties can be used as edible garnishes, but 'Nagoya White' is often named as the best tasting. 'Red Peacock' has thin, feathery leaves that turn deep cherry red. It is especially popular in areas where fall weather is cool and damp.

Colorful Companions

Ornamental kale and cabbage are most striking when grown in the company of fall-blooming flowers, including marigolds, perennial fall asters and chrysanthemums, or with an edging of pansies or violas.

Ornamental kale offers finely frilled leaves.

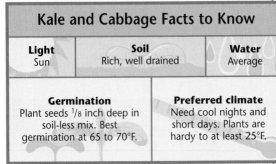

Kale and Cabbage Facts to Know		
Light Sun	**Soil** Rich, well drained	**Water** Average
Germination Plant seeds ⅛ inch deep in soil-less mix. Best germination at 65 to 70°F.		**Preferred climate** Need cool nights and short days. Plants are hardy to at least 25°F.

LANTANA
Lantana camara

Lantana thrives in the hottest, muggiest weather that summer can bring. Flowers form in small clusters, which are often comprised of individual flowers that start out one color and mature to another, giving each cluster a multicolored effect. Butterflies adore the newly opened florets, making lantana a leading plant for any butterfly garden. A tropical verbena cousin from the Caribbean, lantana survives winter in Zones 8 to 10, where the plants grow into large, rambling shrubs. Lantana has escaped cultivation in Florida, where it is often considered a weed.

Lantana flowers change colors as they age, creating a multicolored effect in each cluster.

In the Garden

When handled as an annual, expect lantana to grow less than 2 feet tall and to gradually spread outward 3 feet or more. However, this type of exuberant growth occurs in late summer, after the plants have soaked up plenty of heat, which makes lantana a fine replacement plant for cool-season annuals that expire soon after the weather turns hot. Lantana needs plenty of sun, but in hot climates a little afternoon shade will not hold the plants back.

How to Grow

Lantana is grown from rooted cuttings, which are widely available at garden centers in late spring. Set plants out after the soil has warmed, or keep them in containers placed in warm sun, until you are ready to move them to the garden. Where summers are cool, lantana often grows best in large pots or hanging baskets placed in a warm, sunny spot, protected from cool winds.

Work a complete fertilizer into the soil before planting, and keep the roots moist for 3 weeks after setting out the plants. Once established, lantana needs little care beyond occasional trimming to keep the plants neat. Where summers are long and warm, you can multiply your supply of plants by rooting 6-inch-long stem cuttings in containers filled with moist potting soil.

Selecting Varieties

Numerous named hybrids are available in colors that include yellow, orange, lavender and red. Most plants show a few blooms at an early age, making it easy to choose cultivars based on the colors you want. A few varieties have leaves that are lightly variegated with white, and these are often used in large containers.

Colorful Companions

The dark green foliage of lantana contrasts well when underplanted with 'Marguerite' ornamental sweet potato. Good small plants to grow nearby include ageratum, narrowleaf zinnia and yellow melampodium. Heat-tolerant pentas are often used to frame large plantings of lantana.

Lantana, the all-time favorite of butterflies.

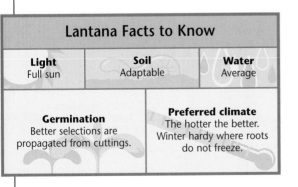

Lantana Facts to Know

Light	Soil	Water
Full sun	Adaptable	Average

Germination	Preferred climate
Better selections are propagated from cuttings.	The hotter the better. Winter hardy where roots do not freeze.

In mild winter areas where lantana is perennial, plants often grow into large shrubs.

LARKSPUR

Consolida ambigua

Cut larkspur for indoor arrangements. The spikes also dry well.

The tall, straight flowering spikes of larkspur are so beautiful in the garden that it can be difficult to cut them for indoor arrangements, but that is what you must do to derive maximum satisfaction from this flower. Also known as annual delphinium, larkspur is not a familiar sight in modern gardens since it cannot be handled as a bedding plant. This is one fine flower that must be direct-sown for best results.

In the Garden

At 2 to 4 feet tall, larkspur is best used as a backdrop for other flowers that share its penchant for cold weather. Grow larkspur in any sunny bed that is very well drained. The plants are prone to rot if left to sit in chronically damp soil. Thin plants to 10 inches apart to help them dry out quickly after heavy rains. Larkspur reseeds itself well, but it is difficult to move misplaced seedlings. Even if you lift the seedlings with soil firmly packed around their roots and transplant them immediately, they usually sulk for weeks afterward.

How to Grow

Sow seeds in the fall in Zones 6 to 9. In colder regions, you can delay sowing until late winter, about a month before your last freeze is expected. Seeds germinate erratically over a period of a month or more.

Whether you plant the seeds in fall or late winter, it's fine to wait until mid-spring to fertilize the plants by top-dressing the soil with an organic or timed-release fertilizer. Mulch lightly, if at all, because mulch tends to keep the plants' crowns damp and promote problems with rotting.

Cut stems freely, but allow some plants to shed mature seeds. Over several seasons, you may lose some colors and wish to start over with fresh seed stock that includes a wide range of pink, purple, lavender and white.

Selecting Varieties

Some varieties grow only to 2 feet, but 'Giant Imperial' usually grows 4 feet tall and includes plants that bloom blue, white, pink and purple. If you like bicolored blossoms, seek out 'Frosted Skies', which has white flowers edged with purple or pink.

Colorful Companions

Corn poppies are the classic bed partner for larkspur, because both species can be planted at the same time and share the same bloom period. Also use larkspur behind pansies, dianthus or other cool-season flowers that bloom in spring.

Larkspur.

Larkspur Facts to Know		
Light Sun to slight shade	**Soil** Fertile, well drained	**Water** Average
Germination Sow when soil is cold, and barely cover seeds with soil.	**Preferred climate** Needs cool weather to germinate and grow. Seedlings are usually hardy to the mid-teens, or lower with snow cover.	

LAVATERA

Lavatera trimestris

'Beauty Mix' is a modern, heavy-flowering lavatera variety that is very easy to grow in rich soil.

The most colorful member of the mallow family, lavatera produces dozens of hibiscus-like flowers with a satiny sheen starting in mid-summer. Sometimes called tree mallow, this native of the Mediterranean positively glows in the garden and makes a pretty but short-lived cut flower as well. Although lavatera is often categorized as a cool-season annual, it is really quite adaptable. Through spring the plants develop extensive roots and abundant maple-like foliage, and then commence heavy blooming in mid-summer. Extremely hot weather may slow flower production, but it often picks up again when more moderate conditions return.

In the Garden

Because of their large size and bushy growth habit, lavatera plants take on a shrub-like appearance, especially when several are grown together. A row of lavatera will form a dense 3-foot-tall hedge, or you can place 3 plants together and let them grow into what appears to be a single large specimen shrub. Give lavatera full sun in all but the hottest climates.

How to Grow

Lavatera can be moody about transplanting, so starting the seeds and handling the seedlings is the hardest part of growing these plants. Start seeds indoors 4 weeks before your last frost, and use peat pots or other plantable containers so the plants can be set out with minimal root disturbance. Or, direct-sow seeds around your last frost date during a period of warm weather. Seeds may take 2 weeks to germinate, so be patient.

Rich well-drained soil that has been fertilized with an organic or timed-release fertilizer will yield the biggest, healthiest plants. Avoid giving lavatera too much nitrogen, which encourages lots of leaves and stems with comparatively few flowers.

Pinch off old flowers and seedpods to help prolong the flowering period. In late summer, cut back tired plants by one-third their size to force out a fresh crop of blooms.

Selecting Varieties

The leading varieties include white 'Mont Blanc', pink 'Mont Rose' and 'Pink Beauty' and deep pink 'Ruby Regis'. 'Silver Cup' bears pink flowers with darker pink veins. Within this species, pink varieties tend to be slightly taller than white ones.

Colorful Companions

The tones of pink seen in lavatera work best with other cool colors. White or pink cosmos are good companions, or you might try tall ageratum. Other prime possibilities include angelonia, pink wax begonia or cleome. Persian shield is an ideal foliage plant to station nearby.

In times past, lavatera went by the common name of tree mallow.

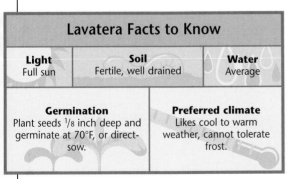

Lavatera Facts to Know		
Light Full sun	**Soil** Fertile, well drained	**Water** Average
Germination Plant seeds 1/8 inch deep and germinate at 70°F, or direct-sow.	**Preferred climate** Likes cool to warm weather, cannot tolerate frost.	

LISIANTHUS
Eustoma grandiflorum

Lisianthus.

Plant breeders took the native southwestern plant known as prairie gentian or Texas bluebell, vastly improved its flower power, and succeeded in turning lisianthus into a very garden-worthy plant. Beautiful tulip-like blooms in pink, blue or white always attract attention in the garden and last for up to 10 days in cut arrangements. Lisianthus is actually a half-hardy biennial, but the improved cultivars rarely survive hard freezes.

In the Garden
The cup-shaped blossoms of lisianthus bring a formal touch to the garden, whether you grow them in beds, planters, or use dwarf varieties as central elements in container bouquets planted in low, broad containers. Lisianthus needs warm sun to flower well and benefits from fertile, well-drained soil. Where summers are very hot, locate lisianthus where the plants will receive a few hours of afternoon shade. Always give lisianthus a prominent place in the front of the garden where you cannot miss every one of its beautiful blossoms.

How to Grow
Bedding plants are widely available in spring, or you can start your own plants from seeds sown 12 weeks before your last frost. Set plants out at about the same time as your last frost, and use cloches if needed to protect them from cold winds. Fertilize the bed with an organic or timed-release fertilizer, and mulch between plants to keep the soil lightly moist. Because the wiry stems often twist or flop as they lengthen and develop buds, it is helpful to use a horizontal trellis made of wire or string to help keep the plants upright.

Purchased plants usually bloom much earlier than homegrown seedlings because they are older, having been held in greenhouses through much of the winter. After the plants commence blooming, cut stems freely to use in indoor arrangements. Alternatively, deadhead the plants regularly to promote a long period of heavy flowering.

Selecting Varieties
'Echo' and 'Heidi' are long-stemmed varieties bred primarily for cutting. 'Echo' has double flowers which always need staking to keep them from toppling when they fill up with rain. 'Heidi' produces single flowers in loose clusters. 'Mermaid' is a heavy-flowering dwarf variety ideal for small containers.

Colorful Companions
The gray-green leaves of lisianthus marry well with dusty miller, ageratum and pink wax begonia. Because of its formal demeanor, lisianthus is a fine flower to grow near boxwoods or other manicured evergreen shrubs.

Lisianthus with bacopa.

Lisianthus Facts to Know		
Light Sun to part shade	**Soil** Fertile, well drained	**Water** Average
Germination Press the tiny seeds into sterile soil-less mix and germinate at 70°F.	**Preferred climate** Adapts to varying weather, but does best when exposed to cool spring conditions followed by summer warmth.	

LOBELIA
Lobelia erinus

The petite leaves and flowers of lobelia turn the plants into vibrant clouds of color. The most common hue is bright blue, but varieties are available in pink or white as well. In any color, lobelia is a valuable little plant for edging or for adding soft color to container bouquets.

Lobelia does a beautiful job of edging beds, and combines well with numerous colors. Companions here include red verbena, gray dusty miller and yellow dwarf marigolds.

In the Garden

A cool-season annual, lobelia thrives when days are warm and nights are cool. However, it is such an enthusiastic bloomer that it often survives hot spells in grand style and remains attractive all the way to frost. Lobelia is very easy to grow and extremely versatile in the garden.

How to Grow

Purchase bedding plants promptly in spring and set them out under cloches at about the time of your last expected freeze. You can also start the tiny seeds indoors in late winter, but the seedlings will not be ready to set out for 2 months. Because the plants are small, you may need a number of them to establish a full, solid edge. Space plants 6 inches apart when using lobelia as an edging, and mulch between plants to discourage weeds and keep the soil moist. Trailing plants are customarily planted just inside the rims of containers or window boxes so they can gracefully cascade down the sides.

Fertilize and water plants regularly, but do allow them to dry out a bit between waterings. Lobelia likes cool, moist roots but cannot tolerate standing water.

In mid-summer, use sharp scissors or pruning shears to cut back the plants by half their size. Water and fertilize them, and they should come back into bloom in a few weeks. Lobelia often puts on a strong new flush of flowers when nights cool down in the fall.

Selecting Varieties

Lobelia varieties fall into two categories: standard and trailing. Both types are available in blue, rose pink or white, with some blue and white bicolors. Choose standard varieties such as 'Blue Moon' or 'Riviera' for edging. 'Crystal Palace', a standard type, has midnight blue flowers and unusual purplish foliage. The 'Cascade', 'Fountain' and 'Regatta' series are trailing types that spread up to 12 inches wide.

Colorful Companions

A robust edging of blue lobelia works like a frame for other white or yellow flowers, or for those with light green foliage. Choose white or pink lobelia to edge walkways that are often used at night. Use trailing lobelia to accessorize containers of geranium, blue salvia or snapdragons. Lobelia is excellent when mixed with hot pink petunias and dusty miller.

Lobelia Facts to Know		
Light Sun to part shade	**Soil** Fertile, well drained	**Water** Average
Germination Press tiny seeds on the surface of damp soil-less mix. Germinate at 70°F, then move seedlings to a cooler location.		**Preferred climate** Prefers cool weather. May wither in mid-summer when grown in hot climates.

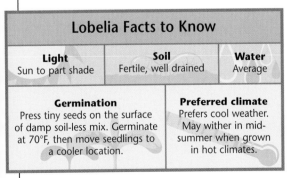

Lobelia cascades from this basket, accompanied by pink petunias.

MARIGOLD

There are three major types of marigolds: large-flowered American or African types, small bushy French marigolds, and ferny signet varieties. All are easy to grow and can be used to fill different niches in your garden.

LARGE-FLOWERED MARIGOLD
Tagetes erecta hybrids

Large-flowered marigolds produce big pompom type flowers more than 3 inches across that are held on stems long enough for cutting. Because of their tropical ancestry, large-flowered marigolds are mildly sensitive to day length, preferring to bloom when days are becoming shorter.

All marigolds need full sun, and large-flowered types that grow more than 18 inches tall benefit from staking or wire support hoops. When grown in a border, these plants rival dahlias for stately stature and the size of their blooms.

Although hybridization has improved things substantially, large-flowered marigolds may be balky about flowering unless they have been exposed to short, 9-hour days. If not exposed to short days at a young age, the plants may spend the summer growing into lanky plants with few blooms. Then, when days shorten in late summer, they produce armloads of beautiful flowers.

Start seeds indoors about 2 weeks before your last frost, or buy bedding plants. Transplant seedlings to the garden after the danger of frost has passed. Work an organic or timed-release fertilizer into the soil before planting, and mulch between plants to retain soil moisture and discourage weeds. Deadhead plants weekly to help keep them in flower for the longest possible time.

Old heirloom strains like 'Crackerjack' grow to 3 feet, but most hybrids grow into shorter, stockier plants. 'Jubilee', 'Antigua', 'Inca', and other varieties described as American or African marigolds are of this type, as are Burpee's white and cream-colored selections.

Compact yellow marigolds edged with ageratum and dusty miller.

Pair orange marigolds with the bold blue spikes of blue salvia, or plant them in the foreground of taller sunflowers. Celosia, lantana, petunia and verbena make good companions for yellow marigolds. Yellow or cream-colored marigolds are easy to work with since they go well with any red, orange or blue flowers.

'First Lady' large-flowered marigolds.

Large-Flowered Marigold Facts to Know		
Light Sun	**Soil** Fertile, well drained	**Water** Average
Germination Germination best at 65°F.	**Preferred climate** Prefers warm weather. Blooms best in late summer to fall after days become shorter.	

FRENCH MARIGOLD
Tagetes patula

French marigolds come in a variety of colors, and are very easy to grow.

Because of their ability to bloom heavily and continuously all summer long, French marigolds are the most popular type for flower beds where nonstop color is the top priority. This species is also useful for starving out rootknot nematodes. In warm climates where nematodes are a recurrent nuisance, French marigolds are often planted in vegetable gardens.

If you live in a cool climate, go ahead and buy bedding plants to get a head start with these trouble-free plants. Where summer lasts longer, direct-seeding is easy because the seedlings are easy to recognize among weeds and germination rates are high. About 2 weeks after your last frost, sow seed in soil that has been enriched with organic matter and a scant amount of fertilizer. Thin seedlings to 12 inches apart, and mulch to limit future weed problems.

'Disco', 'Janie', and 'Hero' are but three of many well-known names in French marigolds. Choose varieties with colors and flower types you find appealing. Depending on variety, French marigolds may pro-duce single flowers, blossoms with tufts of short petals in the centers (called the anemone blossom type), or vivid bicolored blooms marked with deep mahogany red.

'Janie' French marigolds.

SIGNET MARIGOLD
Tagetes tenufolia

You might think of signet marigolds as herbs, for these are the marigolds that produce edible flowers. Their distinctive feathery leaves, which release a citrus scent when touched, also set this species apart from single-flowered French marigolds. This is the marigold of choice for growing in rock gardens or planting around the edges of beds, for the plants grow into up-right, airy mounds. Signet marigolds produce hundreds of small single flowers in yellow, golden orange or deep orange, depending on variety.

You may have trouble locating bedding plants, but signet marigolds are not difficult to start from seeds. Sow indoors in containers 2 weeks before your last frost, and set them out when the seedlings have at least four healthy leaves. You may want to start more plants in late summer, for they make good fall replacements for other annuals on the brink of exhaustion. Plants set 12 inches apart will fill in the spaces between them.

'Lemon Gem', 'Lulu', 'Starfire' or 'Golden Gem' are good varieties to grow in any season. They offer wonderful textural contrast when used as a backup to portulaca.

Signet marigold.

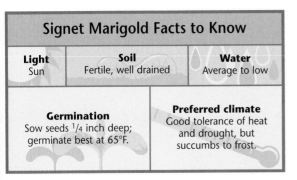

MELAMPODIUM

Melampodium paludosum

Melampodium.

A relative newcomer to American gardens, this vigorous reseeding annual from South Africa has become a top low-maintenance summer flower. Particularly in warm climates, melampodium is justifiably famous for its ability to bloom continuously through summer's worst heat waves. It has no universal nickname that's less cumbersome to pronounce than melampodium, though attempts have been made to call it African zinnia or medallion daisy. A steady producer of small self-cleaning yellow flowers, melampodium asks for little more than sun and warmth to light up the garden with hundreds of bright blossoms the color of the sun.

In the Garden

Melampodium likes full sun and soil that never dries out completely, but any soil that has been adequately fertilized will do. Dwarf varieties fit well into containers, and some are small enough to use as an edging. Full-sized varieties grow to 2 feet tall and are very bushy. Use them to fill beds around a mailbox or lamppost. A fast grower that starts blooming about 60 days after seeds are sown, melampodium can be planted after pansies or other winter annuals for summer-long color.

How to Grow

This flower is so easily grown from seed that you have little to gain by buying bedding plants.

Besides blooming constantly in the hottest weather, melampodium is a strong reseeder too.

Either start seeds indoors 2 weeks before your last frost or direct-seed in the garden in late spring or early summer, after the soil has warmed. Thin dwarf varieties to 10 inches apart, but give larger plants more space. Work a complete organic or timed-release fertilizer into the soil prior to planting, and mulch between plants to retain soil moisture and deter weeds.

Dwarf varieties often need no additional care beyond occasional watering. However, full-sized varieties may grow so large that they need shaping with pruning shears. Although melampodium is a strong reseeder, it is not aggressive. Seedlings appear late in spring, and those that are unwanted are easily pulled out, or you can lift them from beneath and transplant them to where you want them to grow.

Selecting Varieties

If you want a tall selection, look for unnamed varieties sold only by species or common name. 'Showstar' is a popular mid-sized variety that grows to 12 inches tall, while 'Million Gold' is more dwarf in size and habit.

Colorful Companions

Melampodium's bright yellow color and heat tolerance make it a natural for teaming up with red pentas, purple gomphrena, Joseph's coat amaranth that features red or yellow tones, or a multicolored drift of cockscomb or plume celosia.

Melampodium Facts to Know		
Light Full sun	**Soil** Fertile, well drained	**Water** Average
Germination Plant seeds ¼ inch deep and germinate at 70°F. Easy to direct-seed.		**Preferred climate** Wonderfully tolerant of humid heat; cannot stand frost.

MEXICAN SUNFLOWER
Tithonia rotundifolia

A tall, gangly annual second only to giant sunflowers in size, Mexican sunflower features large velvety leaves and bright orange or yellow-orange daisy-type flowers on plants up to 6 feet tall. Mexican sunflower's blooms are not extremely numerous, but they do attract large numbers of butterflies. You can use Mexican sunflower as a cut flower, but it is essential to singe the hollow stem ends in a candle flame immediately after the blooms are harvested to seal in the sap.

Dwarf Mexican sunflower with purple basil.

In the Garden

When grown in the rear in of sunny bed, Mexican sunflowers make a fine backdrop for smaller flowers. Or, locate one or two plants at the edge of the garden where they become eye-catching specimen plants. After the plants reach full size they are prone to toppling over, but they are so heavy that staking is less practical than using pruning loppers to cut off heavy stems that are pulling the plants down with their weight.

How to Grow

Start seeds indoors 2 weeks before your last spring frost or direct-seed soon after the last frost has passed. Work a half ration of organic or timed-release fertilizer into the soil prior to planting. If Mexican sun-

flowers are too well fed, you may get gigantic plants with few flowers. Mexican sunflowers do a good job of shading out weeds, but they may need extra water during hot weather. When the soil becomes too dry, the leaves will wilt sadly until the plants have a chance to drink their fill. To keep tithonia in bloom for a long time, either gather the flowers for arrangements or deadhead the plants about once a week.

Mexican sunflower will reseed, but with restraint. Instead of depending on volunteer plants, it's wiser to gather ripe seeds and store them in a dry place for replanting the next year.

Sun' flowers are an unusual shade of apricot yellow, and the plants grow to about 4 feet. Bright orange 'Goldfinger' and 'Fiesta del Sol' blossoms are produced on 3-foot-tall plants that are more compact and bushy than other varieties.

Colorful Companions

Combine Mexican sunflowers with smaller flowers such as yellow marigolds, melampodium or narrow-leaf zinnias. If space permits, use black-eyed Susan vine as a groundcover beneath plants. Some of the stems will climb up the trunks of the Mexican sunflowers.

Selecting Varieties

Mexican sunflower varieties vary in size and color. 'Torch' grows 6 feet tall and bears dark orange flowers. 'Yellow Torch' is similar, but has yellow petals surrounding orange middles. 'Aztec

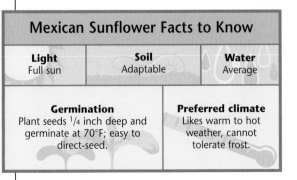

Mexican Sunflower Facts to Know		
Light Full sun	**Soil** Adaptable	**Water** Average
Germination Plant seeds ¼ inch deep and germinate at 70°F; easy to direct-seed.		**Preferred climate** Likes warm to hot weather, cannot tolerate frost.

Mexican sunflower blossom.

MIMULUS
Mimulus hybridus

Mimulus deserves much wider use, particularly in containers where the dramatic blooms can be seen up close. The throats of the tubular blossoms feature downy beards, and the velvety petals are often marked with darker speckles and splotches. If you use your imagination, you may be able to discern how mimulus came to be known as monkey flower. When the splotches are arranged just right, the blooms resemble smiling monkeys' faces.

Mimulus blossom.

In the Garden

Mimulus will grow in shady, well-drained beds, but it is at its best in large containers filled with a rich, peaty potting soil. A location that gets strong sun in spring followed by shade in summer makes an ideal spot. Always grow mimulus within easy reach, because you will need to pinch or snip off old blossoms at least once a week.

How to Grow

You can start mimulus from seed in late winter and move the plants outside after your last frost, but it is simpler to buy stocky bedding plants. Start more seeds in late summer to enjoy mimulus again when the weather cools in the fall.

Allow 3 plants for a 12-inch pot or basket, or space them 6 inches apart in beds. Mature height varies with variety, from 6 to 12 inches. All hybrid mimulus grow into stocky plants with brittle, almost succulent leaves that sometimes block water intended for the plants' roots. If containers become dry, soak them in a tub of water to let them rehydrate completely. Fertilize mimulus every 2 weeks with a soluble fertilizer to keep them well fed. Pinch off the old blossoms regularly. If you miss pinching and numerous seedpods form, pinch back entire stem tips to stimulate reblooming.

Selecting Varieties

Some mail-order companies carry seeds, but the selection is limited. If you want plants of an individual color, buy one already in bloom and propagate stem cuttings from it. At garden centers in the West, two native perennial species also may be sold as monkey flower. These are larger plants that are better grown in beds than in containers.

Colorful Companions

Mimulus blooms may be yellow, orange, mahogany, red, pink or white. They are great plants to place near ferns, or to use as a source of sunny color near shady water features. Try pairing mimulus with blue lobelia in broad, low containers.

'Royal Velvet' mimulus.

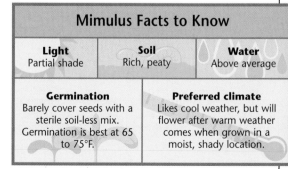

Mimulus Facts to Know		
Light Partial shade	**Soil** Rich, peaty	**Water** Above average
Germination Barely cover seeds with a sterile soil-less mix. Germination is best at 65 to 75°F.		**Preferred climate** Likes cool weather, but will flower after warm weather comes when grown in a moist, shady location.

MOONVINE
Ipomea alba

Moonvine blossom.

This morning glory cousin comes by its name honestly, for its fragrant white flowers open at night and are best seen (and smelled) by the light of the moon. The twining vines are pretty too, heavily clothed in green heart-shaped leaves. Moonvine grows as a perennial in tropical areas, but it is best handled as an annual in places where the ground freezes hard in winter.

In the Garden

Grow moonvine on a chainlink fence or let it twine up a string trellis near your deck or porch. The vines tolerate hot sun and willingly grow into a lovely summer shade screen. In addition to a trellis, you will need a warm, well-drained spot of soil well enriched with or-ganic matter to grow a lush plant. In cool climates where summers are short the vines may grow to only 10 feet or so, but in hot summer areas they sometimes grow to 20 feet or more.

How to Grow

Big moonvine seeds have very hard coats that must be nicked with a sharp knife before they are planted. Otherwise they will remain dormant for months or even years before finally coming to life. You can start seeds indoors in 4-inch pots, or simply sow the scarified seeds where you want the plants to grow just after the last frost has passed. The seedling leaves are huge, twice the size of regular morning glories, so they are easy to distinguish from weeds.

To support strong, early growth, amend the soil with compost and add a complete fertilizer prior to planting seeds or transplanting seedlings. During spells of hot, dry weather, water the plants when the leaves show early signs of wilting. During the second half of summer, feed plants with a soluble liquid fertilizer every 10 days. Gather ripe seeds just before the first fall frost. In Zones 8 to 10, it is wise to watch moonvines carefully to see how prolifically they reseed themselves. Sometimes they get carried away and become weedy.

Selecting Varieties

Variously listed as moonvine or moonflower in seed catalogs, this flower is available only in white and is typically sold by common or botanical name. Beware of wild plants that resemble moonvine. They may be bindweed or another weedy relative.

Colorful Companions

A trellised moonvine forms a cur-tain of green that needs no further accompaniment. For more color, you can mix other morning glories with moonvine on a shared trellis.

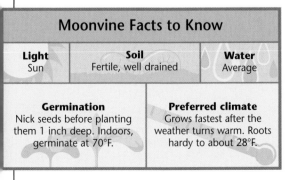

Moonvine Facts to Know

Light	Soil	Water
Sun	Fertile, well drained	Average

Germination	Preferred climate
Nick seeds before planting them 1 inch deep. Indoors, germinate at 70°F.	Grows fastest after the weather turns warm. Roots hardy to about 28°F.

MORNING GLORY
Ipomoea spp.

Morning glory.

Named for the way their flowers open during the early hours of the day, morning glories are the easiest annual vine to grow. The most common type, *I. purpurea*, has heart-shaped leaves and flowers ranging from deep purple to pink to white. But as morning glories have been hybridized to achieve larger, more colorful blossoms, the leaf shape of some varieties has taken on an ivy-leaf silhouette. The color palette now includes many splashy combinations of blue and pink as well as rare reds and pure whites.

Soft purple morning glory lends an elegant touch to the start of each day.

In the Garden

Morning glory vines will twine on any type of wire fence, through open shrubs, or you can use a simple string trellis to coax them to grow into a lush frame around a window or doorway. Morning glories need full sun for at least half a day and will thrive in any reasonably good soil. In fact, the most challenging aspect of growing morning glories is controlling their tendency to rampantly reseed themselves. One safe strategy is to locate morning glories away from vegetable gardens, flower borders or other places where they are likely to become weedy. Instead, grow morning glories near grassy areas so that volunteer plants can be mowed into submission.

How to Grow

Morning glories are warm-season annuals to sow where you want them to grow after the last frost has passed. Enrich the soil with compost and fertilizer before planting, and mulch as needed to keep the soil moist. Seedlings should appear within 2 weeks, with flowers following about 6 weeks later.

After each flower fades, the plants will nurture a small round berry filled with seeds unless you pinch them off. Although time-consuming, this pinching is necessary maintenance for many large-flowered varieties, which will quickly exhaust themselves without your assistance. Fertilizing mature plants every 2 weeks with a liquid fertilizer will also prolong the flowering period.

Selecting Varieties

Sooner or later most gardeners adopt a signature color and stick with it. The field of possibilities includes the giant striped 'Mt. Fuji', the clear sky blue of 'Heavenly Blue' or powder blue 'Blue Silk', or bright white 'Pearly Gates'.

Colorful Companions

The bases of morning glory vines tend to become bare and ragged, but you can hide them from view with numerous small annuals including ageratum, wax begonia, browallia, petunia or vinca.

Cypress vine, a slighty different species (Ipomoea quamoclit) with ferny, finely-cut foliage.

Morning Glory Facts to Know		
Light Sun to partial shade	**Soil** Fertile, well drained	**Water** Average
Germination Soak the hard seeds in water overnight before planting. Some hybrids need scarification.		**Preferred climate** A warm-natured flower that is at its best in mid-summer.

NASTURTIUM
Tropaeolum majus

Easy to grow and infinitely edible, nasturtiums are grown as much for salads as for show. The leaves taste peppery, like watercress, and the flowers have a mild floral flavor. When planting nasturtiums to eat, be careful not to grow them in soil that has been treated with systemic pesticides that are intended for use only on ornamental plants.

In the Garden
Sow fast-growing nasturtiums twice—once in spring, around your last frost date, and again in late summer. Locate them in full sun, or partial shade if you live where summers are hot. Contrary to what some seed catalogs say, nasturtiums grow small

Nasturtiums with variegated foliage display extra ornamental appeal.

and spindly in poor soil and benefit from moderately rich ground that has been improved with organic matter. When well satisfied by the site and soil, nasturtiums grow into spreading mounds. Nasturtiums planted in large containers often spill out gracefully around the edges.

How to Grow
Plant the pebble-sized seeds where you want them to grow. In clay soil, cover the seeds with potting soil to keep a crust from forming at the surface. Thin seedlings to 10 inches apart, and mulch lightly with shredded bark or grass clippings to reduce weeding chores. Frequent picking of flowers for small arrangements or for eating encourages the development of new buds.

Nasturtiums planted in spring may stop flowering during the peak of summer's heat and then come back into bloom in the fall, but nasturtiums do not always make it through summer in good health. Where summers are long, you may opt to pull up tattered plants in mid-summer and sow a second crop as soon as the soil cools a bit. Fall-planted nasturtiums flower continuously until they are killed by freezing weather.

With nasturtiums, you can have a beautiful border and eat it too!

markably well. You can choose other varieties that bloom all red, but most mixtures are dominated by rich orange hues. A closely related species, *T. peregrinum*, best known as canary creeper, is a vigorous annual vine that produces little fringed yellow flowers.

Colorful Companions
The unusual texture of nasturtium foliage and the plant's bright orange, yellow and red flowers pair well with white or purple flowers with comparatively fine texture, such as white sweet alyssum, forget-me-not, ageratum (in warm climates) or purple pansies (where summer are cool). Variegated strains are great for bringing color and texture to herb gardens.

Selecting Varieties
Two varieties with frosty variegated leaves, 'Alaska' and 'Tip Top Alaska', are beautiful accent plants for the corners of beds. In any color, 'Glorious Gleam' seedlings grow into large, sprawling plants that tolerate heat re-

Nasturtium.

Nasturtium Facts to Know

Light	Soil	Water
Full sun to part shade	Moderately fertile	Average

Germination	Preferred climate
Plant seeds ¹/₂ inch deep. Germinates within a week at 60 to 70°F.	Prefers cool-to-warm weather, resents extreme heat. In fall, plants often survive light frost.

NICOTIANA
Nicotiana alata, N. sylvestris

About 95 species of plants are included among the nicotianas, commonly known as tobaccos. Several are beautiful garden flowers, and all tend to exude a sweet fragrance at night. However, plant breeders have been forced to make some tradeoffs in developing forms of nicotiana that grow into very colorful, heavy-blooming plants. As a result, nicotiana varieties with the strongest colors—and the ability to keep their flowers open during the daytime hours—are poor sources of fragrance. They also tend to need quite a bit of sun. More primitive selections grow best in partial shade and feature fragrant flowers that perfume the air from early evening until mid-morning with a sweet scent reminiscent of tuberose.

Nicotiana blossoms are most fragrant from evening until dawn.

In the Garden

Use hybrid nicotianas in sunny display beds or work them into container bouquets. Growing to about 14 inches tall, hybrid varieties have a compact, upright growth habit well suited to formal areas. The color range includes numerous shades of pink, white and red. Selections that produce lime-green flowers are extremely valuable in complicated beds or borders, where they can be used as neutrals to mix with virtually any other flower.

Less refined nicotianas are taller plants that range in height from 2 to 4 feet. They often grow best in partial shade, though they can take full sun where summers are not extremely hot. White and pink are the dominant colors, and some species such as woodland tobacco (*N. sylvestris*) bloom only in white. These nicotianas also may grow as short-lived perennials from Zone 7 southward, and they often reseed when grown in any climate. All nicotianas need rich, well-drained soil.

How to Grow

You can usually buy bedding plants of hybrid varieties, but you will need to grow your own seedlings of old-fashioned nicotianas or hybrids in special colors. Don't be intimidated by the tiny seeds. Once they sprout and begin to grow, very large true leaves develop and growth becomes quite rapid. Nicotianas transplant with ease, so you can grow seedlings in individual containers or in flats.

Work an organic or timed-release fertilizer into the soil, and set plants out at about the time of your last frost. The young plants like cool weather but are easily damaged by heavy frost. With hybrid varieties, pinching back the first flowering spike helps to induce branching, which makes the plants flower more heavily for a longer time.

Cut back nicotianas of all types in mid-summer. By then the leaves will have become ravaged by insects and weather, and flowering will probably decline as well. If you

'Fragrant Cloud' Nicotiana alata.

Nicotiana Facts to Know

Light	Soil	Water
Sun to partial shade	Rich, well drained	Average

Germination	Preferred climate
Press seeds into damp soil-less mix and germinate at about 70°F.	Some strains grow as perennials where winters are mild, with hardiness similar to snapdragons.

fertilize the plants after you prune them, new flowering stems should emerge within a few weeks.

Selecting Varieties

Hybrid nicotianas are often species crosses that involve *N. alata* (the old strain known as jasmine tobacco) and *N. sandarae* (a fragrant pink species sometimes called cranberry tobacco). 'Domino' grows to 14 inches and includes a wide range of colors including rare pink picotee and cool lime green. 'Havana' is quite similar. Dwarf varieties such as 'Merlin' are good for small containers or edging.

If part of your garden receives shade, by all means try some of the old-fashioned nicotianas. Most varieties listed as *N. alata* such as white 'Lumina' or multicolored 'Nicki' are good sources of evening fragrance. Pure species mixes, without variety names, often produce a lovely range of soft pinks, lilac and white flowers that reseed themselves very well.

The flowers of woodland tobacco (*N. sylvestris*) are different in that they are long, tubular, and somewhat drooping. The leading variety name, 'Only the Lonely', echoes the melancholy demeanor of this delightful plant. Unlike the *N. alatas*, *N. sylvestris* selections tend to remain open during the day, though their fragrance is always best at night.

Hybrid nicotianas are bred for vibrant color rather than fragrance.

Colorful Companions

The possibilities for this varied group of flowers is endless. In containers, a single plant of lime-green nicotiana forms a neutral upright pillar around which you can design unique container bouquets. One idea that always delights is a composition that includes other foliage plants in the chartreuse range, such as coleus, ornamental sweet potato and a few sprigs of variegated mint or thyme. Use other hybrid nicotianas as a foil to annuals that produce round blossoms, such as marigolds, petunias or zinnias.

Because of the large size of most species selections, it is usually best to plant them in groups or drifts. Big nicotianas have a coarse texture and loose, rangy growth habit, so it helps to frame them with small, light-textured flowers such as ageratum, nierembergia, dwarf petunias or white narrow-leaf zinnias. In gardens designed to be enjoyed during the evening, you might balance a group of nicotianas in a shady spot with a similar clump of four o'clocks in a sunnier section of the garden.

'Only the Lonely' Nicotiana sylvestris.

'Lime Green' Nicotiana alata.

NIEREMBERGIA
Nierembergia hippomanica

Sometimes called cup flower because of the shape of the blooms, nierembergia is perhaps the best annual to use as an edging along concrete walkways and driveways that heat up dramatically on sunny days. It handles the hot conditions of this niche in champion style, as well as heavy drenchings caused by rain running off of hard surfaces. Best of all, nierembergia often stays in bloom continuously for 3 full months.

'Purple Robe' nierembergia.

In the Garden

Adaptable and easy to please, nierembergia thrives in either full sun or partial shade. Plants grow only to about 8 inches tall and spread 12 inches wide into soft mounds. The foliage and flowers combine to form dense mats which are ideal for broad edgings or for low puddles of color in mixed beds and borders. You also can grow nierembergia in containers, by itself or in combination with other heat-tolerant annuals.

How to Grow

Bedding plants often are available in spring, or you can grow your own seedlings from seed. Start seeds indoors in containers very early in spring, about 2 months before your last frost. The seedlings can tolerate frost, so you can go ahead and set them out, 10 inches apart, while the weather is still chilly. After that, occasional weeding is the only chore you will need to do to help the plants to prosper.

After nierembergia has been in bloom for a month, pinch off old blossoms to help prolong the plants' period of bloom. Continue to pinch off old blooms occasionally for the rest of the summer. In Zones 7 to 9, do not pull up yearling nierembergia when they stop blooming. If you mulch over their roots in winter, plants usually return and bloom well for a second year.

Selecting Varieties

Two varieties are generally available as either plants or seeds: white 'Mont Blanc' and deep purple 'Purple

Robe'. The white form is preferred for edging, especially near walkways that are used at night.

Colorful Companions

White nierembergia goes with everything, which explains its popularity as an edging plant. Its high-contrast company makes bright red geraniums or orange sulphur cosmos look even brighter, or you can use it to intensify the coolness of soft pink petunias or blue fan flower. Purple nierembergia benefits from close proximity to lighter shades, such as pastel vincas, yellow marigolds, apricot celosia or lemony zinnias.

'Mont Blanc' nierembergia.

Nierembergia Facts to Know		
Light Sun to part shade	**Soil** Fertile, well drained	**Water** Average
Germination Plant seeds 1/8 inch deep in soil-less mix. Germinates best at 70°F.		**Preferred climate** Likes a cool start in spring, then tolerates hot weather well. Grows as a short-lived perennial where winters are mild.

NIGELLA
Nigella damascena

Nigella is a curious flower with several special uses. The very thin, threadlike foliage adds fine texture to the garden, and the blue to pink blossoms are strangely exotic. Nigella's common name, love-in-a-mist, refers to the way wiry bracts surround each flower. Nigella blossoms make fine cut flowers, and the balloon-shaped seedpods can be cut and dried. The seeds are edible too, and can be used as a spice in much the same way you might use coriander seeds.

Nigella's exotic blossoms have earned it the common name of love-in-a-mist.

In addition to lovely flowers, nigella produces unusual seedpods that you can dry.

Nigella Facts to Know

Light	Soil	Water
Full sun to part shade	Fertile, sandy	Average

Germination	Preferred climate
Plant seeds ¹/₄ inch deep around your last frost date. Fall planting is possible in mild winter areas.	Resents temperatures above 90°F. Seedlings tolerate light frosts.

In the Garden

Nigella plants that are grown in rich, fertile soil are more robust and productive than those that struggle to grow in less than ideal conditions. Site and soil fertility also affect plant height, which can range from 1 to 3 feet. In most areas, nigella likes full sun, but partial afternoon shade is beneficial where spring gives way to hot summer quickly. High humidity can pose problems too, so try to plant this flower where air circulation is good.

How to Grow

If you are very careful and grow nigella seedlings in peat pots or other plantable containers, you can start them indoors a month before your last frost. But nigella seedlings resent transplanting, so you may elect to plant the seeds in well-prepared soil just before your last spring frost. Thin seedlings to 10 inches apart, and mulch between them to retain soil moisture and discourage weeds.

Give plants a bit of extra fertilizer when they show a few flower buds. This often does not occur until the plants have been growing for more than 2 months. Cut the first flowers promptly, and let the later ones develop mature seeds. The bloom time of nigella is short anyway, but this cutting strategy helps prolong it as long as possible. If encouraged to reseed, nigella often perpetuates itself.

Selecting Varieties

Nigella seed often carries no variety name, but there are a few good ones worth seeking out. Compact 'Miss Jekyll' comes in either blue or pink and is known for its reliability. Taller 'Persian Jewels' is a color mixture that includes varying shades of blue and pink along with white.

Colorful Companions

The blue tones of nigella make a wonderful addition to gardens built around cool color schemes when combined with ageratum, dusty miller, blue fan flower, and any flower that blooms pink. Mixtures that include pink and raspberry tones seem to have a lighter texture in the company of white or pale pink flowers.

PANSIES AND VIOLAS
Viola x *wittrockiana; Viola tricolor* **hybrids**

'Blueberry Sorbet' viola.

Special Winter Care

From Zone 6 northward, pansies and violas benefit from a 2-inch-thick mulch of pine needles or clean straw spread over the bed in early winter. This mulch protects the plants from cold, drying winds, which is important because pansies and violas cannot take up water when the soil is frozen. In all areas, pansies and violas grow very little, if at all, when soil temperatures stay below 45°F.

In the Garden

Pansies and violas are very easy to grow and ask for little more than good drainage and at least a half day of sun. They will thrive in pots or window boxes, make an exceptionally neat edging, and always attract attention when planted in small drifts. These petite flowers also are

Violas.

There are excellent reasons why pansies and violas are the most popular flowers for planting in fall and early spring. All pansies and violas thrive in cool weather, and most strains are quite willing to bloom off and on for up to 8 months, or for however long cool weather lasts. The one thing pansies cannot endure is hot weather. So, in climates where summers are hot, pansies and violas are grown exclusively as winter annuals. Where summers are cool, these flowers often grow as short-lived perennials and bloom well for 2 or even 3 years.

There are subtle differences between pansies and violas. Pansies often have unique "blotches" that make the flowers look like they have faces, while violas often have "tricolor" markings, in which the three petals of individual flowers appear in startlingly contrasting colors. Pansy blooms are at least 1¹/₂ inches across, while violas (also called mini-pansies and johnny jump-ups) have smaller flowers but more of them. Violas also bloom more prolifically in cold weather than do pansies.

Pansy and Viola Facts to Know

Light	Soil	Water
Full sun to partial shade	Moist, slightly acidic, with a pH between 5.4 and 5.8	Above average

Germination		Preferred climate
Refrigerate seeds overnight before planting ¹/₈ inch deep. Best germination at 65 to 70°F. Grow seedlings in a cool place in temperatures between 50 and 60°F.		Best growth between 45 and 80°F. Hardiest varieties survive cold to -10°F.

Pansy blossoms are edible provided they have not been treated with pesticides not intended for use on edible plants.

When planting a large space with pansies, use as many colors as you like. As the plants reach full size, the colors will flow into one another.

ideal for planting among spring-flowering bulbs, such as daffodils, hyacinths or tulips. In the fall, you can color-coordinate pansies or violas with chrysanthemums or ornamental kale. Or, mix and match them with spring-blooming shrubs like azaleas and forsythias.

How to Grow

Pansies and violas started from seed sown in containers are ready to set out in about 8 weeks. Most gardeners save time by starting with bedding plants. Look for compact, dark green plants that have just begun to flower, and avoid those that show long, floppy stems—a sign that the plants have been held in small containers too long under less than ideal conditions. Keep the plants well watered until you plant them.

Prepare a planting site by digging in a 2-inch-deep layer of organic matter to improve drainage and boost the soil's organic matter content. To ensure good drainage, the prepared bed should be at least 3 inches higher than surrounding soil. Most pansies and violas fill in completely when planted 8 inches apart, but you can plant them a little closer together for a more lush effect.

Fertilize pansies with a soluble liquid fertilizer every 2 to 3 weeks whenever they are actively growing. As the weather becomes warmer in spring, you can save time by switching to an organic fertilizer or timed-release fertilizer spread over the surface between plants. Avoid using high-nitrogen fertilizers in warm weather, because they can cause the plants to become stretched-out and leggy. Pull up plants when flowers become small and sparse and the plants lose their deep-green color.

Selecting Varieties

Choose varieties based on the colors you want, and try different ones from year to year to keep things exciting. Children love pansies with faces, as well as the little whiskered markings present on many violas. Pansies in soft pastel shades give a delicate, lacy look to beds and containers.

Colorful Companions

Plant high-contrast colors together in repeating patterns: combinations of yellow and blue, purple and orange and red and white work especially well. Or, play with monochromatic schemes, like edging a bed of lilac pansies with darker purple violas. Light shades usually are preferred since very dark purple or maroon flowers often get lost in the dark-green foliage.

Pansies and violas are natural partners for tulips. You can plant both at the same time in the fall.

PANSIES ACROSS THE LAND

Zones 2 and 3: Hardened-off pansy and viola seedlings set out in early spring survive late frosts and bloom continuously all summer. Flowering stops when temperatures plummet in early winter.

Zones 4 and 5: Very hardy pansy varieties including 'Delta' and 'Sky' can survive winter, as can some violas. When planted in September or April, flowering starts in mid-spring and continues through most of the summer.

Zones 6 and 7: Most pansies and all violas planted in September or early October can survive winter. Violas bloom intermittently through winter, and the plants stay attractive until early summer. Pansies bloom lightly in fall and then become semidormant until early spring. Intense blooming of both types continues until early summer.

Zones 8 and 9: Planted in October or November, pansies and violas produce flowers continuously from fall until mid-spring. Blooms are most numerous in late winter. Plants decline rapidly by early summer, so spring planting is not recommended.

PENTAS
Pentas lanceolata

Extreme heat and humidity can't stop pentas, a tropical perennial from Africa and Arabia now grown as a summer annual in warmer regions of the country. Sometimes called Egyptian star cluster, pentas produces rounded domes of starry flower clusters up to 4 inches wide on tall, shrubby plants. Not too long ago this flower came only in red, but it can now be had in a range of colors including pink, red, white and lavender. Pentas attracts both butterflies and hummingbirds, and the plants bloom continuously from early summer to frost.

In the Garden

Pentas is an ideal summer replacement for cool-season annuals that die out in summer's heat. It grows best in morning sun and afternoon shade, and can be planted in beds or containers. Potted plants can be brought indoors in winter and grown in a bright south or west-facing window. Pentas will grow in any fertile, well-drained soil provided it receives a constant supply of water. In Zones 9 to 11 it can be handled as a perennial.

How to Grow

Start the small seeds indoors 6 weeks before the last frost or buy bedding plants in late spring, after nights have warmed into the 60s. Especially in sandy soil, work in some compost, peat moss, or other soil amendments to improve the soil's moisture-holding capacity.

Mature plants grow into wide mounds about 2 feet tall and 3 to 4 feet wide. Pinch back plants early on to induce branching. As summer gets under way, clip off spent flower clusters and feed plants monthly with a high nitrogen fertilizer. Because pentas needs plenty of water, it is often simplest to fertilize the plants with a soluble liquid fertilizer.

If you want to bring a plant indoors for winter but the ones in your garden are too large, select a few healthy stems and set them to root in damp sand in late summer. Repot them in early fall so they have a chance to become bushy before being brought indoors.

Selecting Varieties

'New Look', which comes in red or pink, is the most widely available pentas to grow from seed. Nurseries sell many other vegeta-

Plant pentas in small groups of three, and the plants will grow together and create a shrublike effect.

tively propagated cultivars in different colors. Among the most reliable and vigorous is 'Nova', which won a University of Georgia gold medal in 1999.

Colorful Companions

Pentas is a natural partner for angelonia or lantana, which have similar cultural needs. Other fine companions include ageratum, wax begonia and white narrow-leaf zinnia.

Pentas always keeps its crisp good looks despite prolonged heat.

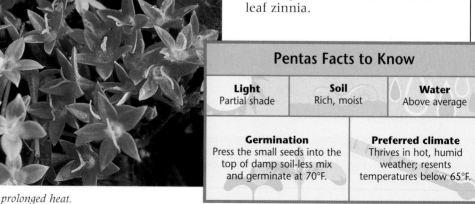

Pentas Facts to Know		
Light Partial shade	**Soil** Rich, moist	**Water** Above average
Germination Press the small seeds into the top of damp soil-less mix and germinate at 70°F.		**Preferred climate** Thrives in hot, humid weather; resents temperatures below 65°F.

PEPPER, ORNAMENTAL
Capsicum annuum

Because of the way the brightly colored fruits adorn dark green plants, ornamental peppers are sometimes called Christmas peppers. Unlike regular peppers, ornamental peppers hold their fruits high above the foliage where they really show. Most varieties are edible yet hot, but the main reason to grow ornamental peppers is for their looks.

In the Garden

Ornamental peppers need warm weather, but they are not difficult to grow.

In sunny beds, try planting them at uniform spacing and surrounding them with a broad band of dwarf yellow or red flowers. You can also grow ornamental peppers in containers and bring them indoors just before the first frost comes for several weeks of sprightly color. Outdoors, plants will keep their good looks after the first frost if you cover them with blankets until mild weather returns.

How to Grow

Either start with purchased plants or grow your own from seeds started indoors about a month before your last frost. Use a sterile soil-less mix, and be careful not to overwater the young seedlings. It's a good practice to add a half ration of soluble fertilizer to the water beginning when the plants are a month old.

Transplant ornamental peppers outdoors at least 2 weeks after your last frost, when the soil is warm. If necessary, use cloches to protect plants from cold winds. Mulch over the soil's surface to retain soil moisture and deter weeds. When set out 12 inches apart, it will take the plants a month or more to fill in the spaces between them.

Most ornamental peppers need no special care beyond occasional fertilizing. If desired, you can clip off old fruit clusters from time to time to stimulate the development of new bearing branches.

Selecting Varieties

'Treasures Red' produces clusters of cone-shaped fruits that start out pale green and ripen to orange and then red. If you want to pick some of your peppers and don't mind having them hot, consider conical 'Prairie Fire', long, pointed 'Riot' or round-fruited 'Marbles'.

Colorful Companions

Most ornamental peppers are red, yellow and orange, and the foliage may be tinted with purple, so it's best to stick with yellow or orange flowers as companions. Some fine bed partners include dwarf melampodium, French marigolds in orange or yellow, or a groundcover of 'Blackie' sweet potato vine.

The fruits of ornamental peppers come in a range of shapes, but they are all small and usually extremely hot if eaten.

Like other peppers, ornamental peppers gradually change colors from green to yellow to orange and finally bright red.

Ornamental Pepper Facts to Know

Light	Soil	Water
Sun	Fertile, well drained	Average

Germination	Preferred climate
Plant seeds ¼ inch deep in sterile planting mix. Germinate at 70 to 75°F. Give seedlings strong supplemental light.	Very adaptable. Likes warm soil and cannot tolerate frost.

PERSIAN SHIELD
Strobilanthes dyerianus

Persian shield's leaf markings are much more subtle when plants are grown in shade.

Any gardener who gets excited about new plants will love discovering Persian shield, a plant native to Burma that's grown primarily for its beautiful foliage. Persian shield's 4- to 6-inch-long pointed leaves are purple veined with green when new and mature to a luminous silvery gray with contrasting green veins. Persian shield is a welcome alternative to coleus or dusty miller, particularly where summers are hot and humid. Since its introduction in 1996, Persian shield has quickly become fashionable in the warm summer climates from Virginia to Texas.

In the Garden
The lush colorful leaves of Persian shield will attract attention in semishady beds or large containers, where it combines easily with other warm-natured annuals. Plants grow into a loose mound about 2 feet tall and equally wide. Locate this plant where it will receive some shade from hot afternoon sun. The site should be well drained and be convenient to water during prolonged dry spells. Except for routine watering, feeding and occasional pinching, Persian shield needs no special care.

How to Grow
A tropical perennial, Persian shield will survive winter only in frost-free areas. Elsewhere it is grown as an annual. Plants grown from cuttings are increasingly available in garden centers in late spring, or you can mail-order them from companies that aggressively seek out new plants.

You can double or triple your supply of plants by pinching back the stock plants you buy when they are about 8 inches tall and rooting the cuttings in clean, damp sand. This operation will improve the bushiness of your plants. If you keep the cuttings in a warm, humid place they will strike roots within 2 weeks.

Persian shield thrives in rich, fertile soil that is well drained and watered regularly. Should your plants become leggy in late summer, simply pinch them back by half their size and follow up with a good drench of a complete fertilizer.

Selecting Varieties
This plant is so new to American gardens that no cultivars have been named at this writing. It is sold under its botanical name or as Persian shield plant.

Colorful Companions
Persian shield combines beautifully with heat-tolerant petunias, chartreuse ornamental sweet potato, pink or white pentas, and many other warm-season flowers that bloom pink. You can also use Persian shield as a neutral in the garden provided the overall color scheme emphasizes soft, cool colors.

Persian shield's purple leaves hide the bases of red salvia in grand style.

Persian Shield Facts to Know

Light Partial shade	**Soil** Rich, well drained	**Water** Average
Germination Not grown from seed. Cuttings root in about 2 weeks with plenty of warmth.		**Preferred climate** Thrives where summers have a warm, tropical feel.

PETUNIA
Petunia hybrids

A bold bed of vigorous petunias.

Today's petunias are so varied that you can garden for a lifetime and never get bored with them. Interest in old-fashioned flowers has brought long-limbed reseeding petunias back into commerce, and plant breeders have succeeded in developing petunias for every niche. There are dwarf varieties for edging, cascading plants for hanging baskets, and a huge range of colors and forms for beds and containers. The box on page 140 summarizes the major types, but a few more comments are in order.

The dominant ancestral color in petunias is pink, so any type of petunia tends to be most vigorous when dressed in pink. The weakest color is red, because red petunias accumulate high levels of sugar in their stems and leaves, which makes them easy targets for various stem and root rots. Some petunias are fragrant, a trait that is more strongly linked to color than to variety name. In general, the most fragrant petunias are purple, pink or white. Petunia fragrance tends to be strongest at night.

Petunia Facts to Know		
Light Full sun to partial shade	**Soil** Fertile, well drained	**Water** Average
Germination Barely cover seeds with soilless mix and germinate at 70 to 75°F.	**Preferred climate** Widely adaptable, tolerant of both cool and hot conditions.	

Petunias.

In the Garden

Petunias need little more than a sunny spot and fertile, well-drained soil. In hot summer climates they benefit from a few hours of afternoon shade. Petunias will bloom their hearts out whether you grow them in beds, pots, baskets or window boxes. A few of the newer petunias such as the 'Wave' series are surprisingly cold hardy and have been known to survive winter in protected spots in Zone 7. However, most petunias are summer annuals to plant in spring and enjoy until frost stops the show.

How to Grow

You can start most petunias from seed 6 weeks before the last frost, but the bedding plant selection is huge and affordable. Look for young plants that have not yet become rootbound, and plant them in soil

'Polo Burgundy Star' petunia.

that has been amended with organic matter to improve texture and drainage. Also work in an organic or timed-release fertilizer before setting out the plants. Petunias normally transplant with ease, but it is important to gently spread the roots and to avoid twisting or breaking the main stems. Mulch between plants to keep the leaves from touching bare soil, which can lead to problems with diseases.

Water petunias before they become extremely dry, preferably early enough in the day so that the leaves will be dry by nightfall. Clip off old flowers from grandifloras to help extend their blooming period. With other types of petunias the blooms are too numerous to clean up, so it's more practical to shear the plants back by one-third once or twice a summer. This shearing back removes green seedpods and stimulates the development of new flowering stems.

Selecting Varieties

Petunias vary somewhat in their adaptation to different regions, and local garden centers take much of the guesswork out of choosing varieties by stocking petunias known to grow well in your area. Use the box (below) to help sort through the many possibilities you encounter when you shop for petunias.

Fancy double-flowered petunias make fine plants for carefully tended containers.

Even though you may be pleased with certain selections, it's great fun to try new ones. Some "must have" award winners include elegant 'Celebrity Chiffon Morn' (AAS 1995), long-vined 'Purple Wave' (AAS 1995) and buttery yellow 'Prism Sunshine' (AAS 1998).

Color Key

Petunias are available in every color except orange, so there is no limit to the ways you can combine them with other plants. Because all petunias have a low, sprawling growth habit, they are perfect for planting near upright flowers such as geraniums. White petunias in particular add a lacy touch to any place where they are grown, and can be used as unifying neutrals in the landscape. Light pink petunias provide an unfailingly fresh accent wherever you grow them.

TYPES OF PETUNIAS

- **Milliflora petunias** are dwarf plants that grow into small mounds only 6 to 8 inches across. The 'Fantasy' series are of this type.

- **Multiflora petunias** are heavy producers of medium sized flowers. They are very vigorous and long-flowering, and include the most popular selections for planting in beds such as 'Madness', 'Celebrity' and 'PrimeTime'. Long-stemmed trailing 'Wave' petunias, which are often grown as groundcovers, fit best into this group.

'Supertunia' cascading petunias.

- **Grandiflora petunias** produce very large flowers, but fewer of them compared to the multiflora type. Velvety singles and frilly double-flowered selections are ideal for containers that receive close attention and include variety names like 'Fluffy Ruffles' and 'Supercascade'.

- **'Supertunia' and 'Surfina'** are product names for certain heavy blooming cascading petunias that are propagated vegetatively rather than from seed. They are ideal for dramatic hanging baskets.

PHLOX
Phlox drummondii

Annual phlox.

There are many types of phlox you might grow in your garden, but none provide the extended bloom you get with the annual form. Each blooming stem is a bouquet in itself, made up of a cluster of small, lightly fragrant flowers. Butterflies visit phlox often to collect the sweet nectar. Today's varieties were developed from a plant found growing in Texas in 1835, but don't assume that phlox is a hot-climate flower. It prospers from spring to early summer in the South, but blooms for a longer time in more moderate summer climates.

In the Garden

You can use dwarf varieties as edging plants, or plant larger ones that grow to 18 inches tall in flowing drifts. Use broad ribbons of phlox to accent walkways, or plant them in wide containers for soft puddles of color. Phlox benefits from full sun, but needs some afternoon shade in warm climates. When plants are set out 10 inches apart in fertile soil, they will develop into a solid mass of color.

How to Grow

Many dwarf varieties are sold as bedding plants, but you may need to start your own seedlings if you want to grow taller varieties with stems long enough for cutting. Start seeds indoors a month before your last frost. Six weeks later, when they are ready to transplant, enrich the bed with organic matter and an organic or timed-release fertilizer.

The plants will quickly gain size as days lengthen in spring. Mulch with shredded bark or clean straw to keep the soil cool and moist, and water phlox deeply during dry spells. If flowering subsides in early summer, you can often coax the plants back into bloom by shearing them back by half their size and then drenching the bed with a soluble fertilizer.

Selecting Varieties

If you like cut flowers, check mail-order seed catalogs for full-sized varieties such as 'Watercolor Memories' or 'Tapestry' (both mixtures of soft pastel shades of pink, blue, lavender and yellow). 'Coral Reef' includes many shades of yellow, salmon and peachy pinks. Many dwarf varieties include bright reds and pinks. Because phlox begin to bloom while the plants are in cellpacks, you can get a good idea of their colors before you buy the plants.

Colorful Companions

Yellow flowers such as black-eyed Susan, calendulas or strawflowers make good company. Where summers are hot, you may need to replace spring-planted phlox with more heat-tolerant annuals in mid-summer. Lantana and pentas may be planted immediately after phlox are removed.

Phlox Facts to Know		
Light Sun or light shade	**Soil** Fertile, well drained	**Water** Average
Germination Plant seeds 1/8 inch deep, germinate in darkness and cool temperatures between 55 and 65°F.		**Preferred climate** Likes cool weather, but established plants can tolerate heat.

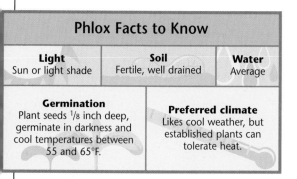

The color range and long bloom time of annual phlox combine to make it a good flower for large mixed plantings.

POPPY
Papaver rhoeas

Whether you call them corn poppies, Shirley poppies, or Flanders poppies, you will be delighted at the delicate blooms produced by these tough, cold-tolerant plants. In addition to their beauty, poppies fill the color gap that often occurs in late spring, when spring-flowering bulbs and shrubs have faded yet summer annuals are not yet ready to bloom.

In the Garden

Corn poppies need a sunny spot where they can grow without being disturbed from fall to late spring. Corn poppies may be planted in the fall from Zone 6 southward, or you can sow them first thing in spring. Following fall seeding, seedlings will appear sporadically through the winter. They have no trouble surviving hard freezes.

How to Grow

Do not attempt to transplant poppies, for they suffer terribly even if they manage to survive having their roots disturbed. Instead, sow the seeds atop cultivated soil, and weed the area regularly to keep the plants from being smothered by weeds. There is little need to fertilize poppies planted in reasonably good soil, but if you grow them in neglected spots it's best to feed them with an organic or timed-release fertilizer in late winter or early spring.

Poppies grow into broad, leafy rosettes that completely cover the ground in a 12- inch circle, so mulching is seldom necessary. A few weeks before they flower, the plants suddenly grow taller. Over a period of a month or so, a single healthy plant may produce up to a dozen pretty blooms. If you want your plants to reseed, be sure to leave some of the flowers on the plants until the petals fall away to reveal lantern-shaped seedpods. Let these dry to medium brown. Gather some pods for replanting in new areas, which is easily done by shaking the seeds out of the holes in the tops of the pods onto the ground below.

Corn poppy.

Selecting Varieties

Most mixtures of this species include red, white, pink and some bicolored flowers. The 'Mother of Pearl' mixture includes soft pastels only, or you can go much brighter will all red 'Legion of Honor'. 'Angels Choir' is a very double form that needs rich soil to flower well.

Colorful Companions

Grow corn poppies with other hardy annuals that grow when the weather is quite chilly and bloom early, such as larkspur and bachelor button. In most areas, there is plenty of time left in the season to grow a warm-weather annual in space vacated by poppies in early summer.

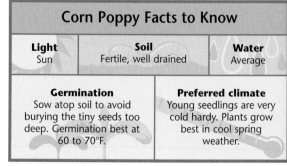

Corn Poppy Facts to Know		
Light Sun	**Soil** Fertile, well drained	**Water** Average
Germination Sow atop soil to avoid burying the tiny seeds too deep. Germination best at 60 to 70°F.		**Preferred climate** Young seedlings are very cold hardy. Plants grow best in cool spring weather.

CALIFORNIA POPPY
Eschscholzia californica

California poppy.

When California poppies are grown in fertile soil and given supplemental water, they will continue to bloom for more than a month. However, plants grown in dry meadows and other neglected places bloom for a few weeks and then dry to a straw-brown color.

The blossoms of this species are predominantly bright orange, but selections have been developed that are deep orange-red ('Red Chief') or a mixture of yellow, red, and or-ange ('Thai Silk'). 'Purple Gleam' is a rare blend of lavender and pink flowers, while the flowers of 'Ivory Castle' are creamy white. In the garden, California poppies mix well with red corn poppies, white ammi or with blue bachelor buttons.

California Poppy Facts to Know		
Light Full sun	**Soil** Well drained	**Water** Below average
Germination Sow the tiny seeds atop the soil. Seeds germinate best when the soil temperature is around 60°F.		**Preferred climate** Plants resent extreme heat, but adapt to most areas when grown during the proper season.

The state flower of California, California poppies are easy to grow from direct-sown seeds. Like other poppies, they are difficult to transplant without serious damage. Fall seeding is best from Zone 7 southward. In other areas, plant just after the last spring frost. If allowed to do so, California poppies often reseed themselves.

In addition to orange, California poppies are now available in creamy yellow and bright red.

OTHER ANNUAL POPPIES

Seed catalogs can't agree on what to call *Papaver somniferum* poppies, which are used to produce three things: brilliantly colored flowers, opium and crunchy edible seeds. It is illegal to grow *P. somniferum* as drug-producing plants, but not as lovely flowers.

Breadseed or opium poppy, Papaver somniferum.

Poppies of this species are grown exactly like corn poppies, though the plants are larger and have distinctive gray-green leaves. They also reseed with great enthusiasm. Once established as residents in your garden, each spring you may need to thin the volunteer seedlings ruthlessly to create 12-inch spacing between plants.

'Danish Flag' has huge crimson blossoms marked with white, and most mixtures include mauve pink. 'Flemish Antique' produces huge frilly blooms packed with petals that are wildly variegated with red and white.

PORTULACA
Portulaca grandiflora

The cactus-like appearance of portulaca fits the places in which you will put it to work—dry, sun-baked places where other flowers refuse to grow. Also known as moss rose, portulaca is a champion annual for growing near concrete surfaces that heat up during the day. The succulent stems spread sideways over the ground, forming low mats of brightly colored flowers much beloved by honeybees. In hospitable sites a few volunteer plants will return year after year.

In the Garden

Portulaca blossoms close up by sunset and during rainy weather, so they are best used in areas seen during the morning hours. In hot climates, try planting portulaca in broad bands along your front walkway. You can also plant portulaca among steppingstones. To assure good root development, use the youngest plants you can find for this purpose.

How to Grow

Start your own seedlings indoors, or look for bedding plants from mid-spring onward. Most modern varieties bloom a little when they are only 6 weeks old, so you can tell which colors the plants are before you buy them. Set plants out after the last frost has passed. Any well-drained soil will satisfy these flowers, but you will get more robust plants if you improve the soil with a 2-inch layer of organic matter prior to setting out the plants. Also work an organic or timed-release fertilizer into the soil before planting. Mulch lightly to discourage weeds.

Portulaca is tremendously heat tolerant, but it is damaged by long periods of drought. Soak the plants well once a week during prolonged dry spells, or whenever the soil becomes completely dry.

If your plants stop blooming and look exhausted, try trimming them back by about one-third their size. Then follow up with a good feeding of soluble liquid fertilizer.

Portulaca.

Selecting Varieties

The double flowers in the 'Sundial' hybrid series stay open longer during the day and the plants are very vigorous. Nonhybrid varieties include both single and double blooms, and they are the best choice if you want to naturalize portulaca in an area of your garden.

Colorful Companions

Portulaca usually stands alone since few other flowers share its ability to adapt to hot, dry sites. Color mixtures have a festive appeal, or you can work with one or two selected colors when using portulaca in formal situations.

Portulacas naturalize easily in sunny beds. These were volunteers that appeared where hybrid portulacas were grown the year before.

Portulaca Facts to Know

Light	Soil	Water
Full sun	Adaptable	Below average

Germination	Preferred climate
Barely cover seed and germinate at 70°F. Can be direct-sown after last frost has passed.	Tolerates hot weather better than most flowers, but succumbs easily to frost.

SALPIGLOSSIS
Salpiglossis sinuata

Salpiglossis.

Also known as painted tongue and velvet flower, salpiglossis is a temperamental beauty that makes a breathtaking cut flower. The trumpet-shaped flowers have exotic veining that makes them look like they have been hand-painted with yellow over darker streaks. But that beauty comes at a price. Unlike its adaptable cousin, the petunia, salpiglossis thrives only when conditions are just right. Those conditions include soil that is neither too heavy nor too light, weather that's neither too cold nor too hot, and a patient gardener willing to work with the tiny seeds.

In the Garden

When well pleased, salpiglossis grows 2 to 3 feet tall and benefits from some kind of horizontal support (see page 55). You can let the lanky stems sprawl, but the blossoms may get lost in the foliage. Flowers are most prolific in full sun, but if you live where summers are hot, by all means locate the plants where they will be shaded during the afternoon.

How to Grow

Salpiglossis seedlings are occasionally sold as bedding plants, but their tendency to transplant poorly limits their popularity. Homegrown seedlings started 8 weeks before the last frost in individual containers fare well when set out at about 6 weeks of age, but do be gentle to avoid damaging the roots. Pinch back seedlings to help induce branching. Start earlier in Zones 6 and 7, and set the plants out under cloches 3 weeks before the last frost. Because

of its cool-weather nature and limited cold hardiness, salpiglossis seldom succeeds south of Zone 7.

Salpiglossis needs perfectly drained soil that has been enriched with plenty of compost or other organic matter. Also mix a little lime into the soil if it tends to be acidic, along with some starter fertilizer. Fertilize plants again in midseason to keep them in flower for as long as possible. Frequent cutting and deadheading also prolong the flowering period.

Selecting Varieties

Only a few named varieties are available, all in mixtures of shades of rust, red, violet, purple and pink veined with yellow. Hybrid varieties such as 'Bolero' and 'Royale' are remarkably vigorous and long flowering.

Colorful Companions

Plant salpiglossis in small masses near plants with a naturally neat growth habit, such as salvia or snapdragon. Pick up the yellow in the etched blossoms with a frame of yellow pansies or dwarf snaps. Salpiglossis grows in the same weather conditions preferred by stocks and phlox.

It's easy to see how salpiglossis became known as "painted tongue."

Salpiglossis Facts to Know

Light	Soil	Water
Full sun to part shade	Rich, well drained	Average

Germination	Preferred climate
Sow atop soil-less mix, cover with black plastic for 5 to 10 days. Germination best in darkness at about 75°F.	Strongly prefers cool nights during the flowering period.

SALVIA
Salvia splendens

If you want to stop traffic with a vivid display and attract humming-birds at the same time, you can do it with bright red salvias. The showiest members of the sage family, bedding salvias adapt to sun or partial shade, and are as at home in large containers as in well-drained beds. For a change of pace, several other colors are available that are almost as vigorous as the classic reds.

In the Garden

Put salvia to work in high-visibility beds that receive at least a half day of sun. Keep in mind that bright red flowers can draw attention from distant viewing points, especially when they are planted in masses or drifts. Salvias need rich, well-drained soil and regular water and fertilizer, so avoid planting them in remote places that are hard to reach with a hose.

How to Grow

Salvia seeds are slow to germinate and sensitive to salt buildup in containers, so bushy bedding plants are a good buy. Before setting out plants 12 inches apart, work a coated timed-release or organic fertilizer into the soil. Water plants well after transplanting, and spread a thin mulch over the soil's surface to safeguard soil moisture and deter weeds.

Don't be alarmed if your salvias show little new growth after transplanting. Many varieties have been bred to bloom a little as young seedlings and then resume vegetative growth for a while before coming back into bloom. Because of sensitivity to day length, plants bloom strongest during the second half of summer.

Every few weeks during the summer, clip off old flower spikes to encourage the development of new ones. Beginning in mid-summer, fertilize plants every 2 weeks with a soluble fertilizer, or spread a booster feeding of organic or timed-release fertilizer over the soil between plants. Water plants often during dry spells to keep the soil lightly moist.

Salvia elegans, *or garden salvia, comes in numerous shades besides the most common one, fire engine red.*

Selecting Varieties

Dwarf varieties such as 'Maestro' grow to only 8 to 10 inches tall, while full-sized 'Flare' and 'Bonfire' grow to 2 feet. Check plant tags to make sure you buy the size you need for your site. The 'Salsa' series has bicolored flowers marked with white.

Colorful Companions

Bright red salvias work well with white flowers such as petunias, geraniums or white vinca, or you can pair them with yellow or blue. Dwarf ageratum makes a

particularly good edging plant for red salvia beds. Use other colors in containers or as accent plants in small spaces. The bicolored salvias are at their best when viewed up close.

Salvia Facts to Know		
Light Sun to partial shade	**Soil** Rich, well drained	**Water** Above average
Germination Seeds need light and 70°F temperatures to germinate. Leach salts from planting medium before planting seeds.		**Preferred climate** Likes warm weather, cannot tolerate frost.

BLUE SALVIA
Salvia farinacea

Salvia farinacea.

Blue Salvia Facts to Know		
Light Sun to partial shade	**Soil** Rich, well drained	**Water** Average
Germination Expose freshly planted seeds to cool temperatures for 2 days, then germinate at 70°F.		**Preferred climate** Thrives in both hot and cool weather.

Commonly known as blue salvia or mealycup sage, *Salvia farinacea* is actually a short-lived perennial. However, it is often badly damaged by cold weather north of Zone 8, so most gardeners grow it as an annual. Bedding plants are widely available in the spring.

This salvia stays in bloom continuously all summer, withstands heat, and produces long, straight, flowering spikes that make valuable additions to summer flower arrangements. 'Victoria' is treasured for its deep purple color, but many devotees have converted to the newer 'Strata' variety, which has bicolored blue and white flowers that give the spikes a cool, frosty look.

Pair this salvia with white flowers if you want to set a cool, relaxing mood. It is also unbeatable used in a red, white and blue color scheme. Few flowers pair as well with orange bloomers such as sulphur cosmos or orange marigolds.

CORAL SAGE
Salvia coccinea

The newest sage to be grown as an annual, Salvia coccinea is less demanding of water and fertilizer than bedding salvias, and it's taller too. Hummingbirds love this flower.

Plants are sometimes offered in cellpacks in the spring, but you may need to start them from seed. Begin by cultivating the soil and adding a 2-inch layer of compost or flower planting mix. Make shallow, 1/2-inch-deep furrows and fill them with potting soil or soil-less mix, and dampen thoroughly. Press seeds into the damp mixture and keep moist for 2 days. Then cover the seeds with 1/4 inch of potting soil or soil-less mix, and keep moist for several more days, or until the seedlings appear. This routine gives the seeds the light they need to trigger germination, and eliminates the possibility that surface soil will dry into an impenetrable crust.

Once established, coral salvia needs little care other than occasional deadheading and watering. The two most popular varieties are 'Lady in Red', which is a uniform coral red color, and 'Coral Nymph', which has coral and white bicolored blooms.

Coral Sage Facts to Know		
Light Sun to partial shade	**Soil** Fertile, well drained	**Water** Average
Germination Germination: Seeds need light and 60 to 70°F temperatures to germinate.		**Preferred climate** Likes warm weather, but can tolerate light frost.

Salvia coccinea, *commonly known as coral sage or red Texas sage.*

SANVITALIA
Sanvitalia procumbens

A native of Mexico that goes by the name of creeping zinnia, sanvitalia is a great little plant for filling holes in the summer garden. A versatile trailing plant, sanvitalia will work as a summer ground-cover, in hanging baskets, or you can use the plants to accent the edges of mixed flower beds. Small yellow to orange flowers with black centers resemble miniature black-eyed Susans or petite zinnias. They pop out profusely from the low, spreading stems.

In the Garden

A resolute summer annual, sanvitalia grows vigorously after the weather becomes warm. Give it well-drained soil and full sun, and sanvitalia can be counted upon for heavy bloom through the hottest part of summer. Where summers are very hot, sanvitalia can handle partial shade. Plants grow to less than 6 inches tall and spread about 14 inches wide.

How to Grow

Start seeds indoors a month before your last frost, or purchase bedding plants if you can find them. Harden off seedlings before setting them out after the soil has warmed. Set three plants in a 12-inch basket, or space plants 10 inches apart if you want a ground-cover effect. Small, young plants transplant better than older ones.

Fertilize sanvitalia lightly unless you are growing it in rich soil, in which case the plants may need no additional nutrients. Plants that do not show healthy medium-green foliage need additional fertilizer, which can be supplied by top-dressing the soil with an organic or timed-release fertilizer, or by feeding plants with a soluble liquid plant food.

Sanvitalia tolerates drought better than most other annuals. After they are well established, the plants can get by on infrequent deep waterings during hot weather. In late summer, after the plants have been blooming for several weeks, trim them back if needed to force out new flowering stems.

Sanvitalia with fan flower.

Selecting Varieties

'Mandarin Orange' and 'Golden Carpet' have yellow-orange petals, while 'Yellow Carpet' is clear lemon yellow. All varieties have contrasting black centers.

Colorful Companions

The sunny hues of sanvitalia contrast beautifully with blue flowers such as ageratum, which is a good match in terms of size and growth habit. You also can use sanvitalia to carpet the ground in front of roses or mid-sized annuals such as narrow-leaf zinnia, blue convolvulus, or trachymene. In baskets or containers, grow sanvitalia alone or in the company of blue fan flower or white petunias.

Most sanvitalias are yellow, but rare whites are great finds for big baskets.

Sanvitalia Facts to Know		
Light Sun to part shade	**Soil** Fertile, well drained	**Water** Average
Germination Press seeds into the top of sterile soil-less mix and germinate at 70°F. Move to intense light immediately after sprouts appear.		**Preferred climate** Likes warm weather and is easily damaged by frost.

SCABIOSA
Scabiosa atropurpurea

Scabiosa.

Often called sweet scabious because of its light fragrance, or pincushion flower because of the way the white-tipped stamens look like little pins stuck in a pincushion, this old-fashioned flower attracts butterflies and makes a long-lasting cut flower. Another old nickname, mourning bride, is more properly used to describe certain old strains that bear only dark maroon flowers. In most seed mixtures, you can expect blooms ranging in color from white to pink to maroon, with numerous shades in between.

In the Garden

Scabiosa blooms appear in flushes, mostly during the second half of summer, on sprawling plants that grow to about 30 inches tall. For the most attractive look, set two or three plants together so they can grow into a lush mound of foliage and flowers. Be sure to allow an access route to the plants so you can easily gather the blossoms for indoor arrangements. Where summers are hot, the plants benefit from partial afternoon shade.

How to Grow

Occasionally bedding plants may be found in spring, but you may need to start your own seedlings indoors a few weeks before your last frost. Set plants out after the last frost has passed, and be watchful that they do not dry out for at least 3 weeks after transplanting.

Scabiosa is an adaptable old-time favorite that will grow in any type of soil provided it is well drained and reasonably fertile, with a near neutral pH. Enrich the soil with compost or rotted manure before planting, or work in a small amount of organic or timed-release fertilizer. Mulch to keep the soil cool and moist. Like many old-fashioned flowers, scabiosa takes its time coming into bloom. Be patient.

Selecting Varieties

Seeds are typically sold in color mixtures. Be sure you buy the annual species. The best perennial forms are propagated vegetatively rather than from seed. In addition to *S. atropurpurea*, another annual species, *Scabiosa stellata*, is grown for its ball-shaped seed clusters, which are lovely when combined with other dried flowers.

Colorful Companions

Because scabiosa is almost always grown in mixed colors and its blooming period is somewhat limited, this is a good flower to flank with neutral gray dusty miller or a subdued white flower such as white petunia, nierembergia, or pastel pink vinca. Blue spikes of blue salvia also make welcome bedfellows.

Scabiosa Facts to Know

Light	Soil	Water
Sun to part shade	Fertile, well drained	Average

Germination	Preferred climate
Cover seed with 1/8 inch of soil-less mix; best germination at about 75°F.	Spring-sown seedlings bloom in late summer. They resent extreme cold and high heat.

SCHIZANTHUS
Schizanthus pinnatus

Schizanthus.

A cool-season flower from Chile, schizanthus or butterfly flower is not well known because its need for consistently cool weather limits the areas in which it can be grown. Schizanthus grows beautifully as a winter annual in the cool maritime climates of the West Coast and makes a great summer flower in the Far North and other climates where hot weather never lasts very long. Wherever it will grow, schizanthus puts on an impressive show of delicate, orchid-like flowers that almost hide the finely cut foliage. The color range includes pink, purple, violet and white, all of which make fine cut flowers. Fragrance in schizanthus is light and fleeting, but it most definitely exists.

In the Garden

Schizanthus needs rich, moist soil, and should be planted in full sun when grown as a winter annual, or in partial shade when grown during the summer. Dwarf varieties are good for window boxes or container bouquets, while larger plants that grow to 2 feet tall are beautiful in a mixed bed or border.

How to Grow

Schizanthus is often sold as a bedding plant in regions where it is known to grow well. In cool climates, you can also grow plants from seed started indoors 10 to 12 weeks before your last spring frost. When handled as a winter annual, try to get the plants situated in September, while days are still long enough to support strong growth.

Schizanthus needs soil that stays constantly moist, so amend the soil if needed to lighten up clay or give sand a little extra bulk. Too little or too much water can spell disaster for this flower. Schizanthus also needs a steady supply of fertilizer, which can be provided in liquid or granular form. To keep plants blooming for a long time, give them an extra feeding just as they come into bloom.

Selecting Varieties

Dwarf varieties include 'Royal Pierrot', which grows to about 7 inches tall. Varieties with 'Parade' in their names are usually heavy bloomers. If you want flowers with intricate markings, look for the variety called 'Sweet Lips'.

Colorful Companions

Almost all schizanthus have contrasting yellow-and-white centers, so it's wise to pair them with solid-colored petunias, verbena, stocks, or pansies to keep the planting from appearing too busy. A small mass planting of schizanthus is always a sure hit.

Schizanthus in a novel color, tangerine orange.

Schizanthus Facts to Know		
Light Part shade to sun	**Soil** Rich, moist	**Water** Above average
Germination Plant seeds $1/16$ inch deep and germinate at 60 to 65°F. Keep dark for 5 days after planting.		**Preferred climate** Requires cool to mild weather, resents high heat.

SNAPDRAGON
Antirrhinum majus

Two thousand years ago, garlands of snapdragons were used to ward off evil spells, but today snapdragons are grown for spellbinding visual effects. Upright spikes covered with flowers make snapdragons great for formal beds, or you can use them as vertical elements in mixed beds or container bouquets. Snapdragons are most dazzling when planted in large groups.

Snapdragons.

In the Garden

Snapdragons grow best in cool weather and often struggle in extreme heat. They generally prefer full sun, but in hot climates they benefit from partial shade. Tall varieties need staking to keep the spikes straight. If allowed to sprawl, the spikes will bend upward toward the sun.

How to Grow

Sow seeds indoors in late winter, or save time by starting with bedding plants. You can set plants out before the last frost, but you will need to protect them from temperatures below 25°F with cloches or cardboard boxes. In Zones 8 and 9, set out snapdragons in the fall. The plants may bloom briefly after planting, but will stop blooming when days become less than 13 hours long.

Work a timed-release fertilizer or organic fertilizer into the soil before setting out the plants. Water well after transplanting, and pinch off any old flower spikes. A light mulch helps control weeds and retains soil moisture.

While snapdragons are in bloom, snip off faded flower spikes promptly to encourage the development of new ones. Shear plants back in mid-summer to help force out a fresh crop of flower spikes.

In mild winter climates, snapdragons often survive winter and bloom well the following spring. However, year-old plants are more susceptible to disease than young ones, so it's best to pull them up after the first flush of spring flowers fades away.

Selecting Varieties

Choose tall varieties like 'Rocket' or 'Bright Butterflies' for cutting. 'Liberty' is a mid-sized snap that grows 20 inches tall and does not need staking. Dwarf varieties are fine for small beds or broad edgings.

Colorful Companions

Snaps come in many bright, clear shades of yellow, red, pink and white. Try edging a planting of mixed colors with fine-textured white or pale yellow pansies, white sweet alyssum, or white nierembergia. Buttery yellow snapdragons are easy to combine with many other flowers in diversified beds.

'Montego Orange Bicolor' snapdragons.

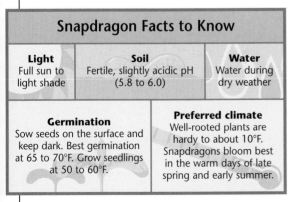

Snapdragon Facts to Know

Light	Soil	Water
Full sun to light shade	Fertile, slightly acidic pH (5.8 to 6.0)	Water during dry weather

Germination	Preferred climate
Sow seeds on the surface and keep dark. Best germination at 65 to 70°F. Grow seedlings at 50 to 60°F.	Well-rooted plants are hardy to about 10°F. Snapdragons bloom best in the warm days of late spring and early summer.

STATICE

Limonium sinuatum

Statice is an essential part of any flower arranger's garden. The flowers make wonderful cut material when they are fresh from the garden, and when dried they can last for years. The blossoms of statice are really a botanical structure called a calyx. Little yellow to white flowers hide inside these bright papery envelopes.

In the Garden

Statice needs bright sun and soil with excellent drainage. The plants grow best when the weather is not extremely hot. Place groups of three to five plants 10 inches apart in mixed beds or borders, or grow statice in a special cutting garden laid out in rows. Until they bloom, statice plants grow into round rosettes of lobed, slightly hairy leaves. At full maturity they are 2 feet tall. It is normal for stems to have flattened "wings" along their length.

How to Grow

Start seedlings indoors about 6 weeks before your last spring frost. Thin seedlings to one per 2-inch container, and move them to a

Statice.

Fresh or dried, statice is always beautiful.

protected cold frame or grow tunnel when they have one true leaf. Transplant at about the same time as your last frost. Before transplanting, enrich the soil with a 2-inch-deep layer of compost or flower-planting mix.

Harvest stems for drying after they are fully opened, but don't let mature stems stay on the plants for long. Frequent harvesting encourages the plants to develop more bud-bearing stems, but go ahead and pull up plants when they stop making new flowers. Where winters are very mild (Zones 8 and 9), plants set out in fall often survive winter and bloom the following spring.

Selecting Varieties

Look to mail-order seed catalogs for the best selection. You can choose between mixtures or individual colors including white, yellow, rose, blue and lavender. All have pale yellow true flowers inside the papery bracts. A mixture called

'Sunset' includes only shades of soft coral pink. The flowers within the 'Soiree' and 'Pacific' series have extra-rich colors, and the plants are very uniform and vigorous.

Colorful Companions

Because of its novel flower form, use statice freely if your garden seems overly dominated by daisy-shaped blossoms. In terms of growth habit and weather preferences, statice is a natural partner for numerous cool-season annuals, including ammi, calendula, bells of Ireland, dianthus, cosmos, larkspur and verbena.

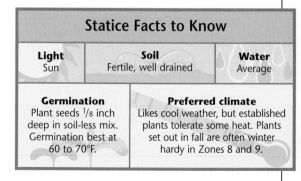

Statice Facts to Know

Light	Soil	Water
Sun	Fertile, well drained	Average

Germination	Preferred climate
Plant seeds 1/8 inch deep in soil-less mix. Germination best at 60 to 70°F.	Likes cool weather, but established plants tolerate some heat. Plants set out in fall are often winter hardy in Zones 8 and 9.

STOCK
Matthiola incana

Any gardener who loves fragrant flowers is bound to fall in love with stocks, which have been fixtures in English cottage gardens for three centuries. Determined cool-season flowers distantly related to cabbage, stocks bloom best when exposed to chilly temperatures followed by gradually increasing warmth.

In the Garden

Where summer remains cool for a long time, you can grow dwarf stocks in sunny beds or use them as edging plants to frame taller flowers. Grow tall stocks for cutting in groups or drifts in a cutting garden or mixed border. Tall stocks reach 2 feet or more when grown in rich, fertile soil with regular water. In windy areas it is helpful to place a number of slender stakes among the plants and weave them together with string to form a supportive matrix for the upright flower spikes.

How to Grow

Unless you are confident that local garden centers will offer bedding plants in early spring, start seeds indoors 8 weeks before your last spring frost. Use individual containers for these fast-growing plants, and keep young seedlings in a cool protected place outdoors such as a cold frame. Set plants out while the weather is still chilly, and use cloches if needed to protect them from late frosts. In Zones 9 and 10 stocks can be grown as winter annuals, but be sure to cover them with boxes or baskets in the event of freezing weather.

Stocks.

Fertilize the site with an organic or timed-release fertilizer prior to planting. After buds appear, feed plants monthly with a liquid plant food to keep them in bloom for the longest possible time. Aggressive cutting also helps to force out late flowers, which have shorter stems than the earliest blooms. Pull out plants when flowering subsides, and replace them with a more heat-tolerant annual.

Selecting Varieties

'Cheerful' produces white or pale yellow double flowers that make the spikes appear especially full and lush. In a range of colors that include pinks, reds, and white, 'Trysomic Giants' are tall plants with a seductively spicy fragrance that are ideal for cutting. Dwarf varieties include fast-growing 'Ten Weeks Mix' and 'Midget', both of which grow to less than 12 inches tall.

Colorful Companions

Stocks planted in early spring often bloom with late tulips. In mixed flower beds, good companions include ammi, forget-me-nots and lobelia. Sweet peas, stocks and sweet alyssum are a classic spring combination in gardens designed to produce maximum fragrance.

Many stocks smell as good as they look.

Stock Facts to Know

Light	Soil	Water
Sun to partial shade	Rich, fertile	Average

Germination	Preferred climate
Press seeds into the top of damp soil-less mix and germinate at 65 to 70°F.	Likes cool weather that gradually warms into the moderate range.

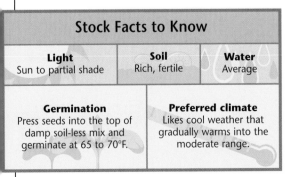

STRAWFLOWER

The common name "strawflower" is usually used for helichrysum, one of the easiest everlastings to grow and dry. But paper daisies (*Acroclinium*) are sometimes called strawflowers too, and both are well worth growing in your garden. Because they have different cultural needs, they are described separately here.

Strawflowers close during wet weather. Always cut them for drying in fair weather, preferably in the morning.

HELICHRYSUM
Helichrysum bracteatum

A half-hardy perennial from Australia, helichrysum is a vigorous member of the aster family. A true cut-and-come-again flower, helichrysum produces blooms steadily from mid-summer to frost on sturdy plants up to 4 feet tall.

In the Garden

Because of its size and longevity, give helichrysum a prominent place near the back of a mixed flower bed or border, but be sure you can reach the plants easily to gather the blossoms. Helichrysum needs full sun, but it can adapt to any soil that's reasonably fertile and well drained. Easy to grow, this is probably the best dried flower for beginners to try.

How to Grow

Start seeds indoors about a month before your last frost. Set the seedlings out after the last frost has passed, and work an organic or timed-release fertilizer into the soil prior to planting. Water as needed to keep the soil lightly moist, and mulch between plants to keep the soil cool and moist.

Expect to see the first blooms about 100 days after planting. Individual flowers close up at night and during wet weather, and then re-open when the sun is bright. To gather them for drying, cut when the blossoms are almost fully open and hang them upside down in a warm place protected from direct sunlight. To reinforce the "necks" of very large blossoms, run a piece of florist wire up the stem and into the base of the blossom before hanging the stems to dry.

Selecting Varieties

'Monstrosum' grows to 3 feet or more and bears very large flowers in the full range of helichrysum colors, while 'Fiery' and 'Salsa' include only hot reds, oranges and yellows. The color range of 'Pastel' is limited to pinks and white. 'Bright Bikini' is a compact variety that fits easily in beds, but its stems are somewhat short for drying.

Colorful Companions

In addition to choosing flowers that coordinate well in terms of color, keep in mind that helichrysum's leathery dark green leaves give it a heavy texture. Ideal companions have a lighter texture and include ageratum, angelonia, portulaca and narrow-leaf zinnia. Yellow marigolds or yellow plume celosia work well with helichrysum too.

Helichrysum.

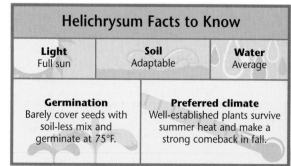

Helichrysum Facts to Know		
Light Full sun	**Soil** Adaptable	**Water** Average
Germination Barely cover seeds with soil-less mix and germinate at 75°F.		**Preferred climate** Well-established plants survive summer heat and make a strong comeback in fall.

ACROCLINIUM
Acroclinium roseum

Dainty paper daisies are sometimes known by their old botanical name of *Helipterum*. These delightful flowers are outstanding in cool climates, where they often bloom continuously all summer. But in other areas acroclinium tends to melt out once temperatures reach the mid 80s. However, you can usually grow a good crop of dried stems before hot weather comes by getting the plants established very early in spring.

In the Garden

Acroclinium is most productive when grown in exceptionally well drained but fertile soil in full sun. Amend heavy clay with plenty of compost or other organic soil amendment before attempting to grow acroclinium. Plants grow 18 to 24 inches tall, and individual plants develop dozens of basal stems, so they need wide 14-inch spacing to ensure good air circulation.

How to Grow

The best way to plant acroclinium is to sow the seeds atop cultivated soil in very early spring. However, if hot weather is likely to cut short the paper daisy show in your garden, start seeds indoors about 6 weeks before the last spring frost. Use individual plantable containers such as peat pots to avoid disturbing the roots during transplanting. Set out as early as you can, and use cloches to protect plants from late frosts. With steady, uninterrupted growth, acroclinium will bloom about 10 weeks after planting.

Acroclinium.

Like other strawflowers, acroclinium blooms close up at night and during wet weather. Cut fresh blossoms in midmorning on a sunny day, and strip off the leaves before hanging them upside down to dry. The thin stems dry very quickly, usually within a week. In most climates acroclinium produces a heavy set of flowers over a period of about 4 weeks and then quickly declines after hot summer weather arrives.

Selecting Varieties

Selections offered in seed catalogs such as 'Best Mix' and 'Sensation Giants' pro-

duce double flowers that bloom in three colors—light pink, dark pink and white, many with sunny yellow centers. A real stunner, 'Pierrot' has icy white blossoms with dark centers surrounded by thin yellow halos. The largest variety, 'Goliath', produces big pink blossoms with dark centers.

Colorful Companions

This flower helps fill the bloom gap between spring perennials and bulbs and most summer annuals. Balance clumps of acroclinium with blue bachelor buttons, pink corn poppies, or a mixed planting of larkspur. Ammi also makes a fine background plant for acroclinium.

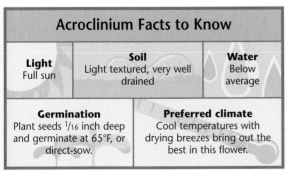

Acroclinium Facts to Know		
Light Full sun	**Soil** Light textured, very well drained	**Water** Below average
Germination Plant seeds ¹/₁₆ inch deep and germinate at 65°F, or direct-sow.		**Preferred climate** Cool temperatures with drying breezes bring out the best in this flower.

SUNFLOWER
Helianthus annuus

Sunflower.

There is no such thing as a sad sunflower. These native "flowers of the sun" are an essential part of any gardener's celebration of summer, and their size and exuberance bring sensational energy to anyplace where they are grown. Depending on variety, sunflowers can be 10-foot-tall giants, big bushes covered with exotically colored flowers, or perky dwarfs that burst into flower when they are still knee high. The big blooms provide lots of pollen for honeybees. As the seeds mature, you can let goldfinches or other seed-eating birds snap them up, or cut and save the heavy seedheads to present to your feathered friends in winter.

In the Garden

Sunflowers demand a warm, sunny spot, and if deprived of sunshine they will twist around to face the direction that offers the most abundant light. If you must grow sunflowers in partial shade, select a spot where they will turn toward the best vantage point from which you can see them. Also, varieties that develop numerous branches are less likely to turn away from you than are upright growers that produce but one or two giant flowers.

Just about any soil will support sunflowers, but modest efforts made to improve the soil will result in bigger, more long-lived plants. Because branching varieties produce new blooms over an extended period of time, they greatly benefit from a high-quality site that might support another heavy feeder such as corn. Sunflowers also are famous for their ability to make themselves at home in old compost heaps.

How to Grow

Start sowing sunflower seeds where you want the plants to grow a week or two after the last frost has passed, or plant seeds indoors in individual containers 2 weeks before the your last frost date. Although sunflowers are warm-season plants, the seedlings are surprisingly hardy and often withstand light frosts that come in late spring. Before planting, enrich the soil with a balanced fertilizer such as 10-10-10. To keep sunflowers blooming in your garden all the way to frost, continue planting more seeds every 3 weeks until mid-summer, or

100 days before you expect your first fall frost to come.

Consider the size and shape of the variety you are growing when thinning seedlings to proper spacing. Upright growers and dwarf varieties can be left as little as 12 inches apart, but allow twice that much space for sunflowers that grow into big, bushy plants. The large leaves of sunflowers often do a good job of shading out weeds, but you may want to use a light mulch to help keep the soil moist between summer showers. In very dry weather, water sunflowers deeply but infrequently.

Many modern cultivars produce a steady parade of blooms for a month or more, but the skyscrapers usually flower once and then get on with the business of nurturing seeds. Flower production is controlled by variety more than any other factor.

Start sunflower seeds in containers or sow them directly in the garden.

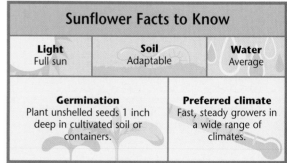

Sunflower Facts to Know

Light	Soil	Water
Full sun	Adaptable	Average

Germination	Preferred climate
Plant unshelled seeds 1 inch deep in cultivated soil or containers.	Fast, steady growers in a wide range of climates.

Bicolored sunflowers are ideal for sowing late (in early summer) so that they bloom in the fall.

Selecting Varieties

There are dozens of sunflower varieties to choose from, and each one has its merits. To simplify the selection process, the varieties here are sorted into four categories: giants, branching sunflowers, low pollen producers for cutting, and dwarf varieties for small spaces.

Giants

These varieties produce a single huge blossom atop a thick stem, followed by fat, edible seeds. Flowers can be more than 12 inches across. Yellow 'Giganteus', 'Mammoth Russian' and 'Paul Bunyan' are of this type.

Branching

Ideal for the back of a border or a big summer hedge, 6-foot-tall branching sunflowers feature abundant blooms, a long flowering period, and a wide range of colors. Flowers are usually about 4 inches across. Yellow-gold 'Holiday', red 'Chianti', multi-colored 'Velvet Tapestry' and creamy 'Italian White' are of this type.

Low pollen

These varieties, bred for cutting, shed little or no pollen and often have long, stiff stems. Flower diameter ranges from 4 to 6 inches. Yellow 'Full Sun', lemony 'Moonbright', and red 'Prado' fall into this category along with 'Sunbeam', which has unusual green centers.

Dwarfs

Stir up some fun by growing some of these lovelies in a small bed or large container. 'Music Box' and 'Sundance' offer a symphony of color, or you can stick with golden yellow by growing 'Sunspot' or 'Elf'.

Colorful Companions

Mask the bases of tall sunflowers with bushy melampodium, or draw attention to sunflowers' strong vertical lines with Joseph's coat type amaranth or plume celosia. Emphasize the wild side of sunflowers by letting them share company with cleome, sulphur cosmos, Mexican sunflower or tall zinnias.

Dwarf sunflowers with white ageratum.

Birds will gather the ripe seeds from sunflower heads left to ripen in the garden. Because of their height, sunflowers make strong vertical accents when grown among smaller flowers such as celosia, marigolds, zinnias and cosmos.

SWEET ALYSSUM

Lobularia maritima

It's difficult to imagine a flower bed or container bouquet that does not benefit from being accessorized with lacy tidbits of sweet alyssum. The fine-textured plants grow into frothy mounds only 4 inches tall and up to 10 inches wide, and most varieties have a light, honey-sweet fragrance.

In the Garden

Use sweet alyssum as an edging for beds, containers, or as a ground-cover in areas planted with spring-flowering bulbs. Plants grow best in cool weather, but they can with-stand heat if they are well rooted and given regular water. Sweet alyssum is very easy to grow.

How to Grow

You can buy plants in cellpacks in the spring, but frequently these are already in bloom and less likely to grow into big, vigorous plants than young seedlings that are just beginning to flower. If you buy seedlings, get them into the ground at the earliest possible time.

A more economical approach is to simply sow seeds in the garden or in flats a few weeks before your last frost. Sow seeds on the surface as they benefit from exposure to light. Flats of sweet alyssum can be cut into brownie-sized chunks with a knife and transplanted to the garden. Thin direct-sown seedlings to 6 inches apart. Feed plants monthly with a soluble fertilizer.

Use scissors or pruning shears to cut back plants by half their size in mid-summer. This rather harsh pruning encourages the development of new basal branches, which will pro-duce new flowers in only a few weeks. Where summers are so hot that sweet alyssum melts into a with-ered mess, start a new crop of plants indoors in late summer and set them out in the fall.

Where winters are mild, allow old plants to stand through the winter, and pull them out in early spring. Beneath the dead foliage you are likely to find volunteer seedlings, which you can leave in place or dig and move to a new location.

Sweet alyssum with white begonia and variegated vinca major.

Selecting Varieties

'Snow Cloth' and 'Snow Crystals' produce pure white blooms on vig-orous plants. 'Easter Bonnet' in-cludes a mix of white, pink, and lilac blossoms. White is usually the strongest color in this species, but you may want to try purple or rose-colored strains, which are available from mail-order seed companies.

Colorful Companions

The airy texture of sweet alyssum works well with numerous flowers and is particularly welcome in the company of purple heliotrope, cal-endulas, or geraniums. Use plants to edge mixed beds or to dress the edges of container bouquets.

Sweet alyssum as a fragrant blooming groundcover.

Sweet Alyssum Facts to Know

Light	Soil	Water
Sun to part shade	Fertile, well drained	Average

Germination	Preferred climate
Sow when the soil temperature is above 50°F; best germination at 70°F.	Grows best under cool conditions.

SWEET PEA
Lathyrus odoratus

A century ago, the new science of plant breeding was applied to sweet peas, and the showy new strains that were created turned sweet peas into a gardening craze. Unfortunately, fragrance was often lost as larger, more colorful blossoms were attained. A revival in the popularity of sweet peas has helped to bring back many of the most fragrant old strains, or you can grow heavy-blooming varieties with only a hint of scent. Either way, sweet peas are one annual that every gardener should grow at least once.

Sweet peas make excellent cut flowers.

In the Garden

Sweet peas need more attention than many other annual flowers. Besides full morning sun, they need fertile soil that has a neutral or slightly alkaline pH. If your soil tends to be acidic, mix a dusting of lime into the bed along with a generous helping of organic matter. Also make plans to trellis your peas. In warm climates sweet peas are short-lived, so a 4-foot-tall trellis of old branches will do. Where summers are cool, sweet peas often grow into heavy vines up to 9 feet long, so they are best trained onto a fence or trellis made of chicken wire or polyester netting attached to secure posts.

Sweet peas accented with a single spire of lavender larkspur.

How to Grow

Most people sow sweet peas in the ground, but you can start them in peat pots if you prefer. Soak the seeds overnight before planting. Plant when cool weather will prevail for at least 3 months: mid-fall in Zones 9 and 10, late winter in Zones 7 and 8, and early spring elsewhere. The young seedlings survive frost and moderate freezes.

Fertilize plants every 3 weeks or so with a water-soluble fertilizer, and mulch between plants to keep the soil cool and moist. Frequent cutting encourages the development of new buds. Pull plants up when they stop flowering and begin to wither. In many areas you can replace spent sweet peas with a more heat-tolerant annual vine, such as morning glory.

Selecting Varieties

'Old Spice' produces fragrant blossoms in a range of colors, and there are dozens of other fragrant old strains to try. In mild winter climates, try "winter" sweet peas such as 'Winter Elegance', which blooms promptly in the spring from fall sowing.

Colorful Companions

Partner sweet peas with small annuals that will help mask the bases of the plants, which are not especially attractive. Sweet alyssum or lobelia do a good job. Pansies and violas are also fine companions for sweet peas.

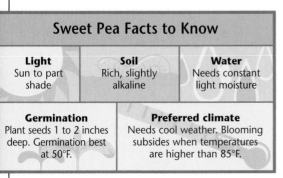

Sweet Pea Facts to Know

Light	Soil	Water
Sun to part shade	Rich, slightly alkaline	Needs constant light moisture

Germination	Preferred climate
Plant seeds 1 to 2 inches deep. Germination best at 50°F.	Needs cool weather. Blooming subsides when temperatures are higher than 85°F.

SWEET POTATO, ORNAMENTAL
Ipomoea batatas

'Blackie' ornamental sweet potato with cobbity daisies and lobelia.

Since making their debut in the gardening world in the mid-1990s, ornamental sweet potato vines have steadily grown in popularity. They feature unique lush foliage, which can be blackish red, lime green, or variegated with white and pink, depending on variety. Vigorous new growth is produced in weather hot enough to make other foliage plants wilt.

In the Garden

Add ornamental sweet potato to large container bouquets or window boxes so the long stems can spill out over the edges. These plants also make great groundcovers in sunny spots. You can grow them beneath taller plants such as roses or between clumps of ornamental grass, or put them to work masking the base of a chainlink fence. Ornamental sweet potato's only hard-and-fast cultural need is plenty of warmth.

How to Grow

Set out purchased plants in late spring, after the last frost has passed and the soil is warm. When used as a groundcover, plants may be set 3 feet apart. In beds and containers, individual plants are typically tucked in between other flowers. As they grow, they fill in any spot of sun they happen to find.

When ornamental sweet potato is grown in the ground in warm climates, the plants form thick tubers, which you can store in a cool place where they will not freeze through the winter. In early spring, place the tubers on their sides in a warm cold frame and cover with 2 inches of weathered straw. As 5-inch-long stems emerge from the tips of the tubers, break them off and transplant them. Whether homegrown or purchased, newly planted sweet potato plants benefit from warm, moist growing conditions.

Warm weather speeds the growth of the vines. Should they ramble too far, simply clip off the tips. If you want more plants to add to late-season containers, set some of your stem cuttings to root in water or moist potting soil.

Selecting Varieties

Nurseries offer three cultivars. 'Blackie' has blackish-red leaves that are broad and pointed, while the leaves of 'Marguerite' are lime green pointed ovals. The leaves of 'Tri-Color' are variegated with white, green and pink.

Colorful Companions

'Blackie' is so dark that it's an ideal counterpoint for light yellow flowers such as yellow marigolds, melampodium, or yellow lantana. Pair chartreuse 'Marguerite' with purple flowers such as 'Purple Wave' petunia, or train the vines to cover the base of a trellis planted with hyacinth bean. Combine 'Tri-Color' with white or light pink lavatera, or pink celosia or gomphrena.

'Marguerite' ornamental sweet potato.

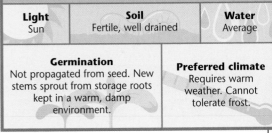

Ornamental Sweet Potato Facts to Know

Light	Soil	Water
Sun	Fertile, well drained	Average

Germination	Preferred climate
Not propagated from seed. New stems sprout from storage roots kept in a warm, damp environment.	Requires warm weather. Cannot tolerate frost.

TORENIA
Torenia fournieri, T. baillonii

From its ancestral home in Vietnam, torenia comes to American gardens with a natural taste for sultry weather. Commonly called wishbone flower, or, along the Gulf Coast, Florida pansy, most torenias bear small white blossoms edged with pink or blue on neat, mounding plants. Torenia thrives in partial shade, just like impatiens, but it is satisfied with slightly less water.

Torenia.

In the Garden

Torenia's ideal niche is a moist spot that receives between 3 and 5 hours of summer sun each day. The plants are small enough to use as an edging, but their 10-inch height also makes them useful for planting in front of taller flowers or growing in containers. To grow torenia beneath trees that have extensive surface roots, plant the torenias in old plastic nursery liners and bury the pots up to their rims in holes dug into the ground. This limits competition for water and nutrients between the tree and the torenias.

How to Grow

In recent years torenias have been added to the roster of bedding plants sold in spring, but not every garden center has them. To grow your own, start the small seeds indoors 6 weeks before your last frost. Move the seedlings outdoors when they have 2 true leaves, and let them grow in a cool, protected place such as a cold frame. Torenia seedlings grow slowly at first, but then they take off after being set out in warm, fertile soil.

Use an organic or timed-release fertilizer when preparing the site, and amend the soil with compost or peat moss if needed to help it retain moisture. A mulch of shredded bark or pine needles is also in order with torenia. Pinch off old seedpods from time to time, and drench plants with a liquid fertilizer every 2 weeks during the second half of summer. Keep in mind that torenia's leaves are naturally a mid-green color, and will not darken when given liberal fertilizer.

Selecting Varieties

The leading torenia variety is 'Clown', which bears white flowers edged with varying shades of blue and pink. Another variety, 'Suzie Wong', is of a different species (*T. baillonii*). It has the same leaf shape as other torenias, but produces yellow-orange flowers on low, spreading plants.

Colorful Companions

Torenia's light colors naturally light up shade, and can be mixed and matched with all of the other annuals that adapt to shade, including bacopa, tuberous begonia, browallia, coleus, impatiens, and touch-me-not. 'Suzie Wong' is great with coleus.

'Summer Wave Blue' torenia.

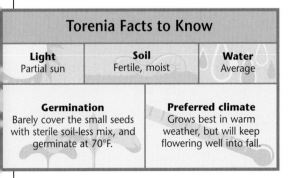

Torenia Facts to Know		
Light Partial sun	**Soil** Fertile, moist	**Water** Average
Germination Barely cover the small seeds with sterile soil-less mix, and germinate at 70°F.		**Preferred climate** Grows best in warm weather, but will keep flowering well into fall.

TOUCH-ME-NOT
Impatiens balsamina

For 150 years this impatiens cousin made a happy home for itself in many a shady dooryard garden. Pretty and persistent but never weedy, the plants willingly reseed themselves year after year. Also known as garden balsam, touch-me-not gets its common name from its pendulous green seedpods, which pop open at the slightest touch when they reach maturity. This jack-in-the-box characteristic makes them a fine flower to share with children.

In the Garden

Touch-me-nots ask for little more than a moist shady spot in which to grow. Unlike impatiens, which carry their blossoms high where they can clearly be seen, touch-me-not blossoms line up along the 2-foot-tall main stem, often sandwiched between layers of leaves that partially hide them from view. This growth habit compromises touch-me-not's worth as a source of color, but its ability to reappear like magic every summer more than makes up for this small imperfection.

The seedpods of touch-me-not pop open when they are touched, and when they become fully ripe.

How to Grow

To establish touch-me-not in a site, start seeds indoors 2 weeks before the last frost. Set the seedlings out a month or so later, after the soil has warmed. Or, direct-seed them in mid-spring. Touch-me-nots need rich, moist soil that contains plenty of organic matter along with a little fertilizer. Space plants about 10 inches apart.

When your touch-me-nots begin to bloom, pull out those that show colors that are not to your liking. This roguing out also delays the number of seasons it will take for the plants to revert to their dominant ancestral color, which is medium pink with a touch of salmon. After fine-tuning for color, just let the plants go. By the time the first frost turns them to mush, they will have shed sufficient seed to serve as a solid foundation for the next generation.

Selecting Varieties

Few seed companies still carry seed, and seed that does remain in commerce usually yields double flowers. Expect them to go back to being singles after a few generations. Many gardeners who save and share seeds handle touch-me-nots, and it can be fun to network with other gardeners through seed swap columns in magazines or through the Seed Savers Exchange (see Resources on page 171).

Rich pink touch-me-nots.

Colorful Companions

Find a coleus with pure pink in its leaves and you have found the perfect partner for touch-me-nots. White browallia and any shade of torenia work well too, or you can simply let touch-me-nots naturalize solo in the shelter of buildings or large foundation shrubs.

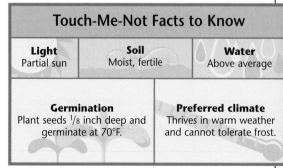

Touch-Me-Not Facts to Know		
Light Partial sun	**Soil** Moist, fertile	**Water** Above average
Germination Plant seeds 1/8 inch deep and germinate at 70°F.		**Preferred climate** Thrives in warm weather and cannot tolerate frost.

TRACHYMENE
Trachymene coerulea

If one of the reasons you garden is to grow flowers that are uniquely beautiful, then you must grow trachymene at least once. Commonly called blue lace flower, this native of Australia produces rounded umbels that resemble Queen Anne's lace or ammi in form, but are soft powder blue. In a fresh arrangement, trachymene provides the perfect counterpoint to big feature flowers like roses or lilies. In the garden, trachymene's cool color creates an irresistible visual oasis.

In the Garden

Trachymene is a cool-season flower to grow in a sunny, well-drained site. Its soft blue color goes with almost everything, and its lacy gray-green foliage further boosts its ability to work well with other plants in mixed beds or border. The plants grow to 20 inches or so in height, and need 14-inch-wide spacing to ensure good air circulation.

Because of its soft color and unusual rounded form, trachymene is a fine filler flower for cut arrangements.

How to Grow

The best way to grow trachymene in most areas is to start seeds early indoors and set them out under cloches in late spring, a week or two before the last frost. As with other annuals with delicate roots, it's wise to transplant trachymene while the plants are quite small. This way they can develop extensive roots while the weather is still cool, and trachymene is never happy spending a long time in containers anyway. In northerly areas where cool nights are common during much of the summer, you can simply sow the seeds in cultivated soil around the time of your last spring frost. Germination problems are usually the result of planting old seed. Buy fresh seed every year, or save and replant your own.

Follow a modest fertilizer regimen with this flower, but provide regular water to keep the soil moist. Where summers are hot, a thick mulch to help keep the roots cool encourages a long, lush succession of blooms.

Selecting Varieties

In seed catalogs, look for this flower by its proper name of trachymene, its now obsolete name of didiscus, or as blue lace flower. One named variety developed especially for cutting is called 'Madonna'. In addition to blue, 'Madonna' comes in pale pink and white.

Colorful Companions

Paint an early summer flower bed blue by planting trachymene near blue forget-me-nots and pansies, supplemented by white sweet alyssum or pink dianthus. Dusty miller is always a welcome bed partner, as are white petunias or richly colored convolvulus.

Trachymene.

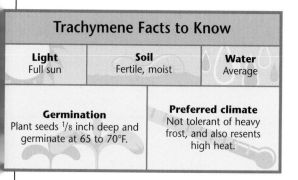

Trachymene Facts to Know

Light	Soil	Water
Full sun	Fertile, moist	Average

Germination	Preferred climate
Plant seeds ⅛ inch deep and germinate at 65 to 70°F.	Not tolerant of heavy frost, and also resents high heat.

VERBENA
Verbena hybrids

Verbenas offer both a beautiful range of colors and long bloom time.

Sorting through verbenas can be confusing due to the introduction of so many new cultivars. There are true annual verbenas to grow from seed, others treated as annuals that are grown from stem cuttings, and perennials that are hardy to Zone 6. Any of these can be handled as an annual in the garden. All verbenas bear rounded clusters of flowers in pink, red, white, or violet, and the plants grow by spreading outward into loose mounds.

In the Garden

Verbenas show surprising vigor when planted in any sunny, well-drained spot. They are most likely to prosper in soil that has been deeply dug and amended with or-ganic matter or in rich loam. Verbena is more weather resilient than many other annu-als, withstanding both cold and heat. Use it almost like a blooming groundcover in beds, or grow it in window boxes, hanging baskets, or large container bouquets.

How to Grow

Seedlings of seed-sown vari-eties are sold as spring bedding plants, or you can start the seeds in-doors 6 weeks be-fore your last frost. Plant extra seeds, because germination rates are often low. Some especially heavy-blooming cultivars are avail-able only as pur-chased plants, but if you live where summers are very hot and humid you will prob-ably find that they are well worth the extra cost. Set verbenas out while the weather is still cool. Add mulch to keep mud from splashing onto the foliage.

Plants stay in bloom longer if you pinch off the old flower clusters. When flowering slows, you can coax out a final flush of blooms by shearing the plants back by half their size and drenching them well with a soluble plant food. When very vig-orous vegetatively propa-gated verbenas are grown in hanging baskets, it is often better to trim them by hand, snipping off leggy or shriv-eled stems as needed to keep the plants nicely balanced.

Selecting Varieties

Outstanding seed-sown hybrids include the 'Quartz' series, which shows better tolerance of powdery mildew than some others. 'Sandy' is available in several colors and makes a very thick 8-inch-tall groundcover. Try 'Peaches and Cream' in containers where you can admire its subtle colors. Superior vegetatively propagated verbenas include 'Tapien' and 'Temari', both available in several colors.

Colorful Companions

Mix and match verbenas with petunias, or use them as a ground-cover in front of any tall flower. Big yellow marigolds, Joseph's coat amaranth, euphorbia and many other upright annuals form a fine backdrop for verbena.

'Pink Bouquet' hybrid verbena.

Verbena Facts to Know		
Light Sun to part shade	**Soil** Rich, fertile	**Water** Average
Germination Plant seeds ⅛ inch deep in sterile soil-less mix and germinate at 70°F.	**Preferred climate** Adaptable. Where summers are long, a second sowing in mid-summer will bloom until frost.	

VINCA
Catharanthus roseus

In a good year, vincas are miracle flowers unmatched for their flower power and vigorous production of glossy green foliage. They are widely used to fill holes in the garden left by expired cool-season plants or for massing in large, low-maintenance beds. These heat-loving plants feature self-cleaning flowers in rich vibrant pinks or soft pastels, which are held at the tips of almost every stem.

In the Garden

Vinca will grow in full sun or partial shade, and needs a well-drained soil that dries out promptly following heavy rains. It is also important not to plant vinca in the same site more than once every 3 years. The reason is a prevalent soil-borne fungus that causes vinca roots to rot, leading to their sudden collapse. Most varieties grow to about 16 inches tall and spread up to 2 feet wide.

How to Grow

State-of-the-art vincas are widely available as bedding plants, which are a good buy when you consider their susceptibility to damping off and other problems. Sterile soil-less mix is mandatory, and you will need very intense light to keep young vincas growing fast and strong. Grow seedlings on the dry side, and never overwater them.

Outdoors, prepare a slightly raised bed, amending the soil as needed to give it a loose, porous texture. Chunky clay simply will not do unless it is well dug and amended with large quantities of

Vinca, also known as Madagascar periwinkle.

organic soil amendments. Mix a light application of any fertilizer into the soil prior to planting.

Water vincas during severe droughts, but under less stressful conditions water the plants little, if at all. Slight yellowing foliage usually can be cured with a soaking of water-soluble plant food. Pull plants up, roots and all, at the end of the season.

Selecting Varieties

Most of the vincas you will find as bedding plants have a compact, uniform growth habit and willingly show you their colors while they are still in cellpacks. The 'Pacifica' series is remarkable for its big flowers in bold colors, while toned-down pastel 'Coolers' glow in filtered shade. White 'Mediterranean' is a vigorous spreader that can almost pass for a

white impatiens, but with much better tolerance of hot sun.

Colorful Companions

A lavish planting of vinca always attracts attention, so you can concentrate on color. The cool pastels work beautifully with ageratum, wax begonia, and other heat-tolerant flowers that bloom in blue, pink or white. With hot pink vinca, stick with sunny yellow companions or calming dusty miller.

Annual vinca.

Vinca Facts to Know		
Light Full sun to part shade	**Soil** Well drained	**Water** Below average
Germination Plant seeds ⅛ inch deep and germinate at 75 to 80°F.	**Preferred climate** Warmth is essential for fast, healthy growth and nonstop flowering.	

ZINNIA

Zinnia species and hybrids

Long-stemmed zinnias are staple summer flowers in any cutting garden, while compact selections provide bright splashes of rich color when planted in large groups in the landscape. Today's zinnias include five major species groups, with a number of interspecies hybrids that have been bred to achieve a wider color range and improved resistance to powdery mildew.

All zinnias are stiff plants that crave warmth and respond to cutting or deadheading by producing more flowers. Where summers last a long time, you often can grow two or three "crops" of these rewarding flowers. Try different types to keep your interest high.

Single-flowered zinnias are of tremendous interest to butterflies. The actual flowers in a zinnia blossom are small yellow structures in the middle of the bloom. Selections that produce a single set of petals that do not crowd out the center are always butterfly favorites.

In the Garden

All zinnias need copious sunshine and warm, well-drained soil. The smallest dwarfs can be used for edging, while mid-sized selections will grow into a colorful low hedge.

Zinnia's velvety petals show endless variation in color.

Locate tall zinnias toward the back of a sunny bed or border where their bases will be well hidden by smaller flowers. You can stake very tall zinnias if you like, or let the plants tumble over. In either posture they will continue to flower to a ripe old age if kept cut or deadheaded regularly.

Small selections that bear single flowers are fine candidates for low-maintenance beds that bake in the summer sun. Petite narrow-leaf zinnias (*Z. angustifolia* or *Z. linearis*) have a fine texture, while those that bear larger flowers have a heavier look that borders on being coarse.

From Zone 6 southward, allow nonhybrid zinnias to reseed themselves from year to year. Once you learn to recognize the seedlings, you will be amazed at the free crop your garden offers up in early summer. Volunteer plants that pop up in awkward spots are easy to dig and move to new locations.

How to Grow

In cool climates, give zinnias a head start by sowing seeds indoors 3 weeks before your last frost, or simply buy bedding plants. Where summers are warmer, direct-seed zinnias where you want them to grow after the last frost has passed and the soil is warm. Thin plants to appropriate spacing, which ranges from 8 inches for the smallest selections to 20 inches or more for 4-foot-tall varieties intended primarily for cutting.

Zinnias need fertile, well-drained soil to achieve maximum size and

'Starbright' narrow-leaf zinnias.

Zinnia Facts to Know		
Light Full sun	**Soil** Fertile, well drained	**Water** Average
Germination Plant seeds ¼ inch deep in warm soil. Indoors, germinate at 75°F.		**Preferred climate** Tremendously heat tolerant, zinnias thrive in both dry and humid climates.

Throughout summer, zinnias stand ready to offer armloads of cut flowers.

'Profusion' zinnias, here in pink, are compact, long blooming and resistant to disease.

produce loads of flowers. So-called Mexican zinnias (classified as *Z. haageana*) prefer slightly dry conditions, but most zinnias respond to regular water by producing a nonstop parade of colorful blooms. Deadhead large-flowered zinnias regularly to keep new blossoms coming. Narrow-leaf zinnias produce so many blooms that it's more efficient to shear them back once or twice a summer than to try to keep up with deadheading.

Selecting Varieties

Large-flowered zinnias (*Z. elegans*) include tall varieties for cutting, such as 4-foot-tall 'Blue Point', a truly outstanding cut flower. Some varieties show festive bicolors, and others have cactus-style rolled petals. If you stick with an individual color, such as deep red or lemon yellow, you will find big zinnias easy to work with in the landscape. The compact 'Dreamland' series makes a fantastic 12-inch-tall flowering hedge.

Mexican zinnias (*Z. haageana*) show outstanding tolerance of heat, drought and disease, but they still need regular care. Blossoms show riveting bicolor combinations of mahogany and yellow-orange. 'Persian Carpet' is a mixture that shows delightful diversity in coloration, or you can emphasize dark mahogany tones by choosing 'Old Mexico' or 'Chippendale'.

Narrow-leaf zinnias (*Z. angustifolia* or *Z. linearis*) are great landscape problem solvers. These thrifty plants can bloom rich orange ('Star Orange'), sunny yellow ('Star Gold'), or white with yellow centers ('Crystal White'). The newer 'Profusion' hybrids have larger flowers and more closely resemble compact large-flowered zinnias.

Peruvian zinnias (*Z. paucifolia*) are old garden treasures worthy of a modern revival. The 'Bonita' series produces simple single flowers with velvety brick red or yellow petals surrounding darker centers.

'Crystal White' narrow-leaf zinnias.

Colorful Companions

As long as you play by the rules, you should have no trouble working zinnias into any landscape. Frame large plantings of mixed-color zinnias with a fine-textured edging of ageratum or nierembergia. Maximize contrast of bright red and orange zinnias by flanking them with blue salvia, white petunias, or yellow plume celosia. Yellow zinnias are very easy to mix and match with other flowers, and the same can be said of soft pinks. The rustic hues of Mexican and Peruvian zinnias look very dramatic when grown in the company of yellow marigolds or mixed portulacas.

The true flowers of zinnia are the small yellow florets. The colorful petals are really bracts.

COMMON AND BOTANICAL NAMES

Abelmoschus   *Abelmoschus moschatus*
- muskmallow,
  silk flower

Ageratum   *Ageratum houstonianum*
- flossflower

Amaranthus   *Amaranthus* spp.
- Joseph's coat,
  fountain plant,
  summer poinsettia   *Amaranthus tricolor*
- love-lies-bleeding,
  chenille plant,
  tassel flower   *Amaranthus caudatus*
- Prince's feather   *Amaranthus cruentus*

Ammi   *Ammi majus*
- bishop's weed,
  white dill

Angelonia   *Angelonia angustifolia*
- angel flower,
  summer snapdragon

Asarina   *Asarina* spp.
- chickabiddy vine,
  climbing snapdragon   *Asarina barclaiana*
- creeping gloxinia   *Asarina erubescens*

Aster, China   *Callistephus chinensis*

Bachelor button   *Centaurea cyanus*
- cornflower,
  bluebonnet

Bacopa   *Sutera cordata*

Begonia, wax   *Begonia semperflorens*

Begonia, tuberous   *Begonia tuberhybrida*

Bells of Ireland   *Moluccella laevis*

Black-eyed Susan   *Rudbeckia hirta*

Black-eyed Susan vine   *Thunbergia alata*
- clock flower

Brachychome   *Brachychome iberidifolia*
- Swan River daisy

Browallia   *Browallia speciosa*
- sapphire flower,
  amethyst flower

Calendula   *Calendula officinalis*
- pot marigold

Candytuft   *Iberis* spp.
- globe candytuft   *Iberis umbellata*
- rocket candytuft   *Iberis amara*

Celosia   *Celosia* spp.
- plume celosia   *Celosia argentea plumosa*
- cockscomb   *Celosia argentea cristata*
- wheat celosia   *Celosia argentea spicata*

Cleome   *Cleome hassleriana*
- spider flower

Cobbity daisy   *Argyranthemum frutescens*
- marguerite daisy

Coleus   *Solenostemon scutellarioides*

Convolvulus   *Convolvulus tricolor*
- bush morning glory

Coreopsis   *Coreopsis tinctoria*
- calliopsis,
  plains coreopsis

Cosmos   *Cosmos* spp.
- common cosmos   *Cosmos bipinnatus*
- sulphur cosmos   *Cosmos sulphureus*

Cup and saucer vine   *Cobaea scandens*
- cathedral bells,
  cobaea,
  Chilean bellflower

Dahlia   *Dahlia* x *hybridus*

Dianthus	*Dianthus* hybrids	**Impatiens**	*Impatiens* spp.
- China pink		- garden impatiens, busy Lizzie	*Impatiens wallerana*
Dusty miller	*Senecio cineraria*	- New Guinea impatiens	*Impatiens hawkeri*
English daisy	*Bellis perennis*	**Kale and cabbage**	*Brassica oleracea*
Euphorbia	*Euphorbia marginata*	**Lantana**	*Lantana camara*
- snow-on-the-mountain		**Larkspur**	*Consolida ambigua*
Fan flower	*Scaevola aemula*	- annual delphinium	
- scaevola		**Lavatera**	*Lavatera trimestris*
Forget-me-not	*Myosotis, Cynoglossum* spp.	- tree mallow	
- common forget-me-not, myosotis	*Myosotis sylvestris*	**Lisianthus**	*Eustoma grandiflorum*
- Chinese forget-me-not	*Cynoglossum amabile*	- prairie gentian, Texas bluebell	
Four o'clock	*Mirabilis jalapa*	**Lobelia**	*Lobelia erinus*
- marvel of Peru		**Marigold**	*Tagetes* spp.
Foxglove	*Digitalis purpurea*	- large-flowered marigold	*Tagetes erecta* hybrids
Fuchsia	*Fuchsia hybrida*	- French marigold	*Tagetes patula*
- ladies' eardrops		- signet marigold	*Tagetes tenufolia*
Gaillardia	*Gaillardia pulchella*	**Melampodium**	*Melampodium paludosum*
- Indian blanket, blanket flower		- African zinnia, medallion daisy	
Gazania	*Gazania linearis*	**Mexican sunflower**	*Tithonia rotundifolia,* aka *T. speciosa*
- treasure flower		- tithonia, torch flower	
Geranium	*Pelargonium* hybrids		
- zonal geranium	*Pelargonium hortorum*	**Mimulus**	*Mimulus hybridus*
- ivy geranium	*Pelargonium peltatum*	- monkey flower	
Gomphrena	*Gomphrena* spp.	**Moonvine**	*Ipomoea alba*
- globe amaranth	*Gomphrena globosa*	**Morning glory**	*Ipomoea* spp. and hybrids
- strawberry gomphrena	*Gomphrena haageana*	- common morning glory	*Ipomoea purpurea*
Heliotrope	*Heliotropium arborescens*	**Nasturtium**	*Tropaeolum majus*
- cherry pie plant		- canary creeper	*Tropaeolum peregrinum*
Hollyhock	*Alcea rosea*	**Nicotiana**	*Nicotiana* spp.
Hyacinth bean	*Dolichos lablab*	- jasmine tobacco	*Nicotiana alata*
		- cranberry tobacco	*Nicotiana sandarae*
		- woodland tobacco	*Nicotiana sylvestris*

Nierembergia	*Nierembergia hippomanica*
- cup flower	

Nigella	*Nigella damascena*
- love-in-a-mist	

Pansy	*Viola* x *wittrockiana*
- viola, mini-pansy, johnny jump-up	*Viola tricolor*

Pentas	*Pentas lanceolata*
- Egyptian star cluster	

Pepper, ornamental	*Capsicum annuum*
- Christmas pepper	

Persian shield	*Strobilanthes dyerianus*

Petunia	*Petunia* x *hybrida*

Phlox	*Phlox drummondii*

Poppy	*Papaver, Eschscholzia* spp.
- corn poppy, Shirley or Flanders poppy	*Papaver rhoeas*
- California poppy	*Eschscholzia californica*
- breadseed poppy, opium poppy	*Papaver somniferum*

Portulaca	*Portulaca grandiflora*
- moss rose	

Salpiglossis	*Salpiglossis sinuata*
- painted tongue, velvet flower	

Salvia	*Salvia* spp.
- garden salvia	*Salvia splendens*
- blue salvia, mealycup sage	*Salvia farinacea*
- coral sage	*Salvia coccinea*

Sanvitalia	*Sanvitalia procumbens*
- creeping zinnia	

Scabiosa	*Scabiosa atropurpurea*
- pincushion flower, mourning bride	

Schizanthus	*Schizanthus pinnatus*
- butterfly flower	

Snapdragon	*Antirrhinum majus*

Statice	*Limonium sinuatum*

Stock	*Matthiola incana*

Strawflower	*Acroclinium, Helichrysum* spp.
- common strawflower	*Helichrysum bracteatum*
- paper daisy	*Acroclinium roseum*

Sunflower	*Helianthus annuus*

Sweet alyssum	*Lobularia maritima*

Sweet pea	*Lathyrus odorata*

Sweet potato vine	*Ipomoea batatas*

Torenia	*Torenia fournieri, T. baillonii*
- wishbone flower, Florida pansy	

Touch-me-not	*Impatiens balsamina*
- garden balsam	

Trachymene (Blue lace flower)	*Trachymene coerulea*
- blue lace flower	

Verbena	*Verbena* x *hybrida*

Vinca	*Catharanthus roseus*
- Madagascar periwinkle	

Viola	*Viola tricolor*
- mini-pansy	
- johnny jump-up	

Zinnia	*Zinnia* species and hybrids
- large-flowered zinnia	*Zinnia elegans*
- Mexican zinnia	*Zinnia haageana*
- narrow-leaf zinnia	*Zinnia angustifolia, Z. linearis*
- Peruvian zinnia	*Zinnia paucifolia*

SOURCES FOR PLANTS, SEEDS AND SUPPLIES

Burpee Seeds
300 Park Avenue
Warminster, PA 18974
800-888-1447
www.burpee.com
Extensive selection of popular flowers with
emphasis on dependable hybrids.

Cook's Garden
P.O. Box 535
Londonderry, VT 05148
800-457-9703
www.cooksgarden.com
Selections include edible flowers and varieties
for cutting and fragrance.

Johnny's Selected Seeds
Foss Hill Road
Albion, ME 04910
207-437-9294
www.johnnyseeds.com
Required reading for cut flower fans.

Nichols Garden Nursery
1190 North Pacific Highway
Albany, OR 97321
541-928-9280
www.gardennursery.com
Distinctive choices among old favorites and
outstanding newer varieties.

Park Seed
1 Parkton Avenue
Greenwood, SC 29647
800-845-3369
www.parkseed.com
A must-have catalog for every flower lover.

Pinetree Garden Seeds
P.O. Box 300
New Gloucester, ME 04260
207-926-3400
www.superseeds.com
Excellent selection of older varieties that are often
hard to find.

Seed Savers Exchange
3076 North Winn Road
Decorah, IA 52101
319-382-5990
web address pending
Historically important heirlooms from around
the world.

Select Seeds Antique Flowers
180 Stickney Hill Road
Union, CT 06076
860-684-9310
www.selectseeds.com
A nostalgic collection of interesting oldies, rare
minor species, and sweet peas galore.

Shepherd's Garden Seeds
30 Irene Street
Torrington, CT 06790
860-482-3638
www.shepherdseeds.com
Cut flowers, edibles, fragrant varieties and much
more.

Stokes Seeds
P.O. Box 548
Buffalo, NY 14240-0548
716-695-6980
www.stokeseeds.com
Color headquarters for outstanding annuals in
every hue.

Territorial Seed Company
P.O. Box 157
Cottage Grove, OR 97424-0061
541-942-9547
www.territorial-seed.com
Stellar selection of flowers for maritime and mild
winter climates.

Wildseed Farms
P.O. Box 3000
Fredericksburg, TX 78624-3000
800-848-0078
www.wildseedfarms.com
High-quality wildflower seeds by the packet or
the pound.

INDEX OF PLANTS

GENERAL INDEX

PHOTO CREDITS

Principal photography by Crandall and Crandall

Barbara Pleasant pp. 13, 15, 27, 38, 39, 41, 50, 58, 59, 60, 65, 66, 67, 68, 69, 70(2), 71 both, 72, 74, 82, 85(2), 86, 87, 92, 93, 100, 102, 104, 113, 115, 117, 119, 123, 131, 134, 142, 144, 146, 148, 162 both

Dency Kane pp. 31, 94, 100, 103 both, 130, 133, 138, 140, 143, 145, 157, 160, 166

Bill Adams pp. 38, 39(2), 66, 73, 84, 123, 140, 161

Bill Johnson pp. 60, 61

Jana Freiband pp. 65, 129, 167

Todd Davis Photography pp. 90, 91, 106, 125, 130, 131, 132, 147, 161